THE MANUAL OF DISCIPLINE

STUDIES ON THE TEXTS OF THE DESERT OF JUDAH

EDITED BY

J. VAN DER PLOEG O.P.

VOLUME I

LEIDEN
E. J. BRILL
1957

THE MANUAL OF DISCIPLINE

TRANSLATED AND ANNOTATED
WITH AN INTRODUCTION

BY

P. WERNBERG-MØLLER
Cand. theol. (Copenhagen), D. phil. (Oxford),
Lecturer in Semitic Languages and Literatures at Manchester University

WM. B. EERDMANS
PUBLISHING COMPANY
GRAND RAPIDS, MICHIGAN
1957

PRINTED IN THE NETHERLANDS

TO SASHA

CONTENTS

PREFACE

The present work is an abridged version of a thesis submitted for the degree of D. phil. at Oxford University. Both the introduction and the commentary have been somewhat curtailed; on the other hand, the bibliography is kept, in the main, in its original form, and reference tables have been added.

For help and advice I am indebted to Professors G. R. DRIVER and H. H. ROWLEY, to Dr S. M. STERN and to Mr P. R. WEIS. I should also like to express my thanks to Professor J. VAN DER PLOEG of Nijmegen, who has accepted this work for publication in a series of studies on the Dead Sea Scrolls published by E. J. BRILL, Leiden, under his editorship.

Some of the present material has already appeared in articles in *Journal of Semitic Studies*, in *Vetus Testamentum*, and in *Studia Theologica*, whose editors have generously consented to my republishing parts of those articles in this volume.

For patient help and encouragement I am deeply thankful to my wife, to whom this book is dedicated.

Manchester, November 1956. P. WERNBERG-MØLLER

INTRODUCTION

The so-called Manual of Discipline (1QS) was found in a cave (now called Cave 1) near Ain Feshkha by the Dead Sea in 1947 together with other scrolls and fragments of manuscripts, the main part of which has been made accessible to scholars in excellent facsimile editions [1]). In order to establish the date for the writing of the Scrolls and their deposit in the cave, scholars have examined the *archaeological* context in which the manuscripts were found, and have considered the *palaeographical*, *orthographical*, and *philological* characteristics of the documents. An introduction to 1QS, however briefly, must naturally deal with all these points.

The original verdict of the *archaeologists*, that the jars in which the Scrolls were deposited were Hellenistic, and that therefore a date later than 100 B.C. for the deposit in the cave would seem unlikely [2]), has had to be altered according to the results of subsequent excavations of Khirbet Qumran which allow for the assumption of a later date for the deposit, and it is now the opinion of the experts that the jars may well be Roman, and that the manuscripts may have been deposited in the cave in the first century A.D., but not later than 70 A.D. [3])

The attempt to establish the age of 1QS and the other manuscripts on *palaeographical* grounds has been made in painstaking detail by Trever [4]) and Birnbaum [5]), and their belief that all the Scrolls palaeographically belong to the pre-Christian era is shared by Albright who has repeatedly declared himself in favour of a Maccabaean or

---

[1]) 1QIsa[a], 1QpHab and 1QS have been published by Burrows of the American Schools of Oriental Research, in *The Dead Sea Scrolls of St. Mark's Monastery*, vol. I (1950) and vol. II, fascicle 2 (1951). 1QH and 1QM, together with other material from Cave 1, have been published in *Discoveries in the Judaean Desert* I (1955), ed. Barthélemy and Milik, and in *Oṣar ham-Megillot hag-Genuzot sheb-bide ha-Universita ha-Ivrit* (1954), ed. Sukenik.

[2]) See e.g. de Vaux, in *RB*, lvi (1949), p. 234; Albright, in *BASOR*, No. 115 (1949), p. 14.

[3]) See e.g. Albright, *ibid.*, No. 126 (1952), p. 2; de Vaux, *op. cit.*, lx (1953), p. 104 f.

[4]) *BASOR*, No. 113 (1949), pp. 6 ff.

[5]) *Ibid.*, No. 113 (1949), pp. 33 ff, No. 115 (1949), pp. 20 ff, and No. 118 (1950), pp. 20 ff; *PEQ* (1949), pp. 140 ff; *ibid.*, (1952), pp. 94 ff; *JBL*, lxviii (1949), pp. 161 ff; *VT*, i (1951), pp. 91 ff; *The Qumran (Dead Sea) Scrolls and Palaeography* (*BASOR*, Supplementary Studies, Nos. 13-14, 1952).

early Herodian dating, cutting out categorically any possibility of some later date [1]). On the other hand, the palaeographers have argued that all the Scrolls cannot possibly have been written at the same time. As compared to 1QIsa[a] and 1QS, whose scripts are very much like one another, 1QpHab was found to have been written in a very different hand, and it was therefore found necessary to assume an interval between the two groups of manuscripts, 1QpHab representing the supposedly more developed and later stage [2]). Furthermore, the notable difference between the script of 1QIsa[a] and 1QS on the one hand and 1QpHab on the other, appeared to justify the view that the two groups of manuscripts were written by scribes of two different schools [3]), 1QpHab representing the later stage in the scribal art of the community.

TREVER and BIRNBAUM used for comparative purposes material dating from 5th century B.C. to 3rd century A.D., the Elephantine papyri denoting the upper, and the Dura-Europos fragment the lower, limit [4]). Although the results of these two scholars are roughly the same [5]), it is to be noted that to TREVER the Nash papyrus gives the clue to the date of the earlier scrolls (1QIsa[a] and 1QS) [6]), whereas BIRNBAUM has never used the fragment that way. The latter scholar compares the letters of the Scrolls with the letters of available material covering the period between the Elephantine papyri and the Dura-Europos fragment, and decides their relative age by a simple process of counting the similarities and differences between the given and the comparative material. In the palaeographical studies of TREVER, however, the reader is left with the impression that the Nash papyrus is regarded *a priori* as constituting the most significant comparative

---

[1]) See e.g. *BASOR*, No. 118 (1950), p. 6.

[2]) BIRNBAUM, *ibid.*, No. 115 (1949), p. 22; TREVER, *ibid.*, No. 111 (1948), p. 14.

[3]) TREVER, *ibid.*, No. 113 (1949), p. 6 and p. 14 f.

[4]) For literature about the comparative material applied (consisting of the following main items: 5th century B.C. Elephantine papyri, 3rd century B.C. documents from Edfu, the Tobias inscription, the Gezer boundary stones, Palestinian ossuaries, the Uzziah plaque, the Queen Helena inscription, the graffiti of the Herodian age, and last, but not least, the Nash papyrus), see ALBRIGHT, in *JBL*, lvi (1937), pp. 145 ff; BIRNBAUM, in *PEQ* (1949), p. 140 f, in *BASOR*, No. 113 (1949), p. 33, and in *JBL*, lxviii (1949), p. 162.

[5]) BIRNBAUM dates 1QIsa[a]: the first half of the second century B.C. (see *BASOR*, No. 113 (1949), p. 35), 1QS: the last quarter of the second pre-Christian century (see *PEQ* (1949), p. 147), and 1QpHab: 1st half of the 1st century B.C. (see *JBL*, lxviii (1949), p. 168). TREVER dates 1QIsa[a]: 125-100 B.C., 1QS: about 75 B.C., and 1QpHab: 25 B.C. to 25 A.D., (see *BASOR*, No. 113 (1949), p. 23).

[6]) *Op. cit.*, *art. cit.*, p. 19. Cf. ALBRIGHT, *ibid.*, No. 115 (1949), p. 17.

material as far as 1QIsa[a] and 1QS are concerned, in the same way as the difference between 1QIsa[a] and 1QS on the one hand and 1QpHab on the other, generally explained by the assumption of the latter being younger than the former, has driven this scholar to the presupposition that the script of 1QpHab is comparable especially to an Aramaic dipinto published by SUKENIK in 1934 [1]).

The results of TREVER and BIRNBAUM have been rejected by other scholars on various grounds. The criticism against the application of the Nash papyrus for dating purposes hits of course TREVER in particular; on the other hand, the objections raised clearly concern the entire material called in for comparison, as well as matters of method in general. LACHEMAN has pointed out that the Nash papyrus was found in Egypt whereas the Scrolls were found in Palestine, and that Egyptian material must not be used for dating Palestinian documents [2]). To this might be added that even with the assumption that no material difference can be presupposed in the scripts of documents from Egypt and Palestine at the time in question, the possibility still exists that the particular script was used longer in one area than in another; perhaps the particular type of script, as we know it from the Nash papyrus and early Aramaic papyri, was still current in Palestine in certain circles at a much later date. This argument is particularly cogent if the view is correct that the Scrolls are written in book-hand by professional scribes belonging to a school, because the probability is that the handwriting used by skilled scribes of a particular school would be in use for a very long time without undergoing any noticeable changes—as opposed to the Nash papyrus which is written in cursive and contains a great variety of letter forms [3]). In fact, not only the Nash papyrus, but also the comparative material as a whole, and even the Scrolls themselves, contain a mixture of forms, and this circumstance is really the main obstacle to placing any reliability on the palaeographical argument in favour of an early dating of the Scrolls; the fact that the types are used promiscuously by the same copyist, appears to discount the value of establishing a line of development in the course of time of any one letter with a view to fixing relative dating of the manuscripts in which the various types are used. Neither is it possible, as BIRNBAUM does, simply to count in each manuscript 'early' and 'late' forms, and then decide

---

[1]) *Op. cit.*, *art. cit.*, p. 22.

[2]) *JQR*, N.S. xl (1949-50), p. 24 f.

[3]) See LACHEMAN, *op. cit.*, *vol. cit.*, pp. 18 ff.

on the question of age by 'weighting' the given material, nor can we, as TEICHER does [1]), assume that the scribes made use of 'archaic' letter forms. It seems odd that a skilled scribe should be inconsistent in his application of old forms if he wanted to archaize. Why, e.g., did the scribe of 1QS use the *Aleph* of 1QpHab, and not that of 1QIsa[a]? Why, indeed, did he use a variety of forms of the same letter? [2]) The two different points of view are of supreme methodological importance, because TEICHER's view that 'old' forms are to be regarded as conscious imitations, entails the view that such 'archaisms' are to be totally disregarded in a discussion of the manuscript concerned, whereas BIRNBAUM's denial of 'old' forms being archaisms, entails the view that such 'old' forms must somehow be considered when deciding the age of the manuscript. In the former case the scholar who wants to establish a late date, rids himself conveniently of any evidence which might point the other way; in the latter case the scholar who wants to establish an early date retains any material which might point that way, and assigns to that material an important part to establish the desired early dating. The palaeographical argument, therefore, cannot be said to offer definite proof of the origin of the Scrolls in pre-Christian times, and evidence other than that derived from the letter forms employed in the manuscripts is needed to prove this.

The *orthographical* peculiarity, which has played an important part in the discussion about the age of 1QS and the other manuscripts from Cave 1, is the profuse application of *matres lectionis*. Indeed, the

---

[1]) *JJS*, ii (1951), p. 83.

[2]) The palaeographical table drawn up by TREVER, as well as his descriptions of each individual letter, *op. cit.*, *art. cit.*, pp. 7 ff, are not careful enough, and therefore misleading. 1QS contains a much greater variety of forms than he presupposes. Thus *Bet*, normally squat, and round in the lower right corner, occurs occasionally with the bottom bar drawn beyond the right vertical (i 16) which presupposes a different ductus and is generally supposed to be late. *Ṭet*, apart from the normal figure 6 form, occurs in the broad, angular form in ii 3 and vii 10. *Mem* (apart from the forms noticed by TREVER) is sometimes a completely closed and oval letter (i 11), sometimes written as a *Samek* (iii 22). *Samek* occurs in various forms: the triangular one (ii 1), the beautifully curved form with the right stroke sloping gently inwards (i 22, v 23, xi 13), the almost completely square form (ii 11), a variation of which is the peculiar, rounded form (ii 15) (the scribe, in ii 24-25, utilized all the last three forms in writing what amounts to little more than one line). *Ayin* is large and carefully drawn (i 3, v 5, vii 14), and small (ii 17, iv 11). *Resh*, normally large, broad, and very distinct, is sometimes small and indistinct, in some places almost like a *Waw* (iv 9, 12, vii 9, 16, viii 25). *Shin* occurs, apart from the most common round form, drawn from left to right, also as a sharply angular letter, drawn by three separate strokes (x 13, 19).

frequent use, especially of *Waw* and *Yod* as vowel letters, is so striking that some scholars have reasoned that the Scrolls on this ground alone must be supposed to be relatively late [1]). The Massoretic rule is that every originally long vowel may be indicated by a vowel letter, and it is not difficult to ascertain that the use of *Waw* and *Yod* in the Scrolls goes far beyond this, those letters being employed there to denote, not only (originally or secondarily) long vowels, but also short ones.

Thus in 1QS we find the following remarkable *plene* writing almost consistently used:

(A) *Waw*

(a) in the singular and plural of segolates of the *quṭl* type, e.g. *ḥwshk* (i 10, ii 7 etc.), *ʿwrp* (v 26), *qwṣr* (vi 26), *qwdsh* (ii 25, iv 5 etc.), *'wzn* (iv 11), *ʿwmq* (xi 19), *rwb* (iv 3), *rwʿ* (iv 11), *twm* (v 24), *ḥwq* (v 7), *kwl* (i 3), *bwr* (ix 15), *ʿwz* (x 25), *rwq* (xi 21), *ṭwhrh* (vi 22), *qwdshw* (viii 16), *qwdshym* (viii 6), *ḥwdshym* (vii 3).

(b) in the construct infinitive Qal, e.g. *ldrwsh* (i 1), *bqwrbw* (vi 16), *wbʿwbrm* (i 18).

(c) in the imperfect Qal: *wypqwd* (ii 6), *yshpwṭ* (viii 25), *yshpwl* (ii 23), *ypqwdhw* (vi 21), *yktwbhw* (vi 22), *ydrwshhw* (vi 17).

(d) in the participle Qal, singular and plural, e.g. *whww'* (xi 4,5), *hʿwbrym* (i 20), *pwqdm* (v 24).

(e) in words where, according to the Massoretes, the short *u* sound is followed by *Dagesh forte* or *silent Shwa*, e.g. *pʿwltm* (iii 16), *pʿwlt* (iv 15), *ḥwqy* (i 7), *ykwprw* (iii 6), *tkwpr* (iii 8), *whwbdl* (viii 24), *wmwbdl* (vii 3, 5), *wlpqwdt* (iii 14), *hshwlḥn* (vi 4).

(f) in the names *mwshh* (i 3) and *'hrwn* (v 21).

(B) *Yod*

(a) in the singular and plural of segolates of the *qiṭl* (*qṭil*) type: *bb'yr* (vii 20, original text), *ngyʿyhm* (iii 14), *hṣdyq* (ix 14).

(b) in words where, according to the Massoretes, the short *i* sound is followed by *Dagesh forte* or *silent Shwa*, e.g. *myswd* (= *msswd*, vii 18), *wkybwd* (iv 11), *myl't* (vi 17, 18), *lnyknʿym* (x 26).

(c) in the imperfect and infinitive Niphal :*yktyb* (ix 2), *'wkyḥ* (x 11), *lhwsyp* (vi 14), *ybdylw* (ix 5).

(d) in the jussive Hiphil: *yby'* (vi 1), *yqym* (v 10).

Both *Waw* and *Yod* may retain their consonantal value by doubling, e.g. *ʿwwnwt* (i 23) and *wnhyyh* (iii 15).

This excessive *plene* spelling is not necessarily to be taken as an

[1]) See Zeitlin, in *JQR*, N.S. xl (1949-50), p. 62; Driver, *ibid.*, *vol. cit.*, p. 130, p. 360 f and p. 370 f; Weis, *ibid.*, N.S. xli (1950-51), p. 125.

indication that the manuscript is late. The free employment of *matres lectionis* is to be found in the Nash papyrus [1]) and in MT [2]); in fact, a close examination of the latter shows that the Massoretes employed the vowel letters at random as denoting only the quality, and not the quantity, of a given vowel sound [3]); besides, from quotations of biblical passages in the Talmud it is clear that in numerous cases rabbinic discussions were based on *plene* spellings which are no longer preserved in MT [4]). It appears possible to argue therefore that the application of vowel letters in some biblical manuscripts of the pre-Massoretic period was different from its application in other manuscripts which eventually came to be officially and exclusively approved. 1QIsa[a] therefore may be regarded as a biblical manuscript from the time before MT was standardized, and the profuse use of vowel letters is to be explained simply by the fact that at the time when it was written vowel signs were not yet invented [5]). If this is so, however, we are brought to the conclusion that 1QIsa[a], and with it 1QS and the other manuscripts, are of considerable antiquity, because the fixation of the standard Bible text originates, as SEGAL has shown, in the time before the destruction of the second Temple, and before the age of the *Sopherim* [6]).

To the assumption of an early date of the manuscripts we are also brought by an examination of their *philological* characteristics. Some scholars do, it is true, maintain a late date of the manuscripts because of purported application of late rabbinic or Karaite expressions and usages [7]), purportedly Arabic influence in the forms of pronouns and suffixes [8]), use of Aramaic forms of words and suffixes [9]), confusion and weakening of gutturals [10]), and purported agreement

---

[1]) COOK, in *PSBA*, xxv (1903), p. 38. — MEYER, in *VT*, iii (1953), p. 227, refers for the use of vowel letters to the Siloam inscription and the Lachish letters.

[2]) *GK*, § 7g.

[3]) See SPERBER, in *HUCA*, xvi (1941), p. 426.

[4]) See SPERBER, *ibid.*, xvii (1942-43), pp. 316 ff.

[5]) Cf. KAHLE, *Die hebräischen Handschriften*, p. 50.

[6]) *JBL*, lxxii (1953), pp. 35 ff. Cf. also LÖFGREN, in *Nyberg Festschrift*, p. 175.

[7]) Cf. DRIVER, *The Hebrew Scrolls*, p. 41 f; ZEITLIN, *op. cit.*, N.S. xxxix (1948-49), p. 237 f and pp. 243 f; WEIS, *ibid.*, N.S. xli (1950-51), p. 135 ff.

[8]) Cf. WEIS, *op. cit.*, *vol. cit.*, pp. 125 ff; DRIVER, in *JTS*, N.S. ii (1951), p. 22; TOURNAY, in *RB*, lvi (1949), p. 210, n. 5. — BÜCHLER, in *JQR*, N.S. iii (1912-13), p. 468 f, assumed late Arabic influence in CD.

[9]) DRIVER, in *JTS*, *vol. cit.*, pp. 21 ff.

[10]) ZEITLIN, *op. cit.*, N.S. xli (1950-51), p. 30, who points to the confusion of *Ayin* and *Ḥet* in the Scrolls and in the language of the common people of Galilee of the Talmudic period.

of 1QIsa[a], not with Sept., but with MT and the late versions [1]).

None of these arguments, however, is cogent. We possess no adequate means of ascertaining whether a word is late or early; our Hebrew dictionaries are incomplete, and a particular word in the Scrolls, which is only recorded in our Talmudic dictionaries, may have been current for centuries before the Talmudic age, and may have been handed down in very ancient literary documents which are no longer existing. As far as 1QS is concerned, this may be said to have happened with such expressions as *srk* ('order', 'regulation', 'rank') and *yḥd* ('community'). The late recording of such isolated words can in no way prejudice the clear evidence which points the other way, and their absence from our records of classical Hebrew may be purely accidental; therefore, rather than being taken as warranting the assumption of a late date of 1QS, they should be regarded as supplementing our fragmentary knowledge of the Hebrew language at an early stage. As for the purportedly late Arabic influence, convincing arguments can be produced for the contention that such forms are in fact to be regarded as genuinely ancient forms which link the language of the Scrolls with classical Hebrew at a pre-Massoretic stage. As far as the occurrence of Aramaisms in the Scrolls is concerned, this is not surprising with scribes whose mother tongue was Aramaic [2]). As for the weakening and confusion of gutturals [3]), this is by no means a late phenomenon; it occurs in MT in numerous cases [4]) and may be traced back to pre-Massoretic times [5]). Finally, the assertion that 1QIsa[a] agrees with MT and the late versions and that, therefore, the manuscript is to be dated somewhere in post-Mishnaic times, can no longer be upheld. A close examination of the variants has made it clear that the manuscript in many cases is based on ancient tradition which points towards the *Vorlage* of Sept. [6]). 1QIsa[a] is therefore, by its differences from MT, to be regarded

---

[1]) Driver, in *JQR*, *vol. cit.*, p. 129 f; — As far as 1QpHab is concerned, see Lehmann, in *PEQ* (1951), pp. 35 ff.

[2]) Aramaic influence may be found in 1QS in i 18 (*whywm*), ii 9 (*'wḥzy 'bwt*), ii 19 (*ywmy*, cf. also iii 5), iii 1 (*lmshwb*); iii 3 (*bmtwr*), iii 9 (*dwky* and *wyhkyn*), v 16 (*m'wm'* (originally)), vii 4 (*yṣḥh*), vii 10 (*yshkwb*), vii 13 (*mtwḥt*).

[3]) In 1QS there are examples of this in i 16, iii 15, v 10, 24, 26, vi 7, 11, 12, 20, 26, 27, vii 3, 14, viii 2, 13, x 1, 2, 6, 10, 12, xi 17, 21. *Aleph* is often omitted (i 7, ii 12, 20, iii 8, v 16, 26, vi 5, 13, vii 7, ix 24, x 1 etc.).

[4]) See Sperber, *op. cit.*, xiv (1939), pp. 161 ff.

[5]) Cf. Kahle, *The Cairo Geniza*, pp. 86 ff, and in *Bertholet Festschrift*, p. 282; Meyer, in *TLZ*, lxxv (1950), col. 722 f.

[6]) Cf. Kahle, in *TLZ*, lxxiv (1949), col. 93; Beegle, in *BASOR*, No. 123

as a *Vulgärtext* which was current in pre-Massoretic times [1]). As we have already seen, MT was fixed before the destruction of the second Temple, and it is therefore reasonable to assume that 1QIsa[a], with its numerous deviations from MT in orthographical respect, is to be dated somewhere in the pre-Christian era, at a time when scribes were allowed to employ *matres lectionis* at their discretion, even in biblical manuscripts.

It may now seem relevant to produce the philological evidence which suggests that all these manuscripts reflect an early stage in the development of the Hebrew language. As will appear from the ensuing analysis, the comparative material is drawn from a variety of literary sources, reflecting a pre-Massoretic pronunciation of Hebrew in, so it seems, a considerable part of Jewry. We add references to passages in 1QS in which the forms concerned occur. This whole argument is possible only because of the extensive *plene* spelling employed which, as we have seen, may in itself be taken to support the assumption of an early date of the manuscript.

(a) Segolates which have the characteristic vowel in the second syllable, e.g. *rḥwb* (iv 9), *shpwl* (ibid.), *qṣwr* (iv 10) *kbwd* (iv 11), *ḥṣdyq* (ix 14), *yshwr* (xi 2). Similar forms may be found in the second column of ORIGEN's *Hexapla* (the 'Secunda'), in Sept., in the transcriptions of Hebrew words in the works of JEROME, and in Samaritan [2]). In those pre-Massoretic writings we find words like *ephesi* (JEROME, = Tiberian *ḥephṣī*), *zemeri* (JEROME, = Tiberian *zimrī*), *cheleki* (Sept., = Tiberian *ḥelqī*), *afara* (JEROME, = Tiberian *'ophrā*), *ylyd* (Samaritan, = Tiberian *yéled*), *'myrh* (Samaritan, = Tiberian *'imrā*), etc. A pronunciation of the segolates according to which the stress was on the second syllable appears then to be a feature which 1QS shares with

---

(1951), pp. 26 ff. Also the Nash papyrus is related to the Hebrew underlying Sept., see COOK, *op. cit.*, *vol. cit.*, p. 45. As far as 1QS is concerned, we find agreement with Sept. in the following passages: i 13 (alluding to Ezra x 3); i 21 (quoting 1 Sam. xii 7); ii 15 f (quoting Deut. xxix 19); v 15 (quoting Exod. xxiii 7); v 19 (quoting Jer. xxiii 17); x 8 (alluding to Hos. xiv 3); xi 14 (alluding to Ps. cxlv 7). — As for the biblical fragments from Cave 4, see SKEHAN, in *BASOR*, No. 136 (1954), pp. 12 ff; CROSS, *ibid.*, No. 132 (1953), pp. 15 ff, and in *JBL*, lxxiv (1955), pp. 165 ff; ALBRIGHT, in *BASOR*, No. 140 (1955), p. 29 f.

[1]) Cf. KAHLE, *Die hebräischen Handschriften*, p. 29. — That our community possessed and knew different biblical manuscripts may be seen from the fact to which KAHLE, *op. cit.*, p. 72 f, has drawn attention, that 1QIsa[a] is really made up of two different manuscripts in which the *plene* spelling is employed to different degrees.

[2]) The ensuing examples are gleaned from SPERBER, *op. cit.*, xii-xiii (1937-38), pp. 136 ff, p. 206 and p. 258.

pre-Massoretic literary sources; that 1QS also contains numerous examples of 'Tiberian' segolates is not surprising, this mixed type of language being, as SPERBER has shown as far as the Secunda, Sept., and JEROME are concerned, 'one of the most significant criteria of the works of those early centuries' [1]).

(b) The use of *yiqṭōlu* and *qᵉṭōlu* forms of the verb in context [2]), cf. *y'bwrw* (i 16), *y'rwkw* (vi 4), *yshqwdw* (vi 7). Imperative forms of the type in question do not occur in 1QS, but are known from 1QIsaª. In MT there are three examples of long *u* in front of the plural ending in the imperfectum: Exod. xviii 26, Ruth ii 8, and Prov. xiv 3, which may perhaps be related to the forms we find in the Scrolls; there are also a couple of examples of stressing the penultimate in front of vocalic ending in the imperative (Judges ix 12 and 1 Sam. xxviii 8). Also in this case can we find parallels in pre-Massoretic sources, namely in the Secunda and in the transcriptions of JEROME where are found the following forms [3]): *yerogou* (= Tiberian *yaḥrᵉgū*), *yephpholou* (= Tiberian *yippᵉlū*), *phthoou* (= Tiberian *pitḥū*), *hedalu* (= Tiberian *ḥidlū*). As has been emphasized by MEYER [4]), the verbal forms of the Scrolls are identical with the pausal forms of MT which rest on old tradition; a natural conclusion, therefore, seems to be that the Scrolls were written at a time in the history of the pronunciation of Hebrew when the original stress on the penultimate syllable and the full vocalization of that syllable were normal features of context forms.

(c) The apparent use of *yᵉquṭ(ṭ)el* forms instead of *yiqṭo/al* forms which may occur in 1QS in forms like *ydwrshhw* (vi 14) and *yshwpṭny* (x 13), and according to YALON [5]) are to be found in 1QIsaª in such forms as *t'wkl*, *t'wmr*, *'dwrshkh*, *wyshwm'wny*, *y'wshqny*, etc., are found also in MT very occasionally, e.g. as YALON draws attention to, in *tᵉ'oklēhū* (Job xx 26), in *to'obdēm* (Exod. xx 5), and in *no'obdēm* (Deut.

---

1) *Op. cit.*, *vol. cit.*, p. 148. — As far as MT is concerned, the *Ketib* and the *Qere* forms represent attempts to combine two different types of text, cf. SPERBER, *op. cit.*, xvii (1942-43), pp. 303 ff. BURROWS, in *BASOR*, No. 111 (1948), p. 20, finds several instances in which 1QIsaª agrees with the *Qere* of MT against the *Ketib*; already REIDER, however, in *JQR*, N.S. xli (1950-51), p. 62, gives examples of 1QIsaª agreeing sometimes with the *Ketib* and sometimes with the *Qere*, and LÖFGREN, in *Nyberg Festschrift*, p. 182, finds that 1QIsaª most often agrees with the *Ketib*, cf. also RABIN, in *JTS*, N.S. vi (1955), p. 180.

2) See MEYER, in *TLZ*, *vol. cit.*, col. 725, and in *VT*, *vol. cit.*, pp. 229 ff.

3) Cf. SPERBER, *op. cit.*, xii-xiii (1937-38), pp. 160 ff.

4) *VT*, *vol. cit.*, p. 231.

5) *KS*, xxvi (1950), p. 241 f.

xiii 3). It may be pertinent to draw attention to Samaritan verbal forms such as *yḥyṣwn* (Exod. xxi 35, MT: *yeḥeṣūn*), *tkyrw* (Deut. ii 6, MT: *tikrū*) [1]), cf. *tkwbh* or *tkybh* for Massoretic *tikbē* in 1QIsa[a] xxxiv 10, and to similar forms in Sept., Secunda, and in the works of JEROME, such as *ibaar* (= Tiberian *yibḥar*), *igaal* (= Tiberian *yig'al*), *isaar* (= Tiberian *yiṣhar*), *ikersou* (= Tiberian *yiqreṣū*), *iesemou* (= Tiberian *yismeḥū*) [2]). In all these cases we seem to have pre-Massoretic forms, presupposing a vocalization and accentuation different from the one which is normally found in MT.

(d) The forms of pronouns and suffixes ending in *-āh*, cf. *hw'h* (iii 17), *hy'h* (ix 5), *'bdkh* (xi 16) [3]). From 1QIsa[a] we can see that the ending was used also in the plural, both of pronouns and of pronominal suffixes [4]). The Samaritan dialect has, by oral tradition, preserved some of these forms unaltered through the centuries [5]), and the fact that we find identical forms in the Scrolls points towards the assumption that the Scrolls were written at a time when the final vowel of these words was pronounced, not only in the Samaritan dialect, but in classical Hebrew as a whole. In the Secunda these forms are not found, because they were forgotten at the time of ORIGEN.

In the case of the pronouns for 3rd pers. sing. (*hw'h* and *hy'h*) an explanation can be offered which links these forms with the corresponding forms in Ugaritic [6]). In that early period the forms of the pronouns for 3rd pers. sing. and plural were *hwt*, *hyt*, and *hmt*; in the same way as *hmt* became *hemāh* in classical Hebrew, thus we should, of *hwt* and *hyt*, expect either *huwāh/hiyāh* or, on the assumption of alternation of *Waw* (*Yod*) and *Aleph*: *hu'āh/hi'āh*, cf. Phoenician *hu'at/hi'at*; the latter forms are closely similar to those found in the Scrolls, whose pronominal forms may thus be ascribed to an early period in which the originally bisyllabic pronoun was fully pronounced [7]).

---

1) See SPERBER, *op. cit.*, xii-xiii (1937-38), p. 257, and *ibid.*, xiv (1939), p. 190, and p. 197, n. 184.

2) See SPERBER, *op. cit.*, xii-xiii (1937-38), pp. 158 ff.

3) The only example of the suffix for 2nd masc. sing. being indicated by *Kaph* only (in the Massoretic fashion) occurs in ii 8, at the end of the line.

4) See BURROWS, in *JBL*, lxviii (1949), p. 208 f; MILIK, in *Biblica*, xxxi (1950), p. 207 f.

5) Cf. GINSBERG, in *BASOR*, No. 112 (1948), p. 20, n. 3; KAHLE, in *TLZ*, lxxiv (1949), col. 92, and *Die hebräischen Handschriften*, p. 41 f.

6) For the following, see ALBRIGHT, in *JAOS*, lxvii (1947), p. 156, n. 31, and in *JCS*, iv (1950), p. 168.

7) Cf. BIRKELAND, in *Mowinckel Festschrift*, p. 28 f; MEYER, in *ZAW*, N.F. xxii

It is only against this background that a fair judgment of the suffix for 2nd masc. sing. (*-kāh*) in the Scrolls is possible. In the Secunda, in the transcriptions of JEROME, and in early manuscripts with Palestinian vocalization, as well as in Samaritan, the suffix is *-āk*, and KAHLE has argued that the Massoretic vocalization is to be regarded as a restitution of the lost final vowel due to Arabic influence [1]). We can now see that the Massoretes, in vocalizing the suffix in the way they did, were dependent on old Hebrew tradition, rather than on loan from Arabic [2]), and MEYER has shown [3]) that the *plene* writing of the suffix, which occurs a few times in MT, originates in the early pre-Massoretic period in which the suffix was still fully pronounced. In complete agreement with this conclusion is also the frequent preservation of the full form of the suffix for 3rd masc. sing. in the Scrolls (in 1QS: *w'ynyhw* (v 5), *bḥwqyhw* (v 11), *rglyhw* (vi 13), *'ḥyhw* (vi 10), *bpyhw* (vii 9), *lpnyhw* (vi 26)), and the spelling of the suffix for 1st pers. sing. as *y'* (in 1QS: *w'py'* (x 19)) which, as GUILLAUME has shown [4]), represents a retention of the ancient Semitic suffix *-iya*.

The conclusion which may be drawn from the above philological investigation is that 1QS (and the other manuscripts) are to be ascribed to a time when forms which later fell into disuse, if not, indeed, into complete oblivion, were still preserved, and the available evidence appears to point towards the assumption of a pre-Christian date. In which other period, if not before the fixation of MT, would a biblical manuscript like 1QIsa[a] be conceivable? At what other time, if not before the Christian era, would it be reasonable to assume the application of forms of verbs, nouns, pronouns and suffixes, some of which link the language of the Scrolls closely with the pronunciation of Hebrew of not only pre-Massoretic, but of early biblical times?

In attempting to fix a more definite date for the composition of 1QS we should no doubt take into account the natural conservatism of religious communities: the ancient stratum of the Hebrew language,

(1951), p. 227. — The spellings *hw'* and *hy'* testify to the originally bisyllabic character of the pronouns, cf. GUILLAUME, in *RB*, lix (1952), p. 185, who refers to *GK*, § 32k. At the time of JEROME the masculine pronoun was *hu*, see SPERBER, *op. cit.*, xii-xiii (1937-38), p. 129.

1) *The Cairo Geniza*, pp. 95 ff.

2) This is realized and acknowledged by KAHLE, *Die hebräischen Handschriften*, p. 73 f, n. 35.

3) *TLZ*, *vol. cit.*, col. 724, and *ZAW*, *vol. cit.*, p. 228 and p. 232.. Cf. BIRKELAND, *op. cit.*, p. 27.

4) *PEQ* (1951), pp. 78 ff.

of which especially 1QIsa[a] is so strikingly representative, may have been preserved through several pre-Christian centuries, and a final conclusion as to the age of the Scrolls, therefore, cannot be reached without regarding additional evidence which may allow us to narrow down the *terminus a quo* within which they have been ultimately composed; we may take it for granted that the manuscripts in our possession are only copies, and that consequently some time must have elapsed between the composition of the non-biblical scrolls and their copying in the documents found in 1947. The *terminus ad quem* for the copying is determined by the archaeological evidence, which precludes the assumption of a date later than 70 A.D., but it is clear that that evidence does not throw any light on the date of the composition of the non-biblical scrolls.

At this stage of our investigation three points are of importance: (a) the definition of the character of the religious circles behind 1QS; (b) the comparison of 1QS with literary documents with which the former shows points of contact; (c) the dating of that comparative material. Only in this way are we able to define the approximate time of the composition of 1QS and to arrive at some conclusion as to the identity of the circles behind our manuscript.

(a) An important figure in the past history of the movement was the 'Teacher of Righteousness', a priest whose authority amongst his followers was derived from his inspired interpretation of the Scriptures. A controversy between him and the 'Impious Priest' (almost certainly the High Priest of the time), during which the Teacher may have suffered a violent death, resulted in a complete breach with official Judaism on the part of our pious who withdrew into the desert (1QS viii 13 f) where they led a secluded life (v 1 f, 14 ff, viii 10, ix 5, 20 f), engaged in the study of the Torah (v 11, vi 6 f, viii 15) and the living of a pious life, according to their particular *halaka*.

They were organized in local units (vi 3), under the leadership of one or several priests, the sons of Zadok (v 1 ff), or the sons of Aaron (v 21, ix 7) who were the Torah students *par excellence*, with complete knowledge of the *halaka* of the society [1]). They alone, therefore, were able to decide whether new halakic suggestions made by the lay members were to be rejected or acknowledged (v 3, ix 7). On the other hand, it is clear from 1QS v 1 ff, vi 1, 13 ff, 24 ff, that the

[1]) The priestly character of the movement from the very beginning is rightly stressed by KAHLE, in *TLZ*, lxxvii (1952), cols. 405 ff.

laity possessed considerable authority in the community, not only with respect to halakic decisions, but also with respect to the important question of admission of new members to the society.

The community was in all respects the frame within which the entire activity of the members was to fall (vi 1 ff), and intimate intercourse with outsiders was strictly forbidden (v 13 ff, ix 6 f). At his entering into the society, the prospective member gave up his personal property which, in the case of his admission as a full member after two years of probation, was pooled with the communal property (vi 13 ff). A particular official, the *Mevaqqer* or *Paqid*, who appears to have had great power in the community, was particularly concerned with the administration of the communal goods and with the supervision of the training of newcomers. At daily sessions (vi 8 ff), as well as at nightly vigils (vi 6 ff), the Torah was recited and expounded. The members sat according to rank (vi 8 f), and submitted their response when called upon to do so; only full members were permitted to take part, and the halakic decisions made must under no circumstance be divulged outside the community (ix 16 f): they were 'secrets' (iv 6), 'revealed' to, or 'found' by, the members (v 11, viii 1 f, 11, ix 13 f); that allegorical interpretation was known and applied is clear from the author's use of scriptural passages, and it is reasonable to assume that the exegesis was done according to certain rules, although these are hard to define [1]).

The sole aim of the Torah study was the detection of the will of God, and the members set themselves the goal of living accordingly (i 3, viii 15 f). In their daily lives with the brethren they strove to realize the ideal of mutual love, humility, and obedience (ii 24, iv 3, v 23; that they were not all of equal standing is clear from i 10, ii 19 ff, v 23, vi 2, 22); to those who failed to live up to this ideal, definite punishments (including excommunications in severe cases) were applied (vi 24-vii 25). In their relationship with outsiders, however, they were allowed, or rather instructed, to harbour feelings of intense hatred (i 10 f, ii 5 ff, 25 ff, v 13 ff, ix 21 ff).

The members were all Jewish and regarded themselves as the true Israel and as the proper heirs of the spiritual inheritance of Israel: they understood the history of Israel and the promises to the

---

[1]) As for the application of biblical passages in 1QS, see the present writer's article in *ST*, ix (1955), pp. 40 ff, where most of the material is collected; as for the exegetical methods applied in 1QpHab, see Brownlee, in *BA*, xiv (1951), pp. 53 ff.

Patriarchs as being fulfilled in them, the actually existing pious community [1]). Throughout 1QS goes a spiritualizing tendency which is particularly clear in the notion of the community as the spiritual Temple (viii 1 ff), in the emphasis placed on true repentance and the living of a perfect life as necessary for obtaining forgiveness for sins (iii 4 ff, viii 3 f, ix 5), and in the preference given to prayer and thanksgiving over sacrificial rites (ix 4 f, x 6 ff). Equally characteristic is the strong intellectualistic ring in many passages (thus e.g. i 11, ii 3, iii 2, iv 3 f, 22, ix 13) and the very frequent use of the word *d't*.

The members celebrated a renewal of the covenant every year, presumably on the Day of Atonement. The first two plates of 1QS describe the ritual in some detail: all the members of the community on that occasion confessed their sins and renewed their undertaking to live according to the will of God. In their daily lives water rites played an important part [2]), and the original text in 1QS vii 20 actually contained an allusion to the well from which the water was drawn for such purposes. Some passages however, warn against a magical conception of water rites (iii 4 ff, v 3 f), which is in line with the spiritualistic tendency mentioned above. The meal described in vi 4 ff may have had sacramental character, and the members may have regarded participation in it as vouchsafing a foretaste of their blissful state in the messianic age to come.

Our pious were deeply concerned about the hereafter. They regarded themselves as strangers in this world (vi 2) and their communal life in the *Yaḥad* was a preparation or training for the fuller life to come (ii 24 f, iii 14 f, iv 20 ff, viii 4 ff, xi 7 ff). They looked forward to the Day of God's Vengeance (i 11, ii 9, 15, iv 12, v 12, ix 23), when God, assisted by the pious (viii 6 f), would destroy evil and re-create the world (iv 25) which was ruled by the Devil (i 18, ii 19), who through his wicked angels caused even the pious to go astray (i 23 f, iii 23 f). They expected two Messiahs (ix 11) [3]), and hoped to live eternally

[1]) A particularly interesting example of this attitude is the identification of the Servant of the Lord with the community, which we find in 1QS iv 6 where Isa. xlii 3 is alluded to, and in 1QS viii 6 where Isa. xlii 1 is quoted.

[2]) Cf. Baumgarten, in *HTR*, xlvi (1953), p. 151 f; Delcor, in *RHR*, cxliv (1953), p. 35 f.

[3]) Cf. Silbermann, in *VT*, v (1955), pp. 77 ff; Otzen, in *ST*, vii (1954), pp. 151 ff; Wieder, in *JJS*, vi (1955), p. 14 f; Kuhn, in *NTS*, i (1955), pp. 168 ff, and in *TLZ*, lxxix (1954), col. 760 f. — Ginzberg, in *MGWJ*, lviii (N.F. xii), (1914), pp. 402 ff, argued that the formula *mshyḥ 'hrn wysr'l* in CD refers to two Messiahs; this view has now been verified by 1QS ix 11: *wmshyḥy 'hrwn wysr'l*. For a discussion of the messianic expectations of the Qumran community, see also Burrows, in *ATR*, xxxiv (1952), pp. 203 ff.

in everlasting peace and joy in the glorious light of heaven, as opposed to the never ending sufferings in the murky depths of hell in store for the impious (iv 6 ff, 11 ff). A certain dualistic way of thought is noticeable, particularly in iii 13-iv 26, but God is supreme: He has arranged everything beforehand, and He will destroy evil when the time is due (iii 23, iv 18 f) [1]).

The name of the community is not given, except that they called themselves 'sons of Light' (i 9, iii 13, 25), 'sons of Righteousness' (iii 20, 22, ix 14), 'sons of Truth' (iv 5), 'men of Holy Perfection' (viii 20), 'men of Holiness' (v 18), 'council of Holiness' (viii 21), 'those who devote themselves' (v 8), the '*Yaḥad*' (i 1 etc.)

The interpretations of the historical allusions in 1QpHab vary a great deal [2]), but a number of scholars find the time of Antiochus Epiphanes reflected in that manuscript [3]), in which case we are brought to the assumption that the Teacher arose somewhere in the first half of the second century B.C., and that the schism took place at that time, but this early dating cannot be accepted unless it is corroborated by other evidence.

(b) We are thus brought to the problem of the literary relationship of the Scrolls, particularly 1QS, with other writings.

That 1QS (and 1QpHab) are closely connected with *CD*, is realized by all scholars and, indeed, the points of contact are so striking that it can hardly be doubted that all these manuscripts originate from the same religious circles [4]). The evidence is overwhelming and need not be given here [5]). Suffice it to say that a fragment of CD has been found in one of the Dead Sea caves [6]), and that the Law Book of the community, the so-called *Sepher Hagu* mentioned in CD, is also referred

---

[1]) As for the eschatology in the Scrolls, see DELCOR, in *RSR*, xciv (1952), pp. 363 ff; COPPENS, in *NC*, v (1953), pp. 5 ff; VAN DER PLOEG, in *VT*, ii (1952), pp. 171 ff; RABINOWITZ, *ibid.*, iii (1953), pp. 175 ff.

[2]) All the theories have been collected and discussed by ELLIGER, *Studien zum Habakkuk-Kommentar vom Toten Meer*, pp. 226 ff. — The references in the *Nahum-Commentary*, published by ALLEGRO in *JBL*, lxxv (1956), pp. 89 ff, are equally obscure and cannot, as the editor thinks, be taken to prove that the persecution of the Teacher of Righteousness took place during the reign of Janneus, see ZEITLIN, in *JQR*, xlvii (1956-57), p. 32, and especially ROWLEY, in *JBL*, lxxv (1956), pp. 188 ff.

[3]) See ROWLEY, *The Zadokite Fragments and the Dead Sea Scrolls*, pp. 64 ff, where ample references to literature are given.

[4]) See ROWLEY, *ibid.*, p. 3 and p. 31, n. 2.

[5]) Some of the parallel passages have been collected and discussed by the present writer, in *JSS*, i (1956), pp. 110 ff.

[6]) Cf. DE VAUX, *op. cit.*, lx (1953), p. 86.

to in 1QSa [1]). Admittedly, there are differences between CD and 1QS, but they are satisfactorily explained on the assumption that CD and 1QS were written at different stages in the development of the movement [2]), although it is hardly possible to say with certainty which of the two reflects the earlier stage.

1QS is also closely connected with the Wisdom literature, especially *Ecclesiasticus* [3]). In both writings the emphasis is put on wisdom gained by study of the Law (Ecclus. vi 37, xxiv 23 ff, xxxii (xxxv) 14 f, cf. 1QS v 11 etc.) [4]); both inculcate virtues like patience, humility, self control, and good table manners (Ecclus. ii 1 ff, iii 17 ff, xviii 21, cf. 1QS ii 24 f; Ecclus. xxxi (xxxiv) 12 f, cf. 1QS vii 13 ff); both insist that ritual acts are of less importance than true piety, and that the ideal sacrifice is living according to the Law and keeping away from wickedness (Ecclus. xxxiv (xxxi) 18 ff, xxxv (xxxii) 1 ff, cf. 1QS ix 4 f, iii 10 f); but in both writings we find at the same time extensive use of sacrificial terminology and interest in the priesthood of Zadok [5]); both warn against hypocrisy, haughtiness, and inconsiderate speech (Ecclus. iv 20 ff, v 9 ff, cf. 1QS iv 9 ff and vii 9), and against association with the wicked (Ecclus. viii 10 f, xi 29 ff, cf. 1QS v 13 ff etc.); both proclaim God's complete control over the world (Ecclus. xlii 15 ff, cf. 1QS iii 15 ff); both teach that secrets can only be received by the humble (Ecclus. iii 19 ff, cf. e.g. 1QS xi 3 ff, iv 5 f). On the other hand, there are significant differences: Ecclesiasticus is void of the half ascetic note which is clear in 1QS; as a matter of fact, Sirach's interest is tied up so firmly with earthly matters that there is no room for eschatology, his conception of the hereafter is that of the Old Testa-

---

[1]) Cf. DE VAUX, *ibid.*, lvii (1950), p. 427.

[2]) Some of these differences have been collected by the present writer, in *ST*, *vol. cit.*, pp. 42 ff.

[3]) The connection between CD and Ecclesiasticus was noted already by LÉVI, in *REJ*, lxi (1911), pp. 165 ff. As for 1QS ,see TRINQUET, in *VT*, i (1951), pp. 287 ff, and WINTER, *ibid.*, v (1955), pp. 315 ff.

[4]) Some scholars would find Gnosticism in the Scrolls, see MARCUS, in *JBL*, lxxiii (1954), pp. 157 ff; SCHOEPS, in *ZRGG*, vi (1954), pp. 1 ff and 276 ff; SCHUBERT, in *TLZ*, lxxviii (1953), cols. 495 ff; SONNE, in *HUCA*, xxiii, part i, (1952), pp. 275 ff; WIEDER, *op. cit.*, iv (1953), p. 165. It is important, however, to realize the intensely practical aspect of 'knowledge' in e.g. 1QS, cf. REICKE, in *SBU*, No. 14 (1952), p. 61, n. 11, and p. 64, n. 23, and in *NTS*, i (1954), pp. 137 ff; DAVIES, in *HTR*, xlvi (1953), pp. 129 ff.

[5]) As far as Ecclesiasticus is concerned, see PFEIFFER, *History of New Testament Times, with an Introduction to the Apocrypha*, p. 367 and p. 374. Cf. 1QS iii 4 ff (alluding to Lev. xvi and xxiii, dealing with the ritual on the Day of Atonement) and v 2 ff (the priests are the sons of Zadok).

ment; accordingly, God rewards and punishes here on earth [1]). It seems, therefore, that our pious shared a number of characteristics with the circles which cherished the Wisdom literature; the lack of the apocalyptic and eschatological aspects in the latter, however, makes it clear that the Qumran community with its intense interest in the hereafter, cannot be identified with the circles from which the Wisdom literature sprang—but the points of contact are nevertheless significant.

For parallels to the eschatology of 1QS we must look in the *Pseudepigraphical literature*. Already, SCHECHTER, in his edition of CD, found the Book of Jubilees mentioned in CD xvi 3 and regarded CD iii 13 ff, vi 18 f as reflecting the same heretical calendar as is proclaimed in Jub. vi 34 ff [2]), and scholars have again and again pointed to the close connection between CD and Pseudepigraphical literature [3]). When the Scrolls were found, it was immediately recognized that they must originate from circles closely related to those which produced the Pseudepigrapha, and this impression is proved beyond dispute by the find of a fragment of the Book of Jubilees in the same cave in which 1QS was found [4]).

(c) The close relationship between 1QS on the one hand and CD, Ecclesiasticus and the Pseudepigraphical literature on the other makes it clear that the former group of writings originate in roughly the same time as the latter. CD has been variously dated, but many scholars have maintained an early Maccabaean dating, and some have placed the origin of the movement in pre-Maccabaean times [5]).

---

[1]) Cf. PFEIFFER, *op. cit.*, p. 385.

[2]) See *Documents of Jewish Sectaries*, I, p. xvi f.

[3]) Thus e.g. BACHER, in *ZHB*, xv (1911), p. 14 f; BERTHOLET, in *Budde Festschrift*, p. 31; MEYER, *Die Gemeinde des Neuen Bundes im Lande Damaskus*, p. 9 f, p. 38 f, and p. 53; SEGAL, in *JQR*, N.S. ii (1911-12), p. 140 f; GRESSMANN, in *ZDMG*, lxvi (1912), p. 499 f; MOORE, in *HTR*, iv (1911), p. 337, p. 348, and p. 359; HVIDBERG, *Menigheden af den nye Pagt i Damascus*, p. 282 f; BARNES, in *JTS*, xii (1910-11), p. 301; REICKE, in *ST*, ii (1949-50), p. 52.

[4]) See DE VAUX, *op. cit.*, lvi (1949), pp. 602 ff. As for the relationship between the Scrolls and Pseudepigraphal literature, see DELCOR, in *RB*, lviii (1951), pp. 535 ff; BROWLEE, in *BASOR*, No. 123 (1951), pp. 30 ff, and *The Dead Sea Manual of Discipline* (*BASOR* Supplementary Studies, No. 10-12, 1951), *passim*; FLUSSER, in *IEJ*, iii (1953), pp. 30 ff; ROWLEY, *The Zadokite Fragments and the Dead Sea Scrolls*, p. 66, n. 3; MOLIN, *Die Söhne des Lichtes*, pp. 158 ff; OTZEN, *op. cit.*, *vol. cit.*, pp. 125 ff.

[5]) BARNES, *op. cit.*, *vol. cit.*, pp. 301 ff; BERTHOLET, *op. cit.*, pp. 31 ff; GRESSMANN, *op. cit.*, *vol. cit.*, pp. 491 ff, and *Die Religion des Judentums*, p. 15; MEYER, *op. cit.*, p. 29; MOORE, *op. cit.*, *vol. cit.*, pp. 330 ff; LEVI, *op. cit.*, lxiii (1912), p. 4; LAUTERBACH, in *JQR*, N.S. vi (1915-16), pp. 47 ff; VOLZ, *Die Eschatologie der jüdischen*

Ecclesiasticus was probably written ca. 180 B.C. [1]; the Book of Jubilees, and therefore also at least the early parts of the Book of Enoch and the Testaments, have been ascribed to pre-Maccabaean, or early Maccabaean, times [2]. It is therefore possible to assume that 1QS reflects the same period, and that the religious circles behind this manuscript existed in pre-Maccabaean times, but were reorganized by the Teacher early in the Maccabaean period [3].

KOHLER [4] identified the circles behind CD as *Samaritan*, but his theory has been rejected on the ground that CD contains numerous allusions to the prophetic writings [5]; that the Scrolls show affinities with the Samaritan dialect is only interesting from a philological point of view, because this circumstance shows that there were religious communities other than the Samaritans, in which old linguistic tradition was preserved, and no religio-historical conclusions may be drawn from this.

G. MARGOLIOUTH [6] identified the circles behind CD as *Christian*, and when the Scrolls were found this theory was vigorously defended by TEICHER [7]. It is contradicted by the general lack of specifically

Gemeinde im neutestamentlichen Zeitalter, p. 15; ROWLEY, *The Relevance of Apocalyptic*, p. 72, and in *BJRL*, xxxv (1952-53), pp. 137 ff; KAHLE, *The Cairo Geniza*, p. 11 f, and in *TLZ*, lxxvii (1952), col. 409.

[1]) See PFEIFFER, *op. cit.*, p. 366 f.

[2]) See CHARLES and COWLEY, in *JQR*, xix (1906-07), p. 567; FINKELSTEIN, in *HTR*, xxxv (1942), p. 312, and xxxvi (1943), pp. 19 ff; MEYER, *Ursprung und Anfänge des Christentums*, ii, pp. 45 ff; ZEITLIN, in *JQR*, N.S. xxx (1939-40), pp. 8 ff; OESTERLEY, *The Jews and Judaism during the Greek Period*, pp. 74 ff; GRESSMANN, *Die Religion des Judentums*, p. 14; ROWLEY, *The Relevance of Apocalyptic*, pp. 54 ff, and *The Zadokite Fragments and the Dead Sea Scrolls*, p. 65, n. 1 and p. 77.

[3]) From the survey of the history of the sect in CD i, it is clear that the circles existed before the rise of the Teacher, and that the work of that great leader consisted of reorganizing those already existing groups on new principles. For this early dating of the non-biblical scrolls and the rise of the movement, see BURROWS, in *OS*, viii (1950), pp. 184 ff; HYATT, in *ATR*, xxxiv (1952), p. 239; AVI-JONAH, in *IEJ*, ii (1952), p. 2 ff; SUKENIK, in *MG*, I, p. 18, n. 6; BLACK, in *JJS*, i (1949), p. 199; DELCOR, in *RHR*, cxliv (1953), p. 13 f; EISSFELDT, in *TLZ*, lxxiv (1949), col. 98; SEGAL, in *JBL*, lxx (1951), p. 145; GINSBERG, in *BASOR*, No. 112 (1948), p. 22; REICKE, in *ST*, ii (1949-50), p. 53 f; ROWLEY, *The Zadokite Fragments and the Dead Sea Scrolls*, pp. 62 ff; for futher literature, see *ibid.*, p. 19, n. 5 and n. 6.

[4]) *AJT*, xv (1911), pp. 404 ff.

[5]) Cf. already MOORE, *op. cit.*, *vol. cit.*, p. 353.

[6]) *Athenaeum*, No. 4335 (November 26th, 1910), pp. 657 ff, and in *Expositor*, 8th series, ii (1911), pp. 499 ff, iii (1912), pp. 213 ff. Cf. also SCHOUSBOE, *La secte juive de l'Alliance Nouvelle au pays de Damas*.

[7]) *JJS*, ii (1951), pp. 67 ff, and pp. 115 ff, iii (1952), pp. 53 ff, pp. 111 ff, pp. 128 ff and pp. 139 ff, iv (1953), pp. 1 ff, pp. 49 ff, pp. 93 ff, and pp. 139 ff, v (1954), p. 38, and in *VT*, v (1955), pp. 189 ff.

Christian ideas in both CD and the Scrolls, and by the archaeological evidence which, on the assumption of a post-Christian date for the composition of the manuscripts, would leave very little time for the history of the community and the writing, copying and deposit of the Scrolls. It is possible that these writings contain material of importance for the understanding of the rise of Christianity, but this belongs to the field of New Testament scholarship and cannot concern us here.

The archaeological evidence also precludes the possibility of assuming that the circles behind CD and the Scrolls were *Karaitic*, and the possible links between our manuscripts and Karaitic writings can be explained by assuming that the former influenced the latter [1]).

There are a great number of similarities between 1QS and the information we get about the *Essenes* from Philo and Josephus [2]). It is therefore not to be wondered at that most scholars are of the opinion that the Scrolls are Essenic, and that consequently 1QS, composed during the first half of the second century B.C., informs us of the life and beliefs of this ancient Jewish sect at an early stage of its history [3]). Pliny, in his *Natural History* v 17, tells us that the

---

[1]) Karaite influence in CD was assumed by Lagrange, in *RB*, ix (1912), p. 330 f, and when the Scrolls appeared his view was taken up by Zeitlin, *op. cit.*, N.S. xli (1950-51), pp. 32 ff, and by Weis, *ibid.*, *vol. cit.*, pp. 125 ff; cf. Szyszman, in *VT*, ii (1952), pp. 343 ff, and iii (1953), p. 411 f, and Wieder, *op. cit.*, vi (1955), p. 14. — As for the theory that the Karaites were influenced by the writings produced by the Qumran circles, see the full account and discussion by Rowley, *The Zadokite Fragments and the Dead Sea Scrolls*, pp. 22 ff. That the CD circles were the precursors of the Karaites is a view held by Lévi, *op. cit.*, lxi (1911), p. 161 f, and by Moore, *op. cit.*, *vol. cit.*, p. 376 f. It may not be irrelevant, however, to draw attention to the fact that Poznanski, an outstanding specialist in Karaitic literarure, in *Jewish Review* (1911), pp. 273 ff and (1912), pp. 443 ff (the articles have not been accessible to the present writer), denied the Karaitic origin of CD, cf. also Revel, in *JQR*, N.S. iii (1912-13), pp. 352 ff, who compares the *halaka* of CD with that of Karaitic writings and reaches the conclusion that there are no points of contact.

[2]) The entire material has been collected by Dupont-Sommer, *Aperçus préliminaires*, pp. 105 ff, and *Observations sur le Manuel de Discipline*. Cf. Moore, *op. cit.*, *vol. cit.*, p. 350, n. 51; Lagrange, *op. cit.*, *vol. cit.*, p. 344 f; Lévi, *op. cit.*, lxiii (1912), p. 9 f; Brownlee, in *BA*, xiii (1950), pp. 56 ff; Burrows, in *OS*, viii (1950), pp. 167 ff; Marcus, *op. cit.*, lxxi (1952), pp. 207 ff; Kahle, in *VT*, i (1951), p. 47; Trinquet, *ibid.*, *vol. cit.*, p. 291; Hyatt, *op. cit.*, *vol. cit.*, p. 238; Vermès, *Les manuscrits du désert de Juda*, pp. 64 ff; Kuhn, in *ET* (1951), pp. 510 ff; Schubert, in *Nötscher Festschrift*, p. 232 f; Mowry, in *BA*, xvii (1954), p. 82. Against this view, see Gottstein, in *VT*, iv (1954), pp. 141 ff; Dhorme, in *CRAI* (1951), p. 194.

[3]) The few points of disagreement between 1QS on the one hand and Philo and Josephus on the other, are easily explained by the fact that 1QS was composed

Essenes lived in settlements on the north west coast of the Dead Sea, which is precisely where Qumran is situated. It is also curious to note that ancient rabbinic tradition has it that the Essenes were the spiritual descendants of the Rechabites, who, at the division of Palestine, were given the area round Jericho [1]), and that 1QS in two passages (vi 2, 14) appears to allude to Jer. xxxv, our only source of information about the Rechabites in the Old Testament; in fact, the possibility is not to be excluded that 1QS, in the frequent use of the root *ndb*, particularly in plates i and v, alludes to the name of the founder of the Rechabite sect.

If we are correct in assuming that the Qumran community felt itself heirs of ancient Rechabite tradition, it is equally indisputable that its *halaka*, as we know it from CD, is closely akin to traditional rabbinic *halaka* [2]), and that some of its practices have exact parallels in what we know from Talmudic sources about the old rabbinic *ḥavurot* [3]). That the various sections of Jewry in the last centuries B.C. had much in common cannot be doubted; tradition has it that there were eight kinds of Pharisees, and that those Pharisees who lived in celibacy were the Essenes [4]), and it has long been suspected by modern scholars that, in fact, the Essenes were a kind of Pharisees[5]). Some scholars have suggested that the name 'Essenes' is the same as '*Ḥasidim*', the pious groups of Maccabaean and pre-Maccabaean times which later developed into the Pharisees [6]). If, therefore, the view that the Qumran community is Essenic is correct, we can, without becoming entangled in logical difficulties, adhere to our dating of 1QS in the first half of the second century B.C., and we

200 years or more before PHILO and JOSEPHUS gave their accounts. It is only reasonable to assume that the sect underwent some changes during that period, cf. ROWLEY, *The Zadokite Fragments and the Dead Sea Scrolls*, p. 82 f, and in *BJRL*, *vol. cit.*, pp. 149 ff. It is also to be noted that both PHILO, JOSEPHUS and PLINY were outsiders, possessing only superficial knowledge of the sect, see MOSBECH, *Essaeismen*, p. 24.

[1]) See KOHLER, in *JQR*, N.S. xi (1920-21), p. 160 f. For the relationship between the Essenes and the Rechabites, see GINSBURG, *The Essenes*, pp. 76 ff; MOSBECH, *op. cit.*, p. 304 f.

[2]) See GINZBERG, *Eine unbekannte jüdische Sekte*, *passim*.

[3]) See LIEBERMAN, in *JBL*, lxxi (1952), pp. 199 ff.

[4]) Cf. GINSBURG, *op. cit.*, p. 22, quoting Aboth de Rabbi Nathan, ch. xxxvii.

[5]) GINSBURG, *op. cit.*, pp. 72 ff.

[6]) As for the view that the Essenes and the *Ḥasidim* are identical, see GINSBURG, *op. cit.*, p. 30; MOSBECH, *op. cit.*, pp. 296 ff; ZEITLIN, *op. cit.*, N.S. xlv (1954-55), pp. 87 ff.

may regard our document as produced by early Essenes of the Maccabaean age, who indulged in Torah studies and apocalyptic speculations [1]).

---

[1]) As for the intense apocalyptic interest of the early Essenes, see especially Kohler, in *JQR*, *vol. cit.*, pp. 145, who claims that the Pseudepigraphical literature originated in the secluded Essenic communities on the north west coast of the Dead Sea.

TRANSLATION

Pl. i

1 .... for his life (?) ...[in
2 the ord]er [1] of the community [2]. He shall seek / God [3] in ... and
3 in ... in order to do what is good and right before Him [4], as / He
commanded through Moses [5] and through all His servants the
4 prophets [6]. He shall love [7] everything / which He has chosen, and
hate everything which He has rejected. He shall keep away from all
5 evil [8] / and adhere to all good action. He shall do truth and right-
6 eousness and justice [9] / in the land, and walk no more in the stub-
7 bornness of a guilty heart [10] and eyes of whoredom [11], / only
doing evil [12]. All those who devote themselves [13] to do the ordinan-
8 ces of God [14], shall be brought [15] / into the covenant of mercy [16] for
the community [17], into the council of God [18]. He shall walk perfectly
9 before Him [19] <according to> all the things / which have been
revealed [20] at the times fixed for their revelations [21]. He shall love
10 each one of the sons of light [22] / according to his lot [23] in the council
of God [24], and hate each one of the sons of darkness [25] according
11 to his guilt / at the time of God's vengeance [26]. All those who devote
themselves to His truth [27], all their discernment and their strength
12 / and their property [28] shall come into God's community, so that
they can clarify their discernment by the truth of God's ordinances
13 [29], and examine their strength [30] / according to His perfect ways,
and all their property according to His righteous counsel [31]. They
14 must not walk [32] away from a single one / of all God's words [33]
in their periods [34]; they must neither rush the times fixed for them,
15 nor flinch from [35] <any> / of the fixed times set down for them [36].
They must not turn aside from His true ordinances by walking
16 either to the right or to the left [37]. / All those who enter into the order
of the community, shall enter [38] into the covenant before God to
17 act / according to everything which He has commanded [39]; they must
not turn back from following after Him [40] because of any terror or
18 dread [41], affliction [42] / or agony [43] during the reign of Belial [44].
When they enter into the covenant [45] the priests / and the levites
19 praise the God of salvation [46] and all His true works [47], and all /
20 those who enter into the covenant say after them: "Amen, amen" [48].

21 Then the priests enumerate God's righteous deeds [49]) together
22 with <His> wondrous acts [50]), / and recount all the merciful acts
23 of grace towards Israel. Then the levites enumerate / the sins of the
children of Israel and all their guilty transgressions and their ini-
24 quities [51]) during the ascendancy / of Belial. [And], after them, [all]
those who enter into the covenant confess [52]) by saying: "We have
25 perverted ourselves, / we [have rebelled], we [have sinned] [53]), we
have acted impiously, we [and] our [fath]ers [54]) before us, by our
26 walking / [contrary to the covenant] [55]); true and righte[ous] is His
punishment of us and our fathers

Pl. ii

1 but His loving mercy He has [bes]towed upon us from eternity
2 and to eternity" [1]). And the priests bless [2]) all / the men of God's
lot [3]) who walk perfectly [4]) in all His ways [5]), and say: "May He
3 bless thee [6]) with every / good [7]) and keep thee from every evil [8]);
may He enlighten thy heart [9]) with immortal wisdom [10]) and favour
4 thee with eternal knowledge [11]). / May He lift up His merciful countenance upon thee for eternal peace" [12]). And then the levites curse [13])
5 all the men / of Belial's lot [14]) and proclaim and say: "Cursed be
thou [15]) because of all thy guilty wicked deeds. May God give thee
6 up / <to> terror [16]) through all those who breathe vengeance [17]).
May He visit upon thee [18]) destruction through all those who take
7 / revenge [19]). Cursed be thou without mercy [20]) <because of>
8 thy deeds of darkness. Damned be thou / in everlasting murky
fire [21]). May God not be merciful unto thee when thou callest [22]).
9 May He not forgive by wiping out thy iniquity [23]) / May He lift
up His angry countenance to wreak His vengeance upon thee [24]).
May there be no peace for thee [25]) at the mouth of any intercessors" [26]).
10 / And all those, who enter into the covenant, say after those who
11 bless and those who curse: "Amen, amen". / Further the priests and
the levites [27]) say [28]): "Cursed because of the idols of his heart which
12 he <worships>[29]) be / he who enters into this covenant and puts the
stumbling-block of his sin [30]) before him so that he backslides, (stum-
13 bling) over it. And if, / when he hears the words [31]) of this covenant [32]),
14 he blesses himself [33]), thinking: "Peace be [34]) with me, / for I walk
in the stubbornness of my heart"—may his spirit be destroyed [35]),
15 thirst as well as saturation [36]), without / forgiveness [37]). May God's
wrath and His angry judgments [38]) flare up [39]) against him [40]) for
16 everlasting destruction [41]), <and> may all / the curses of this

covenant stick to him[42]). May God separate him[43]) for evil, that he may be cut off[44]) from all the sons of light because of his back-
17 sliding / from God[45]) through his idols and the stumbling-block of his sin. May He put his lot among those who are cursed for ever"[46]).
18 / And all those who enter the covenant respond and say after them: "Amen, amen".
19 Thus[47]) they shall do year after year, all the days[48]) of the reign
20 of Belial. First the priests[49]) shall enter / into the order, according to their spiritual quality[50]), one after the other. After them the levites
21 shall enter, / and thirdly the whole people[51]) shall enter into the order, one after the other[52]), (arranged in groups of) thousands, hundreds, /
22 fifties and tens[53]), that every single Israelite[54]) may know his standing
23 place[55]) in God's community / for an eternal council. And no one shall either fall[56]) from his station, or rise from the place of his lot[57]).
24 / For they shall all be[58]) in the community of truth[59]), of virtuous humility[60]), of affectionate love[61]), and of right-minded intention
25 / towards one another, in a holy council[62]), and (shall be) members of an eternal assembly[63]). And every one, who despises[64]) to enter /
26 .....[of G]od in order to walk in the stubbornness of his heart, (shall) not ...... His true community, for his soul has

Pl. iii

1 abhorred instructions[1]) of knowledge of righteous judgments[2]). He is unable to repent, so that he might live[3]), and he is not to be
2 reckoned together with upright ones[4]). / His knowledge, strength and property shall not come into the council of the community[5]), for his cogitation (is done) <with impious sin>[6]), and there is conta-
3 mination / by his sitting[7]). He is not righteous when he walks[8]) in the stubbornness of his heart; in darkness he looks upon the ways
4 of light[9]), and <with>[10]) perfect ones/ he cannot be reckoned. He cannot purify himself[11]) by atonement[12]), nor cleanse himself by
5 water of purification[13]), nor sanctify himself[14]) in streams[15]) / and rivers, nor cleanse himself by any water of ablution[16]). Unclean, unclean
6 he is, as long as he rejects the statutes / of God, so that he cannot be instructed within the community of His council[17]). For it is by the spirit of God's true council[18]) that the ways of man, all his
7 sins, / are atoned[19]), so that he can behold the light of life[20]). It is by the holy spirit of the community in His truth[21]) that he can be
8 cleansed from all / his sins[22]). It is by an upright and humble spirit that his sin can be atoned[23]). It is by humiliating himself under all

9 God's ordinances [24]), that / his flesh can be cleansed [25]), by sprinkling with water of purification [26]), and by sanctifying himself with water of purity [27]). May he establish [28]) his steps for walking [29]) in perfection
10 / in all God's ways [30]), as He commanded [31]) at the fixed time of His revealing (them) [32]), without turning aside, to the right or to the left [33]),
11 and without [34]) / walking contrary to a single one of all His words [35]). Then [36]) he will be accepted by an agreeable atonement before
12 God [37]), and it shall be unto him / a covenant of everlasting community [38]).

13 It is for the wise man [39]) to instruct and teach [40]) all the sons of light [41])
14 concerning the genealogies of all mankind [42]), / with respect to both kinds of their spirits [43]) with the (different) characters of their actions [44]) in their generations [45]), and with respect to their visitation of afflic-
15 tions / together with their times of peace [46]). From the God of knowledge [47]) comes everything which is happening (now) and happens (at any time) [48]). Before they happen He sets down all <their designs>
16 [49]); / and when they come into existence [50]) they carry through their activity according to His glorious design. Nothing can be changed [51]).
17 In His power are / the qualities of all things [52]), He [53]) being the one who sustains them in all their doings [54]). He created man to rule
18 / over the earth [55]), designing two spirits [56]) for him in which to walk until the time fixed for His visitation [57]), namely the spirits
19 / of truth and of deceit. <From a spring>[58]) of light (emanate) the generations of truth [59]) and from a well of darkness (emerge)
20 the generations of deceit. / And in the hand of the prince of lights [60]) is the rule over all the sons of righteousness [61]), and in the ways
21 of light they walk [62]). In the hand of the angel / of darkness [63]) is all the rule over the sons of deceit [64]), and in the ways of darkness
22 they walk [65]). By the angel of darkness (comes) the aberration / of all the sons of righteousness [66]), and all their sins, their offences, their
23 guilt, and their iniquitous deeds (are caused) by his reign, / according to God's mysteries [67]), during the period fixed by Him [68]). All their afflictions and their times of suffering [69]) (are caused) by the ascen-
24 dency of his hostility [70]). / All the spirits which are allotted to him [71]), (strive) to trip up [72]) the sons of light, but Israel's God [73]) and His
25 true angel [74]) help [75]) all / the sons of light. He created the spirits of light and darkness [76]), and upon them [77]) He founded every work [78]), and .... every action, and upon their ways .... [79]). The one God loves for all

Pl. iv

1 eternity [1]), taking pleasure in all its doings for ever; the other—its assembly He loathes [2]), and all its ways He hates for ever.

2 These are their ways [3]) on the earth: to illuminate the heart of man [4]) and to level before him all the ways of righteousness [5]), of truth [6]),
3 and to make his heart fear God's statutes [7]). / A spirit of humility and patience [8]), of great compassion and constant goodness [9]), of prudence, insight, and wonderful wisdom [10]), which is firmly esta-
4 blished in all / God's secrets [11]), leaning on His great mercy [12]). A spirit of knowledge in every action upon which he is intent [13]),
5 zeal for righteous laws [14]), a holy intention / with a steadfast purpose[15]), great affection towards all the sons of truth [16]), and pure <worship> [17]), loathing [18]) all unclean idols, and walking with reservation [19])
6 / by means of wisdom about everything, concealing the truth of the mysteries of knowledge [20]). These are the <basic elements> [21]) of the spirit of the sons of truth of the earth, and the visitation of
7 all those who walk in it will be healing [22]) / and great peace in a long life, multiplication of progeny [23]) together with all everlasting blessings, endless joy [24]) in everlasting life, and a crown of glory [25])
8 / together with a resplendent attire [26]) in eternal light [27]).

9 But (the ways of) the spirit of deceit are: inextinguishable desire [28]) and inertia [29]) in righteous activity [30]), impiety and falsehood, pride
10 and haughtiness [31]), atrocious [32]) disguise and falsehood, / great hypocrisy [33]), fury, great vileness [34]), shameless zeal for abominable doings [35]) in a spirit of fornication [36]), filthy ways in unclean worship[37]))
11 / a tongue of blasphemy [38]), blindness [39]) of eyes and deafness [40], of ear, stiffness [41]) of neck and hardness [42]) of heart, walking in all
12 the ways of darkness [43]), and craft [44]). The visitation / of all those who walk in it will be many afflictions by all the angels of punishment [45]), eternal perdition [46]) by the fury of God's vengeful wrath [47]),
13 everlasting terror / and endless shame, together with disgrace of annihilation [48]) in the fire of murky Hell [49]). And all their times of generations [50]) (will be spent) in woebegone suffering [51]) and <bitter
14 misery> in dark abysses [52]) until / they have been destroyed [53]), there being no remnant and rescue for them [54]).

15 In these (two) are the genealogies [55]) of all mankind, and in their (two) classes [56]) all the hosts of their generations [57]) have a share;
16 in their (two) ways they walk, and the entire work / of their activity [58]) (falls) within their (two) classes, according to everybody's share,

large or small [59]), in all times for ever. For God has set them apart [60])
17 until the last / time [61]), having put eternal enmity [62]) between their (two) classes. (Objects of) abomination are the doings of deceit to truth, and (objects of) abomination are all the ways of truth to de-
18 ceit [63]). There is a fierce / struggle between all their qualities [64]), for they do not walk together. But God, in His mysterious wisdom [65]) and His glorious prudence, has put down a limited time [66]) for the
19 existence of deceit. At the time fixed / for visitation He will destroy it for ever, and then the truth of the earth will appear for ever [67]), for it has polluted itself by the ways of ungodliness [68]) during the
20 ascendency of deceit until / the time which has been decided for judgment [69]). Then God will purify all the doings of man by His truth and purge a part of mankind [70]). He will utterly destroy the spirit of deceit
21 from them [71]) / and clean His flesh [72]) by a holy spirit from all ungodly acts [73]). He will sprinkle upon it a spirit of truth like water of purification [74]), from all the abominations of falsehood and (from) being
22 polluted / by a spirit of impurity [75]), so that upright ones may achieve insight in the knowledge of the Most High [76]) and the wisdom of the sons of Heaven [77]), and the perfect in way [78]) become wise. For those
23 has God chosen for an eternal covenant [79]), / and theirs is all the glory of Adam [80]), without deceit [81]). All false actions will be put to shame. Until now [82]) the spirits of truth and deceit struggle in the heart of
24 man, / (some) walking in wisdom and (some) in vileness [83]). According to his share in truth [84]) and righteousness, thus a man hates deceit, and according to his assignment in the lot of deceit <and ungod-
25 liness>, thus / he loathes truth. For God has set them apart until the time of that which has been decided, and of the making of the
26 New [85]). He knows the work of their actions [86]) in all times / [of eternity], and He allots them [87]) to mankind for knowledge of good [and evil] [88]), [thus de-]ciding the fate [89]) for every living being, according to his spiritual quality .... [90]) visitation.

Pl. v

1 This is the regulation [1]) for the men of the community [2]) who devote themselves [3]) to turn away from every evil [4]) and hold fast [5]) to everything which He has commanded as His pleasure [6]): they shall separate
2 themselves from the assembly [7]) / of the men of deceit [8]). They shall be a community [9]), with Torah study [10]) and property, <submitting response> [11]) according to the sons of Zadok [12]), the priests who keep
3 the covenant, and according to the multitude [13]) of the men / of the

community who hold fast to the covenant [14]). According to them
the norm shall be decided [15]) about everything concerning Torah
study and property and submission of response [16]), so that truth,
4 unity and humility, / righteousness [17]) and integrity and affectionate
love [18]) and circumspect walking in all their ways, can be observed.
No one shall [19]) walk in the stubbornness of his heart, in order to go
5 astray after his heart [20]) / and his eyes [21]) and the thought of his
<guilty> mind [22]). They shall circumcise in the community the
foreskin of the mind [23]) and a stiff neck. They shall lay a foundation
6 of truth [24]) for Israel, for the community of an eternal / covenant [25]).
They shall atone [26]) for all those who devote themselves, for a
sanctuary [27]) in Aaron and for a house of truth in Israel [28]), and (for)
7 those who join them [29]) for a community. In suit and cause / they
shall find guilty all those who transgress (the) covenant [30]). These are
the <norms> of their ways [31]), according to all these statutes, when
they are gathered to the community: every one who enters [32]) into
8 the council of the community, / shall enter into God's covenant [33]) in
the presence of all those who devote themselves. He shall undertake
by a binding oath [34]) to return to the Torah of Moses [35]), according
9 to everything which He has commanded, with all / heart and soul,
according to everything which has been revealed from it [36]) to the
sons of Zadok, the priests who keep the covenant and seek His pleasure [37]), and according to the multitude of the men of their covenant
10 [38]) / who all devote themselves to His truth [39]) and to walking [40]) in
His pleasure. He shall undertake by oath [41]) to separate himself from
11 all the men of deceit who walk / in the way of ungodliness [42]). For they
cannot be reckoned [43]) as being in His covenant, since they have not
sought nor inquired after Him [44]) in His statutes, in order to know
12 the hidden things [45]) in which they go astray / incurring guilt, while
they do the revealed things with a lifted hand [46]), thus arousing
anger for judgment and taking of revenge [47]) by (the) curses of (the)
13 covenant [48]). In them He will execute great / judgments [49]) (resulting
in) eternal destruction without a remnant [50]). He must not enter into
the water [51]) in order to touch the pure thing [52]) of the men of holi-
14 ness [53]), for they cannot be cleansed / unless they turn away from their
wickedness [54]), for impurity [55]) clings to all those who transgress
His words. No one must be united to him [56]) in his possessions and his
15 property [57]), lest he load upon him / guilty sin [58]). But he shall keep
far away from him in everything, for thus it is written [59]): "Keep
16 far away from every false matter" [60]). No one of the men / of the

community must submit response according to them with respect
to any law and commandment [61]). No one must either eat [62]) or drink
anything of their property, or accept anything whatever [63]) from them/
17 without paying for it [64]), as it is written: "Cease ye from man, whose
breath is in his nostrils, for wherein can he be reckoned?" [65]). For /
18 all those who are not reckoned within His covenant, they and everything they have must be excluded. The man of holiness [66]) must not
19 lean on any works / of nothingness [67]), for nothingness are all [68]) who
do not care for His covenant. But all those who spurn His word [69])
He will destroy from the earth, for all their doings are pollution /
20 before Him [70]), and impurity [71]) clings to all their property [72]). When
he enters [73]) into the covenant to do according to all these ordinances,
for the community of a holy congregation [74]), they shall examine /
21 their spiritual qualities in the community, in their mutual relationship,
according to everybody's insight and actions [75]) in the Torah, on
the authority of the sons of Aaron who dedicate themselves in the
22 community to uphold / His covenant [76]) and to scrutinize [77]) all His
ordinances which He has commanded to do, and on the authority
of <the multitude of the children> of Israel[78]) who dedicate
23 themselves to return in the community to His covenant. / They shall
register them [79]) in the order, one before the other, according to his
insight and his doings. They shall all obey [80]) one another, the one in
lower rank the one in higher rank [81]). They shall examine [82]) their
24 spiritual qualities / and their actions year after year, promoting
one according to his insight and his perfect ways [83]), and setting
back another [84]) according to his perverseness [85]). They shall admonish
25 [86]) / one another [87]) in t[ruth], humility, and affectionate love [88]). He
26 must not speak to him [89]) with anger or with a snarl [90]), / or with a
[stiff] neck ... [in] a spirit of ungodliness, and he must not hate him
... of his heart [91]), for he shall admonish him at once [92]), so that he
does not

Pl. vi

1 bear sin because of him [1]); nor must anyone bring up any case against
his neighbour before the Many [2]) without proof [3]) before witnesses.
2 In these / they shall walk in all their exiles [4]), <according to>
everything which is found [5]), in their relationship with each other:
they shall show themselves obedient, the one in lower rank towards
the one in higher rank [6]), with respect to property and money [7]),
3 and they shall eat together, / say benedictions together, and give

counsel together. And in every place, in which there are ten men [8] of the council of the community, a priest [9] must not cease from them [10],
4 / and each member shall sit according to his definite rank [11] before him, and in that order [12] they shall be asked [13] for their counsel concerning every matter [14]. When they arrange the table for eating,
5 or the wine [15] / for drinking, the priest shall first stretch out his hand, in order to bless the bread first [16], or the wine for drinking, the
6 priest shall first stretch out his hand, / in order to bless the bread and the wine first [17]. In a place, where the ten are, there must not fail
7 to be a man [18], who studies the Torah [19] day and night / continually [20], (the members) relieving one another [21]. The Many shall spend the third part of every night of the year together [22], reciting from
8 the Book [23] and studying commandment(s) [24] / and saying benedictions together. This is the regulation for the session [25] of the Many: each member (shall sit) in his definite seat. The priests shall sit in the
9 first seats [26], the elders [27] in the next seats, and the rest / of all the people shall sit, each in his definite seat. In that order they shall be asked concerning judgment [28] and concerning any counsel and matter which the Many may have to discuss, each member submitting his
10 knowledge [29] / to the council of the community. No one must speak in the middle of the speech of another member, (thus interrupting) before he has finished talking [30]. Nor must he speak before the definite
11 rank of the one who is enlisted / before him [31]. The man, who is asked, may (only) speak in his turn [32]. At a session of the Many nobody must say anything which is not according to the pleasure
12 of the Many [33] and, indeed [34], / of the Inspector over the Many [35]. But any one who has something to say to the Many, without <the
13 wish> of the man who asks the council / of the community [36], that man may get on his feet [37] and say: "I have something to say to the Many". If they say [38] to him ("Speak"), then he may speak. <Any
14 one> [39] of Israel [40] <who> devotes himself / to join [41] the council of the community—the Examiner [42] at the head of the Many [43] shall take stock of him [44] with respect to his insight and his actions;
15 if he is amenable to ethics [45], he shall bring [46] him / into the covenant to turn to the truth and to step aside from all deceit [47], and then he shall instruct [48] him in all the laws of the community. Later, when he comes to stand before the Many [49], they shall all be asked /
16 concerning his affairs [50], and according to the counsel which the Many decide to give [51], he shall either draw near [52] or stay away. If he draws near to the council of the community he must not touch the

17 pure thing [53]) / of the Many, until he [54]) has examined him with respect to his spiritual quality and his actions [55]) within the space of a full year [56]); nor must he be mixed with the property of the Many [57]). /
18 When he has spent a year in the community, the Many shall be asked [58]) about his affairs, according to his insight and his actions in Torah. If, according to the priests and the multitude of the men of their
19 covenant [59]), the decision is made / that he should be admitted to the congregation [60]) of the community—then both his property and his
20 possessions shall be submitted [61]) to the hand / of the Inspector, to the possessions of the Many [62]). <And> he shall enter it into the account with his hand [63]), and he must not spend it on [64]) the Many. He must
21 not touch the drink [65]) of the Many until / he has spent a second year among the men of the community. When that second year has elapsed he shall examine him according to the Many [66]). If the decision is
22 made / to bring him near to the community, he [67]) shall enlist him in his definite place [68]) among his brethren, for Torah and law and pure
23 thing [69]), and for pooling of his property [70]). His counsel / and his response [71]) shall belong to the community.
24 These are the rules by which they shall be ruled [72]) by communal study [73]) according to the cases [74]): if there is a man among them who,
25 though he knows, lies / in a matter of property [75]), they (or: he) shall exclude him [76]) from the pure thing [77]) of the Many for one year [78]), and he shall be fined [79]) one fourth of his food [80]). And the one who
26 answers [81]) / his neighbour with a stiff neck <and speaks> with fury, thus refusing [82]) the <guidance> of his associate by rebelling [83]) against the word of his neighbour who is enlisted before
27 him [84]), / his hand has saved him [85]) and shall be fined on[-e] year . . . . [The one w]ho makes an oath [86]) in the honoured name [87]) . . . . .

Pl. vii

1 If anybody curses (God) [1]), either because of being terror-stricken with affliction [2]), or because of any other reason he may have [3]), while reciting from the Book [4]) or saying benedictions [5]) — he
2 (or they) shall exclude him [6]). / He must never again come back to the council of the community [7]); but if it is against one <of> the priests, who are registered in the Book [8]), that he speaks in wrath—he
3 shall be fined for one / year and shall be put into solitary confinement [9]), excluded from the pure thing of the Many; and if it is in thoughtlessness [10]) that he speaks, he shall be fined for six months. The one who lies
4 deliberately [11]), / shall be fined for six months. The man, who scoffs [12])

5 wantonly [13]) at his neighbour < > shall be fined for one year, / and
shall be put into confinement. The one who speaks to his neighbour
with <deceit> [14]), or plays false deliberately [15]) shall be fined for
6 six months; but if / it is against his neighbour that he commits a
fraud [16]), he shall be fined for three months, and if it is with the property of the community that he behaves fraudulently, and he wastes
7 it, then he shall refund it / in full [17]).
8 / If he cannot afford [18]) to refund it, he shall be fined for sixty days.
The one who bears a grudge against his neighbour wantonly [19]), shall
9 be fined for six months, one year [20]), / and the same punishment
applies to him who takes any revenge for himself [21]). The one who
speaks with his mouth an improper word [22]) (shall be fined) for three
months. For the one who interrupts his neighbour's speech [23])
10 (the fine is) / ten days. The one who lies down [24]) and falls asleep
at a session of the Many (shall be fined) for thirty days, and the same
punishment applies to the man who goes away at a session of the
11 Many, / aimlessly and wantonly up to three times at a session, he
12 shall be fined for ten days, but if he gets up / and goes away, then he
shall be fined for thirty days [25]). He who shows himself in public [26])
insufficiently dressed [27]), not being poor [28]), shall be fined for six
13 months, / and the man who spits into the session of the Many [29]),
shall be fined for thirty days. The one who stretches out his hand
14 from under his cloak [30]) so that, he / being clad in rags [31]), his nakedness is seen [32]), shall be fined for thirty days. The one who guffaws
15 improperly [33]), shall be fined for thirty / days. The one who stretches
out his left hand in order to recline on it [34]), shall be fined for ten days.
The man who walks round as a tale-bearer [35]) about his neighbour, /
16 he (or: they) shall exclude him for one year from the pure thing of
the Many, and he shall be fined, but <if>[36]) it is about the Many
that he walks round as a tale-bearer, then he (or: they) shall banish
17 him from them, / and he is never to come back again. The man who
grumbles against the congregation of the community, he (or: they)
shall banish him and he must never come back, but if it is against
18 his neighbour that he grumbles / wantonly, then he shall be fined
for six months [37]). The man whose spirit swerves [38]) from the congregation of the community [39]), by dealing treacherously [40]) with
19 the truth / and by walking in the stubbornness of his heart, if he comes
back he shall be fined for two years: in the first he must not touch
20 the pure thing of the Many, [41]) / and in the second he must not touch
the drink [42]) of the Many, and he shall sit behind all the (other)

21 men of the community. When two years / have elapsed [43]), the Many shall be asked [44]) concerning his affairs. If he (or: they) admit him, he shall be enlisted in his definite place [45]), and afterwards he may be
22 asked concerning judgment [46]). / And [47]) anybody who has been in the council of the community for as long as a period [48]) of ten years,
23 / and whose spirit then backslides by being treacherous [49]) towards
24 the community, and he leaves / the Many [50]) in order to walk in the stubbornness of his heart, (such a one) shall never come back to the council of the community [51]). If one of the men of the commu[-nity
25 has anything] [52]) to do / with him in his pure thing [53]) or his money .... the Many, his punishment shall be the same: he shall be ba[-nished] [54]).

Pl. viii

1 In the council of the community there must be twelve (lay-) men and three priests [1]), perfect in all that has been revealed from the whole
2 / Torah [2]), so that they [3]) can enact truth and righteousness, justice, affectionate love, and circumspect walking [4]) with one another, /
3 keep truth in the land with a steadfast mind [5]) and a broken spirit [6]),
4 pay off [7]) sin by doing justice / and suffering affliction [8]), and walk with everybody [9]) by the measure of truth [10]) and the norm of time [11]).
5 When these become [12]) in Israel / — the council of the community being established in truth—an eternal plant [13]), a holy house [14])
6 consisting of Israel, and a most holy congregation / consisting of Aaron [15]), true witnesses about uprightness [16]), chosen by (divine)
7 pleasure [17]) to atone for the earth [18]) and to punish / the impious [19]) —
8 then that [20]) is the tested wall, the costly cornerstone [21]). / Its foundations [22]) shall neither be shaken [23]) nor be dislodged from their
9 place [24]), a most holy dwelling [25]) / consisting of Aaron, with <eternal> knowledge [26]) of <His> covenant of uprightness [27]), offering up a sweet odour [28]), and a house of integrity and truth [29]) made up
10 of Israel [30]), / upholding the covenant [31]) of eternal ordinances [32]). They will be for acceptance [33]), thus atoning for the earth and deciding judgment over wickedness [34]), separating themselves without deceit [35]), when these have established themselves [36]) in the congregation of the community [37]) for two years in the integrity of a holy
11 way of life / in the council of the men of the community. Everything which has been concealed from Israel and is found [38]) by somebody
12 / who studies [39])—he shall not conceal it from these out of fear of a
13 backsliding spirit [40]). When these become a community / by these

norms in Israel [41]), they shall separate themselves from [42]) the session
of the <men> of deceit [43]) by going out into the wilderness in order
14 to clear His way there [44]); / as it is written: "In the wilderness make
clear the way of ...., level in the desert a highway for our God" [45]).
15 / This alludes to the study of the Torah [46]) [which] He commanded [47])
through Moses to do, according to everything which has been revealed
16 time and again [48]) / and according to that which the prophets have
revealed by His holy spirit [49]). No one of the men of the community,
17 of the covenant / of the community [50]), who abolishes one single
word from the regulations [51]) with a lifted hand, may touch the pure
18 thing of the men of holiness, / or know any of their counsel, until his
actions have become purified from all deceit [52]) by walking in a perfect
19 way of life. / Then he may be admitted into the council [53]) according
to the Many, and afterwards he may be enlisted [54]) in his definite
rank. In this manner [55]) every one who joins the community shall
be treated.

20 And these are the rules [56]) in which <the men of holy integrity>
21 [57]) shall walk with one another: / everyone who enters into the
council of holiness [58]) of those who walk in a perfect way of life,
22 as He commanded—everyone of them [59]) / who transgresses [60])
a word of the Torah of Moses with a lifted hand or a slack hand [61]),
he (or: they) shall banish him from the council of the community /
23 and he shall never come back again [62]). No one of the men of holiness
must mix with his property or with his counsel [63]) concerning
24 / any matter. But if it is in thoughtlessness [64]) that he does it, then he
shall be excluded from the pure thing and from the consultation, and
25 they shall study the rule [65]) / (which runs): "He must neither judge
anybody, nor be asked [66]) for any counsel for two years" [67]). If his
26 behaviour is faultless [68]) / in session, in study, and in consultation
[according to the Man]y [69]), if he does not sin thoughtlessly again
within the space of two years

Pl. ix

1 —for it is (only) because of one thoughtless sin that he can be punished
two years, whilst for the one who acts [1]) with a lifted hand (the punishment is that) he shall not come back again. Only the one who sins
2 thoughtlessly / can be tried for two years as to the integrity of his
way of life and his counsel according to the Many, and afterwards be
3 enlisted [2]) in his definite rank for a holy community [3]). / When these
become [4]) in Israel, according to [5]) all these norms, <a congrega-

4 tion>[6]) of the holy spirit of eternal truth, / they shall atone [7]) for iniquitous guilt and for sinful faithlessness, and <pay off>[8]) (sin) for the earth by means of the flesh of burnt-offerings and from the
5 fat pieces of the sacrifices of right offerings / of lips [9]) as a proper sweetness [10]), and a perfect way of life [11]) as a pleasing freewill offering [12]). At that time the men of the community shall separate them-
6 selves [13]) / as a sanctuary [14]) consisting of Aaron, of the community, as a Holiest of Holy and a house of community consisting of Israel
7 who walk in integrity [15]). / The sons of Aaron alone [16]) shall have control over judgment and property [17]). According to them the decision shall be made [18]) concerning every norm [19]) of the men of the com-
8 munity. / The property of the holy men who walk in integrity—their property must not be mixed with the property of the men of deceit [20]) /
9 who have not purified their way by separating themselves from deceit [21]) and by walking in a perfect way. They must not in any way
10 leave the council of Torah-study [22]), in order to walk / entirely in the stubbornness of their heart. They shall be judged by the first regulations in which in the beginning the men of the community
11 were instructed [23]), / until the coming of a prophet and the Messiahs from Aaron and Israel [24]).
12 These are the ordinances [25]) for the wise man [26]), in which he shall walk in his converse with every living being [27]). According to the
13 norm of every single time [28]) and the weight of every single man / he shall do God's will [29]), according to everything which has been revealed time and again. He shall study [30]) the entire wisdom which has
14 been found in chronological sequence [31]). / He shall set apart the ordinance of time [32]). He shall weigh the sons of righteousness [33]) according to their spiritual qualities [34]). He shall keep hold of the chosen
15 [35]) of time according to / His will as He commanded. He shall give everybody the treatment which is due to him according to his spiritual quality [36]). He shall admit him [37]) according to his cleanness of hands
16 [38]) and bring him near according to his insight. / In this way both the love of him and the hatred of him [39]) (shall be controlled). He
17 must not argue and quarrel [40]) with the men of perdition [41]). / He shall conceal the Torah-counsel <from> the midst of [42]) the men of deceit. He shall admonish [43]) with true knowledge and righteous
18 commandment those who choose / (the) way [44]), each according to his spiritual quality (and) according to the norm of time. He shall guide them with knowledge, and instruct them in the mysteries of
19 wonder and truth [45]) in the midst / of the men of the community,

so that they can walk flawlessly with one another in everything which has been revealed to them [46]). That is the time [47]) for levelling
20 the way / towards the wilderness [48]). He shall instruct them in everything which has been found to be done at the present time [49]). He shall separate himself from every man <of deceit> and <divert>
21 his way / away from all deceit [50]). These are the norms of the way of the wise man in these times, with respect to his love and his hatred:
22 (he shall keep up) eternal hatred / against the men of perdition in the spirit of concealment [51]). He shall leave to them property and labour
23 of hands, as a slave does to the one who rules over him, / (showing) humility before the one who lords it over him [52]). He shall be a man zealous for the ordinance and its time [53]), until the day of vengeance.
24 He shall do pleasure [54]) in all his outstretching of hand [55]) / and in all his reign, as He commanded. Then everything which is done, by that he will be accepted as a free-will offering [56]). Save in God's
25 will he has no delight [57]), / [and in all] the words of His mouth he finds pleasure [58]). Nor does he desire anything which He has not comman[ded, and the command]ment of God he always investigates
26 [59]). / [In affliction and distr]ess he praises his creator [60]). In whatever circumstances which may occur he reh[earses . . . . With the offering] [61]) of lips he praises Him

Pl. x

1 during the periods which He has decreed (?) [1]): at the beginning of the dominion [2]) of light during its coming round [3]); when it with-
2 draws itself to its due dwelling [4]); at the beginning / of the watches [5]) of darkness when He releases its store [6]) and spreads it over <the earth> [7]); as it is coming round whilst it is withdrawing itself from light [8]);
3 when / luminaries <shine forth> from the high abode of holiness [9]); whilst they withdraw themselves to the dwelling of glory; at the entering of the times appointed for the days of the new moon [10]),
4 both when they come round and during / their bonds, one after another [11]); when they are renewed (it means) greatness for the Holiest of Holy and a < > sign [12]) of the release of His eternal mercy [13]); at
5 the beginnings / of appointed times in every occurring period [14]); at the beginning of moons at the times appointed for them [15]); and on holy days [16]) in their fixed order, as a memorial [17]) at the times ap-
6 pointed for them. / With an offering of lips <I> will praise Him [18]) according to an ordinance which is engraved for ever [19]); at the beginnings of years [20]) and at the coming round of the times appointed

for them; at the completion of their definite measure of time [21]),
7 / every day its due, one after another [22]); at the time appointed for
harvest until summer; at the time appointed for sowing until the
time appointed for herbage [23]); at the times appointed for years until
8 their heptads [24]); / at the beginning of their heptads until the time
appointed for liberty [25]). As long as I live there is an engraved ordinance on my tongue for a fruit of praise [26]), the assigned lot of
9 my lips. / I will sing with skill [27]), and all my song is to the glory
of God. The lyre of my harp is (tuned) to the fixed measure of His
holiness [28]), and the flute of my lips I will play [29]) in tune with His
10 justice [30]). / Simultaneously with the entering of day and night I will
enter into the covenant of God, and during the going forth of evening
and morning [31]) I will recite His ordinances. Where they are [32]) I
11 will establish / my boundary without backsliding [33]). <By His
justice> I am chastened according to my perverseness [34]), and my
sins are before my eyes as an ordinance which is engraved. But God
12 I will call my righteousness [35]), / the Most High (I will call) the base
of my happiness, fountain of knowledge [36]), well of holiness, height
of splendour, the power of everything with eternal glory [37]). <I> will
13 choose what / He points out for me, and I will accept the way in
which He governs me [38]). So soon as I stretch hand [39]) and foot I
14 will praise His name [40]). So soon as I go out and come in [41]), / sit
down and get up [42]), and while I lie down on my couch, I will cry out
in exultation to Him. I will praise Him with the offering of the ut-
15 terance of my lips [43]) in the row of men [44]), / and before I lift my hand [45])
to enjoy the dainties of the produce of the earth [46]). In the beginning [47])
of terror and dread, and in the place of affliction and <distress> [48])
16 / I will bless Him by giving thanks distinctly [49]). I will meditate
upon His power [50]), and upon His mercy I will lean the whole day.
17 For I know [51]) that in His hand is the judgment / of every living
being [52]), and that all His actions are truth [53]). When affliction starts [54])
I will praise Him, and also at His salvation I will cry out in exulta-
18 tion [55]). I will not return evil to anybody, / with good I will pursue
mankind [56]). For with God rests the judgment of every living being,
He being the one who repays man [57]). I will not be envious with a
19 godless spirit [58]), / and wealth gained by violence [59]) my soul will
not desire. A man of perdition I will not prosecute [60]) until the day
20 of vengeance. But my anger I will not / turn [61]) away from the men
of deceit, and I will not feel satisfied until He has accomplished
judgment. I will not keep anger [62]) against them that turn away from

21 transgression [63]), and I will not have compassion / for all those who deviate [64]). I will not console [65]) them that are being obstinate [66]) until their way is perfect [67]). Belial [68]) I will not keep in my heart.
22 Neither shall lewdness [69]) / and iniquitous deceit be heard in my mouth, nor shall craftiness and lies be found on my lips. The fruit of holiness
23 shall be on my tongue, and detested words / shall not be found on it [70]). With thanksgiving hymns I will open my mouth [71]), and the righteousness of God shall my tongue enumerate always, together
24 with the faithlessness of man to the point of his complete / sinfulness [72]). Idle words I will remove from my lips, impure and tortuous thoughts from my mind [73]). With the counsel of wisdom I will conceal know-
25 ledge [74]), / and with the prudence of knowledge I will hedge [it] [75]) with a firm wall, keeping faithfulness and the strong decision of
26 God's righteousness [76]). I [will measu]re [77]) / an ordinance by the measuring-line of times .... righteousness, affectionate love towards the lowly [78]), and to strengthen [79]) the hands of the anx[ious] [80]) ....

Pl. xi

1 the erring of spirit understanding; to teach <them that rebel> instruction [1]); to answer with humility [2]) the haughty of spirit;
2 to behave with a broken spirit [3]) towards the men / of oppression [4]) who stretch forth a finger and speak iniquity and acquire wealth [5]). For as for me, the judgment concerning me belongs to God [6]). In His hand is my perfection of way and also my rectitude of heart.
3 / By His righteousness [7]) my sin is wiped out [8]). For from the fountain of His knowledge He has released His light [9]). My eye has beheld His
4 wonders, and the light of my heart [10]) has beheld the secret / of what happens and is happening for ever [11]). A support is at my right hand, on a firm rock is the way of my footstep [12]). It <shall not be
5 shaken> on account of anything [13]), for the truth of God is / the rock of my footstep, and His strength is the staff in my right hand. From the fountain of His righteousness, His justice [14]), a light has come into my heart from His wondrous mysteries. My eye has beheld
6 what is happening for ever, / wisdom which is hidden from man, knowledge and prudent discretion (which is hidden) from mankind,
7 a fountain of righteousness and a well / of strength as well as a spring of glory (which is hidden) from the assembly of humanity [15]). Those whom God has chosen He has established as an eternal possession [16]).
8 He has bestowed upon them a share in the lot / of the holy ones.

With the sons of heaven [17]) He has united their assembly for a council
of community. <Their assembly is a house of holiness> [18]) for an
9 eternal plant during every / occurring period [19]). Certainly [20]) I
belong to wicked mankind [21]); certainly I belong to the assembly of
deceitful humanity [22]). My sins, my iniquities, my transgressions,
10 as well as the perverseness of my mind [23]) / certainly belong to the
assembly of worms [24]) and of them that walk in darkness [25]). For the
way of man is <not>[26]) his (own affair). It is not man who makes
firm his step, but to God belongs the judgment and <in> His
11 hand [27]) is / the perfection of way. By His knowledge everything
happens. Everything which is happening—He fixes it by His design[28]),
and [nothing] happens without His intervention [29]). As for me, when /
12 I totter, the mercy of God is my salvation for ever [30]). When I stumble
over fleshly sin [31]), the judgment concerning me (is passed) by the
13 righteousness of God which stands [32]) for ever. / When my affliction
starts [33]) He rescues my soul from perdition [34]). He makes firm my
steps on the way [35]). In His compassion He draws me near, and in
14 His mercy He brings / my judgment [36]). In the righteousness of His
truth He judges me [37]). In His great goodness [38]) He condones [39])
all my sins. In His righteousness He pronounces me clean of impurity
15 / of man [40]) and (of) sin of mankind, in order that I should praise
God [41]) for His righteousness, and the Most High for His glory [42])
(in the following way): Praised be Thou, my God [43]), who openest
16 the mind of Thy servant unto knowledge [44]). / Direct in righteousness
all his actions. Establish the son of Thy handmaid [45]), as Thou art
17 pleased (to establish) those chosen of mankind to stand / before
Thee [46]) for ever. For without Thy intervention no way can be perfect.
18 Nothing happens without Thy will. Thou has taught [47]) / all knowledge. Everything which happens, happens with Thy will. There is
nobody else besides Thee [48]) to object to [49]) Thy counsel; to compre-
19 hend / anything of Thy holy design; to behold the depth of Thy
mysteries [50]); to understand all Thy wonders [51]), as well as the power /
20 of Thy strength [52]). Who can grasp Thy glory? [53]) What, indeed, is
21 man among Thy wondrous works [54]) ? / Woman-born [55]), <as what
can he be reckoned>[56]) before Thee?—he whose forming (was done)
with dust [57]) and whose dwelling [58]) is food for worms [59]), he, who
22 is saliva which has been emitted, / clay which has been nipped off [60]),
he whose longing [61]) is for the dust! As what can clay and that which
is shaped by hand <be reckoned>, and what counsel [62]) does it
understand?

TEXTUAL NOTES

(MS and MB refer to the photographs and the transcription in the edition by Burrows).

Pl. i

L. 1. MS reads ל[..........]שים, with a lacuna of 13-14 letters. Restore [בסר]ך היחד, cf. l. 16. — L. 2. MS reads ב[....] וב [....]. — L. 5. Emend מעשי to מעשה (Sukenik). — L. 8. Read להיחד (MB: להוחד). Emend כול to ככול, cf. viii 15, ix 13. — L. 11. Read יבואו (MB: יביאו), cf. iii 2 where MS reads יבואו. — L. 13. Read מכול (MB: בכול). — L. 14 f. Emend להתאחר מכול to להתאחר אחד מכול. — L. 16. An original יאבורו corrected to יעבורו. An original אלפני corrected to לפני. — L. 18. Read והיום. — L. 21. Emend גבורתום to גבורתו. — L. 22. Read חסדי רחמים, with MB. — L. 24. Restore [וכול] (van der Ploeg). — L. 25. Restore [פשענו חט]אנו הרשענו אנו [ואב]ותינו, with most scholars. An original בהלכתנו corrected to בלכתנו. — L. 26. Restore [קרי בברית] (Dupont-Sommer), cf. CD xx 29. Restore ובאבות[ינו]. Restore וצדי[ק].

Pl. ii

L. 1. Restore [ג]מל (Brownlee), cf. Isa. lxiii 7. — L. 5. An original מעשר corrected to מעשי. — L. 6. Emend אל זעוה to אל לזעוה (Iwry). — L. 7. Emend כחושך to בחושך, cf. l. 5. — L. 11. Emend לעבור to לעבוד. — L. 14. Read ונספתה (Brownlee). Read הרויה, with MB. — L. 15. Emend ידבקו to ודבקו, cf. Sept. — L. 24. Restore [ו]אהבת. — L. 25. Restore [אי]ש. An original בבעצת corrected to בעצת. — L. 26. Restore [בעצת א]ל (Habermann) or [בברית א]ל (Brownlee). Restore [יעבור ביח]ד (Brownlee).

Pl. iii

L. 1. Read למשוב (Milik; MB: למשיב). — L. 2. Read יבואו (Habermann; MB: יביאו). An original בבאון corrected; emend to באון (Ginsberg). An original וגולים corrected to וגאולים. — L. 3. Read בשיבתו (MB: בשובתו) and במתור (MB: במתיר). Emend וחושך to בחושך. Emend בעין to ועם (Barthélemy). — L. 9. Read דוכי (MB: דוכו). — L. 14. MS appears to read נגועיהם (MB: נגיעיהם). — L. 15. Emend מהשבתם (Barthélemy; MB: מחשבתם) to מחשבתם. — L. 19. Emend מעון to מעין. — L. 20. Read וביד (Habermann; MB: ביד).

Pl. iv

L. 5. Emend כבוד to עבוד. — L. 6. Read יחבא (MB: וחבא). Emend סודי to יסודי. — L. 12. An original נקמות corrected to נקמת (Barthélemy). — L. 13. Emend ורעת מרורים to ורע תמרורים. Read בהוות, with MB. — L. 18. Read perhaps להוית (Yalon; MB: להיות). — L. 23. Read והיה (Milik; MB: יהיה). — L. 24. An original ישנה corrected to ישנא. Emend ירשע to ורשע (Brownlee) and delete בו as a dittograph. — L. 26. Restore [עולמים] (Dupont-Sommer). Restore [ורע]. Restore לה[פיל] (Dupont-Sommer).

Pl. v

L. 2. Emend ומשובים to ומשיבים. — L. 4. An original והצצע corrected to והצנע. — L. 5. Emend ואאם to אשם (Burrows). — L. 7. Emend תכון to תכוני. — L. 10. Read יקים (Brownlee; MB: יקום). — L. 11. An original דרשו corrected to דרשהו. — L. 12. Emend לאששמה to לאשמה (Milik). An original משפטים corrected to שפטים (Brownlee). — L. 13. An original הנשי corrected to אנשי. — L. 14. Read ייחד (MB: יוחד). An original ובהושו corrected to ובהונו — L. 15. Read ישיב (MB: ישוב). — L. 16. An original מומא corrected to מאומה. — L. 20. An original הונום corrected to הונם (Milik). Read להיחד (MB: להוחד). — L. 22. An original רוב corrected to ר:ב (Barthélemy). — L. 24. An original להוגי corrected to להוכיח. — L. 25. Restore בא[מת], cf. ii 24. — L. 26. Restore וב[רוח.....קשה] בעורף. Between the restored letters 5-6 letters are lost. Read ישנאהו (MB: ישנא הו). Restore perhaps [בעורלת] לבבו (Brownlee). An original ביומור corrected to ביום.

Pl. vi

L. 2. Restore [כ]כול. — L. 3. An original לאחד corrected to ויחד. Emend החיד to היחיד or היחד. — L. 7. Emend על יפות to חליפות (Yalon). — L. 8. An original הזה corrected to וזה. — L. 11. Emend להפץ to לחפץ. — L. 12. Emend במעמד to במחמד. L. 13. Emend וכולה מתנדב to וכול המתנדב. — L. 14. Read ידורשהו (MB: ודורשהו), cf. l. 17. — L. 15. An original ולבינהו corrected to והבינהו (van der Ploeg). — L. 18. Read ישאלו (MB: ושאלו). — L. 19. An original יקריבו corrected to יקרבו. — L. 20. Read אל (Habermann; MB: על). — L. 20. Emend יכתבו to וכתבו. — L. 26. Emend ידבר to ודבר. Restore ל[פר]וע (Brownlee). Emend יסוד to יסור (Brownlee). — L. 27. An original ונאנעש corrected to וננעש; emend to ונענש. Restore א[ח]ת. After the restored *Ḥet* a gap of ca. 9 letters. Restore [אש]ר.

Pl. vii

L. 2. Emend על to אל. Emend בן to מן. — L. 3. An original על corrected to אל. Emend יכחס to יכחש. — L. 4. Read בלו (Milik; MB: בלי). Delete בדעהא as a dittograph. — L. 8. Read יטור (MB: יטיר). An original המשפט corrected to במשפט. — L. 9. Read ולמדבר (MB: ולמדבר). — L. 14. Read נרעתה (MB: נראתה); emend to נראתה. An original ישגק corrected to ישחק. — L. 16. Emend ואיש to ואם. — L. 17. Emend יסוד to סוד. — L. 19. An original אלוא corrected to לוא (MB: ולוא). — L. 20. An original בבאיר corrected to משקה. — L. 21. Emend אל to על. — L. 22. An original כול corrected to וכול. Above בעצת an *Ayin* was added, but later effaced. —. L. 23. Read ויצא מלפני (Milik; MB: יוצא·לפני). — L. 24. Restore איש מאנשי היח[ד אשר ית]ערב. — L. 25. Restore לש[לח הואה] (cf. l. 16) or לש[לח אותו].

Pl. viii

L. 1. Read תמימים (MB: תמימים). — L. 2. Emend אם to עם. — L. 4. An original ביסדת corrected to במדת. — L. 5. An original העצת corrected to עצת (Barthélemy). — L. 6. An original ובוחרי corrected to ובחירי. — L. 8. An original יזדעו corrected to יזדעזעו. Read מסקומם (Barthélemy; MB: ממקומם). — L. 9. Emend כולם to עולם (Iwry). Emend משפט ולקריב to משפטו לקריב. — L. 10. An original לחוחת corrected to לחוקות. Emend בהכין to בהכון. Emend ביסוד to בסוד. — L. 11. An original תסתר corrected to הנסתר. — L. 13. Emend הנשי to אנשי. — L. 14. Emend בערכה (Barthélemy; MB: בערבה) to בערבה. — L. 15. Restore [אשר]. — L. 17. Read יסיר (van der Ploeg; MB: יסור). — L. 19. An original יכתיו corrected to יכתב. — L. 20. Emend אנשי התמים קודש to אנשי תמים הקודש. — L. 21. Read מהמה (Barthélemy; MB: מהמה). — L. 26. Restore ם[על פי הרבי] (Milik).

Pl. ix

L. 2. Read יכתיב (MB: יכתוב). — L. 3. Emend ליסוד to לסוד. — L. 4. Emend ולרצון to ולרצת. Read זבחי תרומת (MB: זבח ותרומת). — L. 6. Read להיחד (MB: להוחד). — L. 11. An original ניא corrected to נביא. — L. 14. Read הצדיק (MB: הצדוק). — L. 17. Emend בתוך to מתוך. — L. 18. An original להנחום corrected to להנחותם. — L. 19. An original להולך corrected to להלך .An original ההיאה corrected to היאה. — L. 20. Emend איש ולוא הסר to איש עול ולהסר. — L. 25. Restore [ובכול]. Restore צו[ה ולמ]שפט. — L. 26. Restore [בצרה וצו]קה, cf. x 15 f. Restore יס[פר..........תרומת].

Pl. x

L. 2. Emend עלת to על תבל (VAN DER PLOEG). Emend באופיע to בהופיע. — L. 3. Delete נ. — L. 6. Emend הברכנו to אברכנו. An original ישנים corrected to שנים. — L. 10. An original אבוה corrected to אבואה. — L. 11. Emend ומשפטו to במשפטו. — L. 12. Emend מכין to מכון. Read מעין (BROWNLEE; MB: מעון). Read עולמ (MB: עולם). Emend הבחרה to אבחרה. — L. 13. An original ברששית corrected to בראשית. — L. 14. Read תרומת (BARTHÉLEMY; MB: תרומת). Read במערכת (BAUMGARTEN; MB: ממערכת). — L. 15. Emend בוקה to צוקה (BROWNLEE). — L. 19. An original אנש חת corrected to אנש שחת. An original לוא אפיא באף לשבי corrected to לוא אתפוש עד יום. — L. 24. An original אסתר corrected to אספר. — L. 25. Restore [בעד]ה (REICKE). Restore א[חלק]ה (MILIK). — L. 26. Read לניכנעים (MB: לנוכנעים). Restore לנמה[רי לב] (VAN DER PLOEG).

Pl. xi

L. 1. Emend רוכנים to רוגנים (GINSBERG). — L. 4. Emend יוד עוזע to יודעוע. — L. 5. Read משפטו (MB: משפטי). — L. 7. Read מעין (MB: מעון). Read נתנמ (MB: נתנם). — L. 8. Emend וסוד מבנית קודש to וסודם בית קודש. — L. 10. Emend לאדם to לוא לאדם. Emend מידו to בידו. — L. 11. Restore [כול]. — L. 13. Read יפתח (DRIVER; MB: יפטח). Read יביא (MB: יבוא). — L. 17. An original הודיתה corrected to הוריתה. — L. 21. Emend מה:ישב to מה יחשב. Read מדורו (HABERMANN; MB: סדורו). Read מצי רוק (MB: מצור רק). — L. 22. Emend מה ישיב to מה יחשיב.

COMMENTARY

Pl. i

[1]) Hebr. *srk*, typical of 1QS and CD (1QS i 16, ii 20, v 1, 23, vi 8, 22; CD vii 6, 8, x 4, xii 19, 22, xiii 7, xiv 3, 12). In rabbinic literature the word means 'habit' (see JASTROW's *Dictionary*, II, p. 1028). In the Greek version of an original source of the Testaments τάξις is used for *srk* (see CHARLES, *The Apocrypha and Pseudepigrapha*, II, p. 815), and it appears that in 1QS *srk* is used with the same shades of meaning as τάξις (see LIDELL and SCOTT's *Lexicon*, s.v.), viz. (a) (battle) array, order (i 16); (b) post or place in the array (vi 22); (c) ordinance, prescription (v 1, vi 8). In the latter meaning it is roughly synonymous with *ḥōq*, cf. CD vii 6, as compared with xix 2 f.

[2]) Hebr. *yḥd*. Perhaps it is meant to be one of the names of the sect (YALON). In the meaning 'community' the word has a biblical foundation (TALMON). 1QS viii 19, as compared with the parallel phrase in CD xiii 11, suggests that the word was used of the community as a whole (*yḥd* = *ʿdh*); it is the same as *yḥyd* in CD xx 1, 14, 32 (STERN). Several nouns of the *qaṭl* type appear in the Scrolls as belonging to the *qṭil* or *qṭul* types, and it is reasonable to assume that we have a similar case of alternative pronunciation in *yḥd*/*yḥyd*. MARCUS connects *yḥd* in 1QS with ὅμιλος, used in PHILO's and JOSEPHUS' descriptions of the Essenes.

[3]) *Drsh* is in Isa. viii 19, xi 10, Job v 8 constructed with the preposition *'l* (cf. VAN DER PLOEG), but Exod. xviii 15; 1 Sam. ix 9 etc., as well as the phraseology in 1QS v 11, recommends the taking of *'l* here as 'God'. The verb, in most of the passages in which it occurs in 1QS and CD (also CD i 10), has the connotation of seeking God by studying the Scriptures, cf. Targ. in Isa. lviii 2 and in Ps. cxix 10. The Tetragrammaton is constantly avoided in 1QS, in the commentary part of 1QpHab, and in CD. LÉVI argues that the tendency to avoid the Tetragrammaton may be found already in the Old Testament, and that therefore the frequent use of *'l* is not to be taken as a sign of a late date. —With *ldrwsh* starts a sequence of infinitives which all, except in cases of clear subordination, are to be translated as finite forms: they are the promises, to which the members of the community pledged themselves on renewing the covenant (BURROWS).

[4]) Cf. Deut. vi 18 (BROWNLEE), xii 28 where MT has *bʿyny* (*YHWH*) which Targ. and Pesh., for fear of anthropomorphism, render by

qdm (cf. Sept. ἐναντίον), corresponding to *lpnyw* in our passage. For *ldrwsh—lʿśwt*, cf. Ezra vii 10.

[5]) Cf. e.g. Joshua xxi 8. The name of Moses is spelt *plene* according to the usual habit of the scribes of the Scrolls who apply the *plene* writing to an excessive degree. The name is never spelt *plene* in MT (YALON). Cf. CD v 21 (BROWNLEE).

[6]) Cf. 2 Kings xvii 23, xxi 10, xxiv 2; Dan. ix 10; Ezra ix 11. — It is to be noted that in the Old Testament Moses and the prophets are never mentioned together; they are so in our passage and in CD v 21 f. This may be taken as an indication of the high esteem in which both the Torah and the prophetic writings were held by the religious circles behind the Scrolls and CD.

[7]) For ll. 3b-4a, cf. CD ii 15; 1Q22 i 5 f. The phraseology is biblically inspired, cf. Isa. vii 15, 16; Amos v 15; *kwl*, the object of 'love' and 'hate', has been taken as referring to things (MILIK) and persons (DUPONT-SOMMER). The latter interpretation is influenced by JOSEPHUS' *Jewish War* II 8, where we are told about the Essenes that they undertook μισήσειν δ'ἀεὶ τοὺς ἀδίκους καὶ συναγωνεῖσθαι τοῖς δικαίοις. This passage is, however, no exact equivalent to our text, and the continuation in ll.4-5 (*mkwl rʿ-bkwl mʿśy ṭwb*) appears to favour the impersonal interpretation of *kwl* in our passage.

[8]) Ll. 4b-5a, to which no parallel can be found in the Old Testament, seems to be an echo of a 'golden rule', used by both Jewish and Christian moral teachers, cf. e.g. Test. Asher iii 1 f (BROWNLEE); Test. Benj. viii 1; Rom. xii 9; 1 Thess. v 21 f.

[9]) Cf. v 3 f, viii 2, and the very close parallel in Test. Benj. x 3 where, as in our passage, 'truth', 'righteousness' and 'judgment' are objects of 'to do'. Cf. Jer. ix 23, with the Lord as subject, and Jer. xxiii 5, with the Davidic Messiah as subject.

[10]) 'Stubbornness of heart' also ii 26, vii 24, ix 10; CD ii 17 f, iii 5, 11 f, xix 19 (BROWNLEE), a favourite expression in Jer. (vii 24, ix 13, xi 8, xiii 10 etc.), cf. Deut. xxix 18. *'shmh* may be taken as an adjective (*'ashēmāh*), or as a substantive (*'ashmāh*); in either case it belongs to *lb*. The root *'shm* is frequent in 1QS (i 23, iii 22, v 15) and CD (i 9, ii 16, ix 12, xv 4).

[11]) Hebr. *ʿyny znwt*, cf. Ezek. vi 9; Num. xv 39 (BROWNLEE); in Targ. at the latter passage the verb *znh* is taken figuratively and is rendered by *ṭʿʾ* 'go astray', which agrees with the figurative usage of 'whoredom' in Jer., Ezek., in Hos., as an expression for faithlessness and backsliding, cf. CD ii 16: *wʿny znwt ky rbym tʿw bm*.

[12]) Cf. Isa. lvi 2.

[13]) Hebr. *hndbym*. The word has been read as participle Qal (HABERMANN), as *nedhābhīm* (KUHN), and as participle Niphal (BROWNLEE). For the latter interpretation, cf. the Hitpael forms in pl. v. — The use of the root *ndb* in 1QS is closely related to that of Targ. in Ps. cx 3 (*dmtndbyn l'wryyt'*), and to the Midrashic interpretation of *ndyb* (Num. xxi 18) in CD vi 8 ff. Both *ndbym* in pl. i and *mtndbym* in pl. v should be taken as designations for the community as a whole (BROWNLEE), and not for a group within it, viz. the newcomers applying for membership (against DUPONT-SOMMER). All the members renewed the covenant every year, cf. ii 19 and note.

[14]) Cf. e.g. Deut. xxvii 10, xxviii 15.

[15]) Hebr. *lhby*, translated as passive (BURROWS). This fits the context, as in this section the community as a whole is envisaged, and not only the Overseer whose responsibility it was to admit new members (cf. vi 14 f). For the omission of *Aleph*, cf. *GK* § 74k. It would be syntactically possible to regard *l'śwt* as governed by *lhby* (VAN DER PLOEG): 'and to bring all .... to do (i.e. make them do)' etc. The parallel phrase in vi 14 f, however, speaks against that interpretation.

[16]) Cf. Deut. vii 9 (BROWNLEE), quoted in CD xix 1 f. None of the versions supports the rendering in 1QS. *Ḥsd* here, as in the biblical passage, means the divine mercy (DUPONT-SOMMER), rather than any human virtue (against BROWNLEE).

[17]) All scholars take *lhyḥd* (by many read as *lhwḥd*) as a verb (Niphal or Hitpael). The dependence of the immediately preceding words on Deut. vii 9, suggests that *lhyḥd* in 1QS is our author's interpretation of *l'hbyw* of the biblical passage which in this way was applied to the community exclusively. In favour of this interpretation we may also refer to the usual biblical construction according to which *hbryt whḥsd* is followed by the preposition *l*, thus introducing the group for which the divine mercy is meant (see 1 Kings viii 23; Dan. ix 4; Neh. i 5; 2 Chron. vi 14). For the retention of *He* of the article after *l*, see *GK* § 35n.

[18]) Or: 'in the counsel of God' (SUTCLIFFE). The word *'ṣh* is used in the meaning 'counsel' in i 13 and xi 18, but in other passages (ii 25, iii 2, 6, vi 16, vii 2, viii 1, 5) it appears to be the equivalent of *'dh* and *swd*. In this meaning the word is used in Aramaic and Christian-Palestinian (YALON).

[19]) Cf. Gen. xvii 1 (BROWNLEE); Jub. xxi 2; Test. Issach. iii 2 (RABIN, in note on CD ii 16).

[20]) Hebr. *hnglwt*. The question whether this word refers to the Torah (VAN DER PLOEG) or to the revelations of the hidden meanings of the Torah (SUKENIK) is tied up with the interpretation of the phrase following.

[21]) Hebr. *lmwʿdy tʿwdwtm*, cf. iii 10. *Mwʿd* has been taken in the meaning 'assembly' (SUKENIK), but Num. xvi 22 and Ps. lxxiv 8, in which passages the word has this meaning, offer no parallel to the phraseology of our passage, and the suffix in *tʿwdwtm* does not necessarily refer to the members of the community, but may go back to *hnglwt* (cf. *GK* § 135o); furthermore, an interesting parallel to our passage is contained in CD iii 14 f: *wmwʿdy kbwdw ʿydwt ṣdqw* where *ʿydwt* is to be read as *ʿddwt* ('periods' = *ʿttwt*). DRIVER, in a letter, agreeing to this interpretation, draws my attention to Jer. xi 14; Ezek. xxii 4, where *ʿd* is taken by the versions as 'period'. So there seem to be good reasons for retaining the usual meaning of *mwʿd* also in our passage, and this may be supported by reference to viii 15, ix 13 where *ʿt* seems to correspond to *mwʿd* of i 9. YALON also takes *mwʿd* here as 'time', and paraphrases: 'everything which is revealed for Israel in the times of the covenants', finding an allusion to an old rabbinic tradition (*Berakot* 48b, bottom), that the Torah was given at three covenants. However, the idea of a constant stream of revelations, gained by the study of the Torah, appears to be something fundamentally characteristic of the spiritual activity of the society, cf. viii 11 f.

[22]) I.e. the members of the community, also ii 16, iii 13, 25, not in CD. Cf. Luke xvi 8; John xii 36; 1 Thess. v 5; Eph. v 8 (BROWNLEE); Enoch cviii 11 (*tewweld 'enta berhān*).

[23]) As in CD xiii 12 *gwrl* is in 1QS often used with a reference to the different ranks of the members within the society (DELCOR). DUPONT-SOMMER finds in the word a strong fatalistic note, as we know it from Zoroastrian way of thought.

[24]) Or: 'by the counsel of God', cf. note 18 above.

[25]) Cf. Wisd. of Sol. xvii 2: 'prisoners of darkness'.

[26]) Cf. e.g. Num. xxxi 3; Jer. l 15. — *bnqmt* does not belong to the preceding *k'shmtw* (against BROWNLEE), nor is it necessarily parallel to *bʿṣt* in l. 10 (against MOLIN). The preposition is best taken as indicating time.

[27]) YALON regards *'mt* as being used here in the meaning of *bryt*. The word is better taken as a synonym of the Torah, cf. the parallel phrase in l. 7, and Ps. cxix 142.

[28]) Hebr. *hwn*. JOHNSON draws attention to the similarity to the Jerusalem Church (Acts ii 44 f, iv 34 ff).—The word should be taken in its Hebrew sense, and not in the Aramaic meaning 'ability' (against SUKENIK and MARCUS).

[29]) Hebr. *b'mt ḥwqy 'l*. MILIK takes *'mt* in the meaning 'fidelity' and regards *ḥwqy 'l* as an objective genitive, but l. 15 (*ḥwqy 'mtw*) recommends the objective interpretation of *'mt* here.

[30]) Hebr. *wkwḥm ltkn*. For syntax, cf. e.g. ix 14.

[31]) Cf. Ezra x 3, according to Sept., Vulg., Pesh.

[32]) The text here uses the verb *ṣ'd* which cannot mean 'transgress'. YALON explains *lṣ'wd* by *l'bwr*, and refers for this interpretation to an ancient hymn in which occurs the phrase *lhzhr pn tkw hṣw'd*, which is an allusion to the warning in Tamid vi 3: "Take heed that thou begin not in front of thee lest thou be burnt" (the words are directed to the priest officiating at the bringing of incense on to the altar: *hwy zhyr shl' tthyl lpnyk shl' tkwh*). According to YALON *hṣw'd* of the hymn must be taken as alluding to the one who *transgresses* (the warning). This interpretation, however, is very doubtful. The verb *ṣ'd* (Arab. 'to ascend') is used in classical Hebrew of the particular gait employed in religious processions, cf. 2 Sam. vi 13, and assumed later the simple meaning 'to walk', see Prov. vii 8; Ecclus. ix 13, but we have no evidence that the word ever assumed the meaning 'to transgress'. In the hymn, to which YALON refers as a support for his contention, it would be in line with all evidence available to interpret *hṣw'd* as alluding to the officiating priest (lit.: 'the one who ascends, or advances solemnly towards, the altar').

[33]) Cf. e.g. Jer. xxxvi 4.

[34]) Hebr. *bqṣyhm*, cf. CD ii 9, xvi 2 where the suffix, as in our passage, alludes to persons (against YALON who suggests that *qṣym* is used here in the meaning '*parashiyyot*' (cf. Samaritan *qaṣin*), the suffix going back to *dbry 'l*). The meaning 'time' of *qṣ* can be traced already in the Old Testament, cf. RABIN, in note on CD i 5. BROWNLEE goes a step further and suggests that the word be taken as alluding to periods of worship, but this usage is without parallel, and his references to 1QS x 1; 1QpHab xi 6; CD xvi 2, as well as our context, cannot be said to confirm his view. In CD xvi 2 the word clearly means 'epoch'; in 1QS x 1 the word denotes the various periods set down by divine decision: day, night, season, year etc.; in 1QpHab xi 6 *qṣ* does not in itself mean 'a period of worship', but the period, the space of time, taken up by *mw'd mnwḥt ywm hkpwrym*.

[35]) Hebr. *ht'ḥr*, cf. Ecclus. vii 34, xxxviii 16 where the verb means 'to flinch' (SMEND). The context of CD xi 23, where Hitpael of *'ḥr* also occurs, is obscure.

[36]) The dependence of this phrase on 2 Sam. xx 5 suggests that it does not, as it is commonly assumed, allude to the festival calendar of the community. The meanings of *qṣ*, *'t*, and *mw'd* are, to all intents and purposes, identical, and the injunction may stem from a view similar to that expressed in viii 4, ix 14, cf. ix 23, that an action, in order to be morally perfect, should not only formally comply with a commandment, but should also take place at the right time. An exact parallel to this is Jub. xvii 18 where it is said about Abraham: 'Neither was his soul impatient, nor was he slow to act'.

[37]) Cf. Deut. xvii 20, xxviii 14; 1QS iii 10.

[38]) Hebr. *y'bwrw*. From the *plene* writing it is clear that the pausal form was used as an ordinary context form, one of the striking philological features of the Scrolls (cf. the Introduction). Although this feature is not the common thing in CD, there are a few examples: i 20 (*y'byrw* = *y'bwrw*), vi 3, x 18. For *'br b*, cf. Deut. xxix 11 (BROWNLEE), not in CD which always uses *bw'*. BARTHÉLEMY points out that 'entrance into the covenant' is a strange expression, because all the members belong *de jure* to the Mosaic covenant, even before entering into the community, and he draws attention to the use of 'covenant' in monastic circles, in the meaning of 'a special and solemn undertaking given by the new members', and compares v 9, vi 19 with Syriac ܒܢܝ ܩܝܡܐ (children of the covenant).

[39]) Cf. Gen. vii 5 (BROWNLEE); Deut. i 3, 41; Jer. xxxv 18.

[40]) Cf. Num. xiv 43, xxxii 15; Joshua xxii 16 etc. (BROWNLEE). The spelling *m'ḥrw* (also in 1QSa i 17, 18, 22) is remarkable with a scribe who otherwise makes frequent use of the *plene* writing, and YALON therefore suggests that the defective spelling be taken as an indication of the pronunciation *-ō* instead of *-āw*, of the suffix; for an explanation of this he points to the Samaritan dialect. Same orthography in CD x 9.

[41]) Also x 15; 1QpHab iii 4, iv 7. Cf. Exod. xv 16 (STERN).

[42]) The word *mṣrp* in classical Hebrew means 'crucible' (Prov. xvii 3, xxvii 21), but we need an abstract noun in our passage. In Syriac the root *ṣrp* means 'to afflict', and this meaning suits the context (cf. VAN DER PLOEG and YALON).

[43]) The translation is based on the Syriac meaning 'terror' of *hym*'. The word occurs in the Syriac codices A, B, C in Luke xxii 44. As a

translation of γενόμενος ἐν ἀγωνίᾳ we read there: ܐܬܟܬܫ ܗܘܐ ܒܗܘܡܠܐ (cod. A and C) or ܒܗܘܡܠܐ (cod. B); for the word, cf. also JACOB, in *ZAW*, xxii (1902), p. 96.

[44]) I.e. the present age until the coming of Messiah; cf. 'the kingdom of the enemy' in Test. Dan vi 2, 4 (KUHN). *Bly'l* (also l. 24, ii 5, 19; CD iv 13, 15, v 18, viii 2) = Βελίαρ of the Testaments and Jubilees (GRESSMANN, in *ZDMG*, lxvi (1912), p. 493).

[45]) Hebr. *b'wbrm bbryt*, followed by *yhyw* which is an interesting change of MT at Deut. xxix 11: *l'brk bbryt YHWH*. In order to avoid the Tetragrammaton our author changed it into a form of the verb *hyh*! The dependence on Deut. xxix 11 here accounts satisfactorily for *yhyw* in our passage; consequently, the participles in the following lines are not to be regarded as dependent on this one finite form (against BROWNLEE); they are rather to be taken as the equivalents of finite forms in themselves and are best translated by present, i.e. we have here a description of the ritual followed at the renewal of the covenant, rather than instructions of the same (cf. MILIK).

[46]) Cf. Isa. xii 2.

[47]) Cf. Enoch lxiii 8; Ps. xxxiii 4 (?).

[48]) The following ritual is inspired by Deut. xxvii ff, although in Deut. xxvii the response of the people consists of a single 'Amen' (BROWNLEE). Our author seems to be somewhat dependent on Neh. viii 6 (BROWNLEE) in which scriptural passage he appears to have regarded *kl h'm* as suggestive of *kwl h'wbrym*.

[49]) In 1 Sam. xii 7 Sept. has read a verb for 'recount' in front of *'t kl ṣdqwt YHWH*. BH suggests the insertion of *w'gydh lkm* into MT, but our passage, using the root *spr*, may be taken to presuppose *w'sprh lkm 't kl ṣdqwt YHWH* as the text on which Sept. is based, cf. Ps. lxxi 15.

[50]) Biblical passages like Deut. iii 24; Ps. lxxi 16, cxlv 4; Esther x 2 show that the suffix in *gbwrtwm* goes back to *'l*, and not to *ṣdqwt*.

[51]) Hebr. *wḥṭ'tm*, taken as a defectively written plural, co-ordinate with the preceding *'wwnwt* and *psh'y*, cf. Lev. xvi 21; from the obvious allusion to this biblical passage we may conclude that the annual ceremony, which is here described, took place on the Day of Atonement (cf. BROWNLEE). It is interesting to notice that *htwdh* of the biblical passage has been replaced by *msprym*, the oral confession being the concern of the whole community, and not only that of the priest(s), acting on behalf of the laity.

[52]) Hebr. *mwdym*; CD xx 28: *wytwdh*, agreeing with Lev. xvi 21.

The following confession is, in a slightly different form, handed down also in CD xx 28-30 where, however, its ceremonial character does not appear. The confession is modelled on 1 Kings viii 47; Ps. cvi 6; Dan. ix 5 (DUPONT-SOMMER); cf. Neh. ix 33; Ezek. ii 3; Jub. i 22 (BROWNLEE); 2 Chron. vi 37; Yoma iii 8, iv 2, vi 2. For a discussion of the arrangement of the verbs, see BAUMGARTEN, in *HTR*, xlvi (1953), p. 158 f.

[53]) 1 Kings viii 47; Ps. cvi 6; Dan. ix 5 support the restoration (BROWNLEE).

[54]) For consciousness of the sins of the forefathers, cf. Jub. i 22 (BROWNLEE); Jer. iii 25; Dan. ix 16.

[55]) HABERMANN, restoring [*qry bbryt*] takes *bryt* as belonging to the following which he reads as *'mt wṣdq* ('the covenant of truth and righteousness'), but (a) the expression does not otherwise occur in any of the Scrolls; (b) the parallel text in CD shows that *'mt wṣd(y)q* belongs to what follows and should be taken as predicate of *mishpṭw*. This last mentioned objection also applies to the suggestion that *'mt* be taken to what precedes, and *wṣdyq* to what follows (against MILIK). The latter word must be taken as the equivalent of *wṣdq* (see note on ix 14), and must not be separated from *'mt*. A literal translation would be :'truth and righteousness is His punishment'.

Pl. ii

[1]) VERMÈS refers to *Berakot* ix 5 as an explanation of the formula here; in the Mishnah mentioned the use of the phrase at the end of a benediction is said to be due to the view of some heretics that there was only one *'wlm*. It is to be noted, however, that the expression is biblical (Ps. xl 2 and ciii 17), and there is no reason why our author should be reflecting a polemical attitude here.

[2]) To the following pattern of blessing and cursing (ll. 1 ff and ll. 4 ff), cf. Deut. xxvii 12 f. In accordance with Deut. xxi 5 (BROWNLEE) the priests (and not representatives of the people as in Deut. xxvii 12) do the blessing, whilst the levites are in charge of the cursing, cf. Deut. xxvii 14.

[3]) As opposed to 'the men of Belial's lot' (l. 4 f), cf. Lev. xvi 8-10 which our author may, by some peculiar interpretation, have taken as alluding to the two irreconcilable groups.

[4]) Cf. CD i 20 f.

[5]) Cf. e.g. Deut. x 12, xi 22.

[6]) The following benediction is an expanded version of Num.

vi 24-26, with orthographic variations from MT, characteristic of the Scrolls. All versions follow MT slavishly. For another example of free use of the Aaronitic blessing, see 1QSb *passim*, and Jub. xii 29. As for the suffix for 2nd masc. sing. (*-kh*), see the Introduction.

[7]) Cf. Test. Joseph xviii 1; perhaps a reminiscence of Ps. xxi 4.

[8]) Ps. cxxi 7; Jub. xii 29, xxxi 24.

[9]) A variation of Num. vi 25 which is typical of our community: the biblical phrase has been turned in subjective, mystic direction, but by this particular interpretation the parallelism between *y'r pnyw* and *wyḥnk* of the biblical verse is lost. For the idea, cf. iv 2, xi 3, 5.

[10]) Hebr. *śkl ḥyym*, lit. 'wisdom of life'. i.e. wisdom which gives life (Brownlee), 'life' being used here, as very often in the Pseudepigrapha and the New Testament in the meaning of 'eternal life' (see Bauer, *Wörterbuch zum Neuen Testament*, s.v. ζωή), Cf. Prov. xvi 22 (Lambert).

[11]) Cf. viii 9, as emended.

[12]) Cf. Test. Dan. v 11 (Brownlee), 'peace' being used here in the meaning of the blissful state of the pious in heaven. For the combination of 'life' and 'peace', cf. Rom. viii 6.

[13]) Cf. Deut. xxvii 14 f, of which l. 4b-5a is clearly dependent. It appears that our author, in *qwl* of the biblical passage, has found an allusion to cursing, hence *mqllym*.—For execration of the impious, cf. CD xx 8 (Dupont-Sommer) where, however, *kl qdwshy ʿlywn* is most naturally understood as referring to angels (Hvidberg).

[14]) For *'nshy blyʿl*, cf. *'nshym bny blyʿl* (Deut. xiii 14), and *'nshy bny blyʿl* (Judges xix 22). Cf. Jub. xv 33.

[15]) Cf., besides Deut. xxvii 15, also Deut. xxviii 16, 19. These passages show that the full stop should not be put after *'th* (against Schubert).

[16]) Cf. Jer. xxix 18. The spelling *zʿwh* agrees with *Qere* of the biblical *zwʿh* (Gottstein). The verb is best taken as jussive, expressive of the powerful wish or command, a mood one would expect in a curse (S. R. Driver, *Hebrew Tenses*, p. 55).

[17]) For this particular function of the angels, cf. Test. Levi iii 2 f; Enoch lxii 11; Targ. in Lev. xxvi 25.

[18]) Hebr. *'ḥrykh*, cf. Jer. xxix 18 from where the preceding sentence was taken. *Pqd klh* is not biblical, but is used also in CD viii 2 (xix 14) in a context which is closely related to ours: both texts deal with the disastrous fate of the backsliders.

19) Hebr. *mshlmy gmwlym*, lit. 'those who pay rewards', i.e. the angels. For the idiom, cf. e.g. Isa. lix 18; 1QpHab xii 3.

20) Cf. Enoch v 5.

21) Cf. iv 13; Enoch ciii 8 (Brownlee). For 'eternal fire', cf. Matt. xviii 8, xxv 41; Jude 7 (Kuhn); Test. Jud. xxv 3; Test. Zeb. x 3.

22) For the combination of *ḥnn* and *qr'*, see Ps. iv 2, lxxxvi 3. The spelling *yḥwnkh* here, as in l. 3, agrees with the pronunciation given by the Massoretes in Num. vi 25. Of *l'* with the jussive there are a few examples in the Old Testament, see *GK* § 109d; S. R. Driver, *Hebrew Tenses*, p. 54.

23) For the combination of *slḥ* and *kpr*, cf. Lev. iv 26, 31 etc. *'wwnyk* is either plural (Milik) or singular (van der Ploeg). In i 23, iii 7, 22, xi 9 *'wn* has the normal feminine ending in plural, and singular is probably intended in our passage. Similar cases of *plene* spelling in front of the suffix are found in the Samaritan Pentateuch and in the *Ketib* forms of MT, see Sperber, in *HUCA*, xiv (1939), p. 211 f; cf. *GK* § 124 k. The writing of the suffix for 2nd masc. sing. as *-k* is unique in 1QS.

24) Hebr. *lnqmtkh*, the genitive being objective. For Qal of *nqm* with the accusative in this meaning, see Joshua x 13.

25) Cf. Isa. xlviii 22, lvii 21; Enoch v 4, xii 5 f, xiii 1, xvi 4, xciv 6 etc.

26) Hebr. *'wḥzy 'bwt*, cf. Syriac ܐܚܕ ܐܒܘܬܐ 'to intercede'. The phrase occurs in a hymn by Ephraem Syrus (see Bickell, *Ephraemi Syri Carmina Nisibena*, No. lxvii, at the end), where we read: ܢܐܚܘܕ܆ ܐܒܘܬܝ ܠܐܒܘܗܝ, which Bickell translates: 'occludat delicta mea patri suo', but this translation has rightly been corrected by Payne Smith, *Thesaurus Syriacus*, col. 12, to: 'obferat patrocinia mea patri suo'. The Syriac idiom goes back to Accadian *abūta ṣabātu*, or *abūta aḥāzu*, see the examples I have quoted in *VT*, iii (1953), p. 196 f, n. 5. Driver, in a letter, has also drawn my attention to a particularly instructive occurrence of the phrase in Thureau-Dangin, *Rituels Accadiens*, p. 135, l. 258, where we read about the Goddess Sarpanitum that she was *ākilat qarṣū ṣābitat abūtu*: 'accuser and advocate'. The mention here of *ṣābitat abūtu* side by side with *ākilat qarṣū* is significant because, as the latter idiom occurs in Aramaic, it may be suspected that the single, late occurrence of ܐܚܕ ܐܒܘܬܐ in a hymn by Ephraem Syrus may be due to accident; so no conclusion as to the age of our text may be drawn from the use of *'wḥzy 'bwt* in our passage; the expression may have existed in Aramaic for centuries, and its occurrence in 1QS may be taken as one of the many signs of Aramaic

influence in the language of the scroll (thus DRIVER, in a letter).—The interpretation given makes excellent sense in our passage, the meaning being: 'not even by intercession will the impious obtain 'peace'', the intercessors being angels (counterparts of the punishing angels in l. 6 f), cf. Test. Dan vi 1; Test. Levi iii 5, v 6 f, and numerous passages in Enoch (ix 3, xv 2, xxxix 5, xlvii 2 etc.), see CHARLES' note on Enoch ix 10.

[27]) Cf. Pesh. in Deut. xxvii 9. Similarly the text of CD iii 21 agrees with Pesh. in Ezek. xliv 15 (RABIN).

[28]) Hebr. *whwsypw* ... *w'mrw*. There are no instances in the Old Testament of *hwsyp* being followed by the perfect consecutive when the verb is used complementarily; the construction is, however, used with *shwb* (Isa. vi 3).

[29]) The following lines are an almost word by word quotation of Deut. xxix 18-20 which deals with the worshippers of idols, the noun *glwlym* being used in Deut. xxix 16 and the verb *'bd* in the immediately following verse. There can be little doubt, therefore, that the emendation proposed is justified: the meaning becomes clear and the translation given is in accordance with the biblical context on which our passage is dependent. The author, having Deut. xxix 16 ff in mind, coined the expression *glwly lbw* under the influence of the picture language of Ezek. xiv 3, 4, 7.

[30]) Cf. Ezek. xiv 3; CD xx 8-10 (BROWNLEE).

[31]) I.e. the stipulations.

[32]) Hebr. *hbryt*, MT: *h'lh*, cf., however, Deut. xxix 8.

[33]) Hebr. *ytbrk*, MT: *whtbrk*.

[34]) Hebr. *yhy*, MT: *yhyh*. LAMBERT translates by future indicative which can hardly be the meaning intended by the jussive here, in spite of some exceptional cases in the Old Testament where the jussive appears to state a fact, cf. S. R. DRIVER, *Hebrew Tenses*, p. 213.

[35]) The use of consecutive perfect after jussive is in accordance with Hebrew syntax (cf. S. R. DRIVER, *Hebrew Tenses*, p. 126 f). The verb is therefore to be translated by jussive (cf. MILIK). It alludes to *spwt* of MT which Targ. and Pesh. have connected with *ysp* 'to add'; the subject is the following *rwḥw* which is not in MT, but may have been suggested to the author by the following *hrwh*.

[36]) Loose quotation of Deut. xxix 18 which has 'the watered with the thirsty'. Our translation is supported by 1QpHab xi 13 f where no doubt two substantives are intended, but the application of the biblical phrase both in 1QpHab and in our text is obscure. Is it an

expression for 'entirely' (cf. *BDB*, s.v. רוה), or are 'thirst' and 'saturation' (alternatively 'dry' and 'saturated') meant in some figurative way, somehow describing the double position of the person concerned (VAN DER PLOEG)?

[37]) Hebr. *l'yn slyḥh*, MT: *l' y'bh YHWH slḥ lw*.

[38]) Hebr. *'p 'l wqn't mshpṭyw*, MT: *'p YHWH wqn'tw*.

[39]) Hebr. *yb'rw*, MT: *y'shn*. Cf. Sept.: ἐκκαυθήσεται.

[40]) MT: 'against that man'.

[41]) Also v 13; the Hebrew equivalent of *hagᵘel la'ālam* in Enoch lxxxiv 5.

[42]) Word by word agreeing with Sept. Cf. CD i 17 (BROWNLEE).

[43]) Hebr. *wybdylhw*, MT: *whbdylw*. Cf. Enoch xxii 11.

[44]) Hebr. *wnkrt*, not in MT or any of the versions.

[45]) Cf. Zeph. i 6a. The rest of that biblical verse is quoted in v 11. The preposition in *bhswgw* is best taken causally (cf. VAN DER PLOEG).

[46]) To this phrase there is an exact parallel in Enoch xxvii 2: *reggūmān 'eska la'ālam* ('those who are cursed for ever'), and that same book often speaks of the execration of the godless, see v 5 (BROWNLEE), 6, xxii 11, cii 3, and cf. also Jub. xxxvi 10 (BROWNLEE), xxiv 32. The Hebrew permits of various interpretations; thus e.g. *wmkshwl 'wwnw* may be taken to what follows, either as the subject (BROWNLEE), or as the object (SCHUBERT). The dependence of the phraseology on Ezek. xiv 3, 4, 7 favours the taking of *bglwly wmkshwl 'wwnw* as one phrase (cf. VAN DER PLOEG). The dropping of *b* in front of *mkshwl* provides no valid objection to this interpretation, cf. *GK* § 119hh.

[47]) Hebr. *kkh*. For the phraseology of our passage, cf. 1 Sam. i 7 and Job i 5, of which passages the beginning of the line is made up. Both biblical passages deal with ritual acts (the offering up of sacrifices). Job i 5 shows that *kkh* of our passage should be taken retrospectively: the section starting with l. 19 is to be regarded as continuing the description of the renewal of the covenant (cf. VAN DER PLOEG), and not as describing a different ceremony (against e.g. DUPONT-SOMMER). The question is important, because if we are right in our assumption that the two sections belong together and describe the same ceremony, it is obvious that the annual entering into the covenant was a thing in which the whole community took part. DUPONT-SOMMER, however, thinks that the two sections deal with two different ceremonies, i 1-ii 18 describing the admission of novices into the community.—It is to be noted that the following passage is

held in the imperfect tense, which indicates the customary repetition of actions from time to time (*GK* § 107g; S. R. Driver, *Hebrew Tenses*, p. 27), whilst in the previous passage, with its sequence of participles, emphasis was placed on the various activities as happening during the ceremony (*ibid.*, p. 35 f).

[48]) Hebr. *ywmy*. For the form, which may be due to Aramaic influence, cf. also 1QSa i 7; 1QIsa[a] i 1.

[49]) Three classes are mentioned here: priests, levites, and laity; in vi 8 f 'elders' take the place of 'levites'. This small discrepancy appears to favour the view that 1QS has been compiled from different sources; still another tradition is contained in CD xiv 3 ff, according to which the community was divided into four classes: priests, levites, Israelites, and proselytes (these last mentioned were recruited from the *Jews*, cf. Rowley, *The Zadokite Fragments and the Dead Sea Scrolls*, p. 35 f, n. 8).

[50]) Hebr. *lpy rwḥwtm*, cf. iv 26, ix 15, 18; CD xx 24. No similar phrase is found in the Old Testament.

[51]) Cf. Exod. xviii 21, *'m* meaning the lay members of the community.

[52]) Sanhedrin ii 1 shows that the custom of 'passing by, one after the other' was well known among the Jews and used on occasions other than the one here mentioned. The very close verbal similarity of the passage in Sanhedrin ii 1 to ours might suggest that we should translate by 'pass by', if it were not for 1QS i 16 which favours the combination of the verb with the following *bsrk* in the meaning 'enter into'.

[53]) Cf. Exod. xviii 21, 25 (Brownlee); 1QSa i 14 f; Enoch vi 8, lxix 3, lxxxii 17, 20. In CD xiii 1 f (Brownlee) Exod. xviii 21, 25 is alluded to as a proof that a community must consist of at least ten members; in 1QS, however, the division into 'thousands, hundreds, fifties, and tens' seems to indicate, not the number of members of the different local units (against Reicke), but groups of different standing within the community.

[54]) From the context it is clear that 'Israel' here means the community as the spiritual and true Israel (Davies).

[55]) Hebr. *byt m'md*. Rabin, in note on CD xx 5, draws attention to the Mishnaic meaning of *m'md*: 'assembly for religious purposes' and refers for this meaning to our passage. The application, however, of the suffix for 3rd pers. masc. sing. appears to exclude that sense here. The word also occurs in CD ii 9, iv 5, to which passages Brown-

LEE, maintaining the sense 'office', refers; in these two passages, however, it is generally translated by 'existence' which seems the most natural rendering (cf. HVIDBERG). In our passage the word alludes to the particular rank, or 'station', of each member, see the parallelism of *byt m'mdw* and *mqwm gwrlw* in l. 23. Cf. ἀνάστημα in Test. Levi xvi 3.

[56]) Hebr. *yshpwl* = Tiberian *yishpal*; another case of *yiph'ol* for *yiph'al* in vii 10.

[57]) Cf. Exod. xviii 23, in which passage our author appears to have found a scriptural basis for the classification of the members of the community. For *yshpwl 'ysh*, cf. Isa. ii 9.

[58]) Hebr. *hkwl yhyw*, *constructio ad sensum*, cf. Joshua xxiii 14, and RABIN's note on CD viii 19.

[59]) Hebr. *byḥd 'mt*, cf. l. 26. The translation follows LAMBERT who regards *byḥd* as governing the following abstracts.

[60]) Hebr. *'nwt ṭwb*, the latter word perhaps being a reminiscence of Mic. vi 8 from where the following phrase is taken. The demand for 'humility' plays a central part in later Wisdom literature, cf. e.g. Ecclus. iii 17 and ch. x.

[61]) Hebr. *'hbt ḥsd*, cf. Mic. vi 8, but whereas in the biblical passage *'hbt* is meant as an infinitive of which *ḥsd* is the object, the context of our passage appears to suggest the taking of *'hbt* as a substantive of which *ḥsd* is a qualification (cf. BROWNLEE). For an examination of the use of the phrase *'hbt ḥsd* in 1QS, see HYATT, in *ATR*, xxxiv (1952) pp. 232 ff.

[62]) Hebr. *b'ṣt qwdsh* (cf. CD xx 24 f), a general term for the whole community (against HVIDBERG and RABIN).

[63]) Hebr. *swd 'wlmym*, perhaps a title which the members applied to their community (SCHUBERT). For the expression, see DELCOR, in *RSR*, xciv (1952), pp. 377 ff. KUHN compares οἱ ἐπουράνιοι in 1 Cor. xv 48.

[64]) Hebr. *wkwl hmw's*, cf. CD viii 19. The verb is taken from Lev. xxvi 43, as is *g'lh npshw* in the following.

Pl. iii

[1]) Hebr. *byswry*, cf. Ps. Sol. iii 4 where the peculiar text of the Greek version οὐκ ὀλιγωρήσει δίκαιος παιδαγόμενος ὑπο Κυρίου is almost certainly due to the translator's misunderstanding of *l' ym's ṣdyq yswr YHWH*: he took *yswr* as the passive participle of *ysr* and not, as he should have done, as the substantive *yissur*.—BROWNLEE

emends to *yswr wd't* and refers to the poetic context which, to his mind, suggests the alteration, as it offers us two terms in poetic parallelism. There is no doubt that BROWNLEE is right in assuming a certain rhythm here, and his suggestion has the advantage of breaking up what otherwise appears to be a series of construct states. On the other hand, the parallel phrase in l. 5 f, where the object of *m's* is *mshpṭy 'l*, and CD xix 5 f where the objects are *mṣwt* and *ḥqym*, appears to suggest that plural should be read also in our passage. YALON suggests ii 26-iii 1 be interpreted in the light of Hos. vii 15 and Job iv 3. His argument hinges on the occurrence of *ysr* and *ḥzq* in both these two passages and in 1QS iii 1, and he suggests that the text in the latter is important for the right understanding of the two scriptural passages mentioned, because we are now to his mind able to see that *ysr* there means 'to bind', in the same way as *ḥzq* there also means 'to bind', and not, as is generally assumed, 'to strenghten'. He finds the support for this in 1QS iii 1 by translating *byswry d't* ... *l' ḥzq*: 'he does not tie upon himself the belt of knowledge' (cf. Isa. xi 5). But (a) *ysr* does not make sense in the meaning 'to bind' in either Hos. vii 15 or Job iv 3; (b) the parallel passages from 1QS and CD produced above suggest that *byswry d't* should be taken to what precedes.

[2]) Hebr. *mshpṭy ṣdq* (also iv 4, cf. ix 17; CD xx 30 f), cf. Isa. lviii 2; Ps. cxix 7, 62 etc. For 'knowledge of righteous judgments', cf. Ps. Sol. ii 12, v 1, viii 8.

[3]) Hebr. *lw' ḥzq lmshwb ḥyw*, cf. 4 Ezra vii 81 f: 'spreverunt legem Altissimi .... non possunt reversionem bonam facere ut vivant'. The similarity between the two passages is almost verbal and suggests that *ḥzq* in 1QS means 'to be able to'; *mshwb*, then, is an Aramaic infinitive (VAN DER PLOEG). The use of *ḥzq* in this way is not biblical. For the phrase 'to return to his life', i.e. 'to repent so that he might live', cf. Acts xi 8.

[4]) Hebr. *yshrym*, cf. iv 22; CD xx 2.

[5]) Hebr. *'ṣt yḥd*. The community as a whole is meant; the expression is quite frequent in 1QS (v 7 etc., also vi 3; cf. 1QpHab xii 4), but does not occur in CD.

[6]) Hebr. *rsh' mḥrshw* which appears to be dependent on Hos. x 13 (*ḥrshtm rsh'*), the verb having been taken, not in the meaning 'to plough' (which is the meaning intended in the passage, cf. the parallelism), but in the meaning 'to devise', 'to think', cf. Prov. iii 29. The object *rsh'* seems to have prompted this interpretation.

[7]) For the spelling *bshybtw*, cf. 2 Sam. xix 33. The context appears to allude to the sessions of the society.

[8]) Same verb (*twr*) applied in CD ii 16 and iii 11. The form *mtwr* in our passage is due to Aramaic influence. We should have expected a preposition in front of *shryrwt*, and YALON suggests the reading, either *bshryrwt* or *'ḥry shryrwt*.

[9]) This sentence may contain an allusion to Isa. v 30 which our author, ignoring the *Ṣade* in *l'rṣ*, may have translated: 'And he looks unto light, but behold it is darkness'. The translation given is closely akin to the suggestion by STINESPRING that *ḥwshk* is not the object of *ybyṭ* (against VAN DER PLOEG), but should be taken as an adverbial accusative.

[10]) The emendation proposed may be supported by a reference to *w'm yshrym lw' ytḥshb* in l. 1 f which appears to be an exact parallel to our passage. The manuscript appears to favour the reading of the original text as *b'wn*, and YALON suggests *'wn* be taken, not in the meaning 'sin', but in the meaning 'band', 'connection'. For *'wn* in this meaning he refers to Lev. Rabbah, xvii 1 where *'wnwt* is parallel to *ṣybym* ('thin threads'), and to the obscure passage in Hos. x 10 where *'wnwtm* occurs in connection with the verb *'sr*. This last mentioned reference is particularly interesting for the biblical scholar, but unfortunately YALON has not explained further how that biblical passage is then to be understood; even on the assumption of *'wnwt* being used there in the sense he suggests, the meaning of the passage is not clear. As we have already seen (see note 1 above) YALON takes the roots *ysr* and *ḥzq* in l. 1 in the meaning 'to bind', the idea of tying together and unifying being, to his mind, the thought dominating the first lines of this plate; he even suggests the verb *ytḥshb* be taken in the meaning 'to bind', and draws attention to Syriac ܚܫܒ. As we now see, he carries his idea through also in l. 3 f by connecting *'wn* with the same idea of 'tying', and he translates *b'wn tmymym lw' ytḥshb* in the following way: 'he is not to be united with the perfect'. This is, to be sure, a most interesting and ingenious interpretation of the passage, but as we have already seen, there are other and, so it seems, more obvious ways of interpreting l. 1; besides, it is a little strange to read a doubtful Syriac meaning into the verb *ytḥshb*, as it is most naturally taken in the meaning in which it is used in classical Hebrew.

[11]) Hebr. *yzkh* which is probably meant to be Hitpael, like the ensuing *yṭhr* and *ytqdsh*; for the form, cf. *GK* § 54 2b Rem.—The

decidedly spiritualistic attitude expressed in the following lines seems very different from the levitic rules of CD x. On the other hand, 1QS v 13 as well as the very phrasing of our section shows that the community did practice certain water-rites, but apparently stressed the inadequacy of the rites themselves. WIESENBERG, by way of parallel to this attitude, compares Tos. Taanit i 8.—The section is hardly polemical, and perhaps we have here a lesson delivered to the members of the community before the participation in the water-rites which seem to have played a special part at the renewal of the covenant which is reported in the context.

[12]) Hebr. *bkpwrym* which naturally suggests that the Day of Atonement (cf. Lev. xxiii 27) was the day κατ' ἐξοχήν for the water rites here mentioned, cf. the phrase *tplh lywm kpwrym* in 1Q34bis 5, and the mention of *ywm tʿnyt* in CD vi 19; in the same direction we are lead by the use of *ṭhr* and *qdsh* in l. 4, cf. Lev. xvi 19, of *bʿnwt npshw* in l. 8, cf. Lev. xxiii 27, and of *my rḥṣ* in l. 5, cf. Lev. xvi 4, 24, 26. That the annual renewal of the covenant was enacted on this particular day is in itself a reasonable assumption when it is considered that the occasion concerned revolved round repentance and confession of sins, as did the Day of Atonement. It is only to be expected that a thoroughly Jewish body, which is what we are dealing with here, would, on this important point, continue Jewish tradition.

[13]) Hebr. *my ndh*, lit. 'water of impurity' (also iii 9, iv 21), cf. Num. xix 9, 13 etc. (BROWNLEE).

[14]) Hebr. *ytqdsh*, frequently used in the Old Testament in connection with ablutions (e.g. 2 Sam. xi 4; Isa. lxvi 17).

[15]) Hebr. *ymym*. 'Seas' would seem to be the obvious rendering of this word. There are, however, two passages in the Old Testament in which the word occurs in parallelism with *nhr* 'river' (Isa. xix 5 and Ezek. xxxii 2), obviously just being a poetical variation of that word; the same seems to be the case in our passage, and it is at least questionable whether our community performed water rites in 'seas'.

[16]) Hebr. *my rḥṣ*. The expression is not biblical, but is modelled on *rḥṣ bmym* in Lev. xvi 4, 24 etc.

[17]) There is a strong spiritualistic note here, and it is interesting to notice that the foundation of our particular line is Lev. xiii 45 f (BROWNLEE) which our author has interpreted in a spiritual way. Lev. xiii 45 f deals with the leper who, being unclean, must live outside the camp; from this regulation is elicited that a man who 'rejects the

statutes of God' (same vocabulary as Lev. xxvi 43, cf. CD viii 19 (xix 32)) is to be regarded as an outcast without access to the instruction given within the community. The frequent combination of *yḥd* and *'ṣh* in the expression *'ṣt hyḥd* (cf. iii 2, vi 16, vii 2, viii 1, 5) suggests that *yḥd 'ṣtw* of our passage is to be taken as a variation of that expression (against VAN DER PLOEG who takes *'ṣtw* as the subject of *htysr*). *Mshpṭy 'l* are different from *mshpṭy hyḥd* in vi 15 (DELCOR): the former expression alludes to the Mosaic Law, the latter to the regulations of the sect.

[18]) Hebr. *brwḥ 'ṣt 'mt 'l*. BROWNLEE has seen that *rwḥ 'ṣh* is from Isa. xi 2, and he translates accordingly: 'through the spirit of God's true counsel'. It has escaped his notice that our author, although borrowing the expression from Isa. xi 2, has taken it to mean 'spirit of council' (cf. REICKE's translation). That this is so becomes clear when the following facts are considered: (a) the phrase is parallelled in the following line by *wbrwḥ qdwshh lyḥd b'mtw*: 'by the holy spirit of the community in His truth'; (b) the exposition starting with *ky'* in l. 6b gives the reason for the statement in l. 5b-6a, carrying on the interpretation of Lev. xiii 45 f (see previous note). The idea is: by his rejection of God's statutes the impious is like a leper, unclean and banished from the camp (l. 5b = Lev. xiii 46a); so, he cannot be instructed within the community because the spirit is within the community (l. 6a = Lev. xiii 46b). Accordingly, *'mt* belongs to *'ṣt*, not to *rwḥ*.

[19]) Cf. Isa. xxii 14, xxvii 9. In *ykwprw Waw* is used as indicating short *u* in front of *Dagesh forte*. The preceding *drky 'ysh* has been taken in a variety of ways. BROWNLEE, following a suggestion of DANIELS, restores a *Lamed* in front of the expression; as however this reconstruction presupposes the taking of *'ṣh* as 'counsel' we may dispose of it. The translation follows VAN DER PLOEG and may be suppported by a reference to Prov. xvi 6 f.

[20]) For 'light of life', cf. John viii 12 (BROWNLEE). An interesting parallel is contained in 1QIsa[a] liii 11, where the scroll agrees with Sept. in reading *'wr* after *yr'h*. In Job xxxiii 30 Pesh. contains a similar phrase.

[21]) Hebr. *brwḥ qdwshh lyḥd b'mtw*. As we have seen, the expression is parallel with *brwḥ 'ṣt 'mt 'l* of the previous line (cf. note 18 above). So, neither should *lyḥd* be taken as the object of *lhbyṭ* (against VAN DER PLOEG), nor should *yḥd* be taken in the meaning 'unity' (against BROWNLEE), still less should it be taken as a verb (against MILIK);

b'mt belongs to *lyḥd*. AUDET examines the expression 'holy spirit' in CD and 1QS and stresses its appellative character. Cf. 1QSb ii 24.—Our passage provides us with the clue to the understanding of CD ii 12 f, a passage which is full of problems to which scholars have sought various solutions. The text there reads: *wywdy'm byd mshyḥw rwḥ qdshw* ... *'mt wprwsh shmw shmwtyhm*. The questions discussed may be summed up in the following way: (a) should *mshyḥw* be taken as the noun *mshyḥ* in the singular + suffix? If so, should it be interpreted as alluding to the Messiah of the community (SCHECHTER), or to some person in the past, e.g. Enoch or Moses (LÉVI), or to the founder of the sect (LAGRANGE)—or should it be taken as equal to *mshyḥyw*, alluding to the prophets (LESZYNSKY)? (b) Is *rwḥ qdshw* to be taken as second object of *wywdy'm* (SCHECHTER), or as apposition to *mshyḥw* (LÉVI)? (c) Should the word at the end of l. 12 be read as *whw'* (SCHECHTER), or as *wḥwh* (RABIN)? (d) Should *bprwsh* be taken adverbially (GINZBERG), or in the meaning: 'in the interpretation of ..' (WARD)? (e) Should *shmw* be deleted as a dittograph (SCHECHTER, referring to CD iv 4 f), or should it be kept, and if so, should it be taken as a noun (LAGRANGE), or as a verb (WARD)?—There are two passages which help us to appreciate the meaning of this difficult passage. One is CD v 21 f, and the other is our passage here in 1QS iii 7. In CD v 21 f we read: *ky dbrw srh 'l mṣwt 'l byd mshh wgm bmshyḥw hqwdsh*. The similarity in phraseology between *byd mshyḥw rwḥ qdshw* in CD ii 12 and *bmshyḥw hqwdsh* in CD vi 1 is clear. In the passage preceding the latter Moses was mentioned (*byd mshh*), and it might therefore be reasonably assumed that the continuation *wgm bmshyḥw hqwdsh* should be understood as alluding to the prophets (cf. 1QS i 3), in other words, the phrase should be taken parallel with *byd mshh*. But how can *b* be parallel with *byd*, and how can *mshyḥw* be taken as alluding to the prophets? The first of these two questions is easily answered: *b* is either an abbrevation for *byd* (that the scribe of CD makes use of this abbrevation in ii 6 and vi 1 has already been noticed by RABIN), or we have here simply one of those cases where a preposition is resumed by a different one. As for *bmshyḥw*, the interpretation of this expression as alluding to the prophets has already been suggested by some scholars (cf. above), and RABIN draws attention to Ps. cv 15 where *bmshyḥy* is parallel with *wlnby'y*. There can be no doubt, therefore, that in CD ii 12, as well as in vi 1, the word is meant as plural, not singular. Now, it is interesting to notice that the scribe at vi 1 left a space between *bmshyḥw* and *hqwdsh*. The parallel in ii 12 has *byd mshyḥw rwḥ qdshw*, and it is reasonable to believe that the text before the scribe at vi 1 had exactly the same wording, but being puzzled by *rwḥ* which, with the reading *mshyḥw*, could not be taken to belong anywhere, he consequently left it out. In ii 12 he did not do so because, like many modern scholars (cf. above) he took *rwḥ qdshw* as the second object of *wywdyʿm*. Presupposing that originally ii 12 and vi 1 read the same words, viz. *mshyḥw rwḥ qdshw*, it is not difficult to see that this is simply to be emended to *mshyḥy rwḥ qdshw*: 'those who were anointed with the holy spirit' which, as we shall see, makes excellent sense not only in vi 1, but also in ii 12 (for 'anointment with spirit' as a figure of speech alluding to prophetic inspiration, cf. Isa. lxi 1); in that passage the taking of *rwḥ qdshw* as the second object of *wywdyʿm* is to be dismissed, as the phrase is *nomen rectus* of *mshyḥy*; so, the taking of *rwḥ qdshw* as apposition is equally impossible. But what, then, is the second object of *wywdyʿm*? There is a close similarity in phraseology between CD ii 12 f and our passage here in 1QS iii 7. It might, therefore, be expected that the latter passage might help us to solve the problem of the former. In our passage we read: *wbrwḥ qdwshh lyḥd bʾmtw*, and in CD ii 12 f we read: *rwḥ qdshw . . . ʾmt*. The contexts of the two passages are admittedly different, but the similarity of the two phrases is striking. As we have seen 1QS iii 7 is to be translated: 'by the holy spirit of the community in His truth', parallel with 'the spirit of God's true council' of the previous line. That the word *yḥd* occurs in CD in the form *yḥyd* (man. B: xx 1, 14, 32) is recognized by most scholars, and the suggestion of the present author is that this word should be read also in CD ii 12. SCHECHTER's reading is not justifiable, as the second letter is clearly a *Ḥet*, not a *He*, and the last letter cannot in any way be read as an *Aleph*. RABIN, therefore, reads *wḥwh*, but the slight stain suggesting the left vertical stroke of a *He*, may be a smudge on the manuscript, and the word may be transcribed as *wḥwd* = *yḥyd*. The parallel in our passage (1QS iii 7) shows that the suffix in *qdshw* is a dittograph and should be deleted, and suggests that the *Waw* in front of *bprwsh* should be joined to the preceding word. Thus we get: *byd mshyḥy rwḥ qdsh yḥyd ʾmtw*: 'through those who were anointed with the holy spirit of his true community', which is only a slight variation of the expression in our passage: 'by the holy spirit of the community in His truth'. The following *bprwsh* of the CD passage is without difficulty taken as the second object of *wywdyʿm* and *shmw* should be deleted as a dittograph. The emended text in CD ii 12 f then reads: *wywdyʿm byd mshyḥy rwḥ qdsh yḥyd 'mtw bprwsh shmwtyhm*, and it means: 'and He made known to them, through those who were anointed with the holy spirit of His true community, the exact meaning of their names'.

22) Cf. Jer. xxxiii 8.

23) Cf. Isa. vi 7.

24) Cf. Lev. xvi 31 in which passage our author has taken *ḥqt 'wlm* as a second object of *'nytm*, thus spiritualizing the meaning of 'humble oneself' which of course in the biblical passage means 'to fast'; cf. Vulg.

25) Cf. 2 Kings v 10. That our author here lapses into the terminology belonging to the sphere of leprosy agrees with his exposition of Lev. xiii 45 f in l. 5 f. Hebr. x 22, alluding to baptism, is an interesting parallel.

26) Hebr. *lhzwt bmy ndh*. BROWNLEE proposes the emendation of *lhzwt* to *lhzkwt* because (a) the regular usage is to sprinkle water *upon* a person; here, however, the usage is to sprinkle a person *with* water; this is ungrammatical; (b) the emendation brings into parallel structure two Hitpael infinitives: 'so that he may purify himself .... and sanctify himself ...'. Neither of these reasons is compelling; a slight difference from biblical usage is not surprising with an author who writes in a language different from the one he speaks; besides, our passage is dependent on Num. xix 21, and it is reasonable to assume that our author has been influenced by *bmy ndh* occurring in the second half of that verse. Num. xix 21 also shows that the verb is Hiphil, not Hophal (against REICKE).

27) Cf. Syriac ܕܘܟܝܐ 'purity' (YALON), see PAYNE SMITH's *Thesaurus Syriacus*, I, col. 895.

28) Hebr. *wyhkyn*. The retention of *He* in the imperfect Hiphil is not unknown in the Old Testament (cf *GK* § 53q), although this feature is characteristic of biblical Aramaic (see MARTI, *Kurzgefasste Grammatik der Biblisch-Aramäischen Sprache*, p. 37). For the phrase (also xi 13), cf. Ps. cxix 133.

29) Hebr. *lhlkt* which should perhaps be equated with *lhlykt* (HABERMANN); on the other hand, the defective writing is strange, and the word may be meant as an infinitive Qal, cf. the original text in i 25. For 'walking in perfection', cf. Prov. xxviii 18; Ps. lxxxiv 12.

30) For 'God's ways', cf. Deut. x 12, xi 22 etc. (CD xx 18 sing.).

31) *Drk* as an object of *ṣwh* is deuteronomistic, see e.g. Deut. x 12, 16, xiii 6. No version supports *k'shr* for *'shr* of MT in any of the passages concerned; the author is here influenced by the frequent phrase *k'shr ṣwh* (Gen. xlvii 11; Exod. vii 10 etc.).

[32]) See note on i 9. YALON suggests that *t'wdtyw* should not be pronounced *te'ūdotāw*, but *te'ūdātāw*: the word is plural, and the defective writing is due to influence from Aramaic where the plural ending is *-āt*; for this he refers to Isa. xxvi 19 and xlvii 13.

[33]) Cf. i 15.

[34]) For the use of the infinitive with *'yn*, cf. S. R. DRIVER, *Hebrew Tenses*, p. 274.

[35]) See notes on i 13 f.

[36]) Hebr. *'z*, expressing logical sequence.

[37]) Hebr. *yrṣh bkpwry nyḥwḥ lpny 'l.* None of the translators has taken into account that the phraseology of this passage is modelled on Ezek. xx 41: *bryḥ nyḥwḥ 'rṣh 'tkm*, where the verb is used in the meaning 'accept', with God as the subject. The verb is used in the same meaning in our passage, and the subject, although not formally, is virtually God: our author, for fear of anthropomorphism, has turned the sentence into passive in a manner reminiscent of the Targums: 'he will *be accepted* as an agreeable atonement *before God*', i.e. the verb should be read as Niphal (cf. HABERMANN). The general spiritualistic outlook of our author, of which the whole passage is a typical example, accounts for the replacement of *ryḥ* in the biblical passage by *kpwry* in our passage. That this particular word has been chosen is satisfactorily explained by the fact that the whole of iii 4 ff is strongly influenced by the phraseology of Lev. xvi and xxiii, dealing with the Day of Atonement. The idea of the perfect lives of the members as being the 'sacrifice', by which forgiveness for sins is procured, is expressed also in viii 3, and especially in ix 24: *wkwl hn'śh bw yrṣh bndbh* whose meaning may now be considered as established: as in our passage the verb is to be read as Niphal and taken in the meaning 'accept', and *bndbh* occupies a position similar to that of *bkpwry nyḥwḥ* in our passage; *kwl hn'śh* is *casus pendens*, resumed by the suffix in *bw*, and the passage is to be translated: 'Then everything which is done, by that he will be accepted as a free-will offering'.

[38]) This is an allusion to Num. xxv 13 (quoted also in Ecclus. xlv 15), with two interesting differences: (a) *wlzr'w 'ḥryw* has been left out because of not being in keeping with the strictly individualistic attitude of our author; (b) *khnt* has been replaced by *yḥd*—a small, but significant change of the scriptural passage which appears to exclude an identification of the community with any shade of Sadduceism (cf., however, *bryt khwnt 'wlm* in 1QSb iii 26).—The dependence on Num. xxv 13 makes it clear that *'wlmym* should be connected with

yḥd (cf. MILIK), and not with *bryt*; furthermore, the deliberate replacement of *khnt* by *yḥd* appears to favour the taking of this word in its usual meaning 'community', rather than in the abstract sense 'communion' (against MILIK), cf. also v 5 f, where the translation 'community' is the only one to apply.

[39]) Hebr. *lmśkyl* (also 1QSb i 1, iii 13, v 20). We now enter upon an essay which takes up the rest of this, and the whole of the next, plate. The governing thought is that of the two spirits ruling in man and dividing mankind into two sharply distinguished sections, the children of righteousness and the children of deceit, these two groups being in the power of the angel of light and the angel of darkness respectively. The dualism however, is not consistent: God is the one who created the spirits, and consequently also the one who bestowed the power over mankind on the two angels. A strong foreign influence has been noticed here by DUPONT-SOMMER, BROWNLEE, and KUHN, the doctrine of the two spirits apparently being Zoroastrian, but there is nothing in our section of the consistent dualism, so characteristic of Zoroastrian thought; the insistence on Yahweh as the only God to whom no equal counterpart can possibly exist, permeates the whole of our section, in full harmony with traditional Jewish thought.—The style of the first two lines of the essay is stilted and turgid and has given rise to a variety of translations.—The designation *mśkyl* also occurs in ix 12, 21; CD xii 21. HVIDBERG suggests it is used in a general way and correspondingly some students of 1QS simply translate 'wise man' (cf. e.g. BURROWS). Others take the word as referring to a particular teacher (e.g. DUPONT-SOMMER), perhaps even the *Mevaqqer* (VAN DER PLOEG). Attention might perhaps be drawn to the use of *mśkyl* in the Old Testament (Dan. xi 33, xii 3), and of 'wise' in Pseudepigraphical literature (e.g. Enoch c 6, civ 12). Both in Daniel and in Pseudepigraphal literature the designation 'wise' is used in a general sense about a member of the pious community, and this is probably the meaning in which the word is used also in 1QS and CD, cf. especially 1QS ix 12 where the ensuing injunctions are most naturally taken as applying to the community as a whole, and not only to the teacher of the society.

[40]) Hebr. *lhbyn wllmd*. The two roots are used in other passages both in 1QS and CD (cf. 1QS iv 3, 22, xi 1; CD i 8, ii 14, xiii 5 (*byn*); 1QS ix 13; CD xx 4 (*lmd*)). Cf. Isa. xl 14 (VAN DER PLOEG).

[41]) Cf. i 9.

[42]) Hebr. *btwldwt kwl bny 'ysh*. The preposition introduces the

object of *lhbyn* and *llmd*: the origin and history of mankind, told on a metaphysical basis, is exactly the gist of the following essay. The echo of biblical phraseology is not confined to the word *twldwt* (LAMBERT), but the use of words like *myn* (l. 14), *br'* (l. 17), and *ld't ṭwb* [*wr'*] (iv 26) suggests that the whole of the essay is based on Gen. i ff. In these chapters, which deal with the Creation and Fall, our author found a basis for his metaphysical speculations, and it is an interesting fact that he found no difficulty in fusing Zoroastrian speculations with the old biblical narratives in the opening chapters of Genesis; so it seems that we are here dealing with a community which, in spite of the foreign ideas which it harboured, managed to maintain itself as being in accordance with Jewish, biblical tradition.

43) There is no doubt that *rwḥ* in this essay is used in both a metaphysical and a psychological way, designating at the same time the governing principle of either good or evil *and* the individual spirit of every man; the former meaning is clear in iii 18, and the latter appears to be presupposed in iv 23; in our passage *rwḥ* is to be taken in its metaphysical sense; on the other hand, it must be supposed that various degrees were contained within the two main groups.

44) Hebr. *b'wtwtm lm'śyhm* which alludes to the two kinds of actions in which the spirits reveal themselves. The translation is based on the assumption that we have a periphrastic genitive construction here; for this philologically interesting feature, which occurs also in CD, see RABIN in note on CD ii 9. The characteristic of this construction is that the *nomen rectus* is anticipated by a suffix and introduced by the preposition *l*. None of the translators of 1QS has realized the occurrence of the construction here and in l. 16, although in both passages the assumption of the construction concerned clarifies the meaning considerably. The word *'wt* occurs in Deut. xi 3, as in our passage, in connection with *m'śh*; whereas, however, the word in Deut. xi 3 means 'sign', 'miracle', it is used in our passage in the meaning 'characteristic'.

45) Hebr. *bdwrwtm*. Some scholars take *dwr* here in the meaning 'category', 'class', 'society' (DUPONT-SOMMER, BARDTKE, and BROWNLEE, respectively). Here again, as often in 1QS, the realization of the biblical foundation of the phraseology helps us to hit the right meaning; the expression is used in the same way as *bdwrwtyw* in Gen. vi 9, and a straightforward translation is to be preferred to any of the suggestions mentioned above (cf. HABERMANN). *Btwldwt* in the

preceding line presents no difficulty for this interpretation of *bdwrwtm* because, as we have seen, that expression does not mean 'in their generations'; so, BROWNLEE's objection to the translation given is invalid, and his translation cannot be supported by reference to NEUBERG's article in *JNES*, ix (1950), pp. 215 ff.

[46]) Cf. Hos. ix 7. In the biblical passage the punishment of the people is forecast, and *hpqdh* and *hshlm* are synonyms, both to be taken *in malam partem*. Our author, however, by reading *hashshālōm* for *hashshillūm* took the passage to forecast the punishment in store for the sons of darkness, and the blissful state in the hereafter in store for the sons of light: the suffixes in *ngyʿyhm* and *shlwmm* refer to the two opposite groups (cf. MILIK). This interpretation suits the ensuing descriptions in iv 6-8 and iv 11-14 which describe the peace of those ruled by the 'true' spirit, and the afflictions of those ruled by the 'wicked' spirit.—The reference to Hos. ix 7 has already been given by HABERMANN, but according to the biblical passage he reads the word in our passage as *hashshillūm*, in which case, of course, there can be no question of distributing the suffixes on different groups.

[47]) Cf. 1 Sam. ii 3. No gnosticism should be traced in the application of this expression (against SCHUBERT).

[48]) Hebr. *kwl hwwh wnhyyh*. Scholars are divided on the question of time aspect in *nhyyh*; MILIK translates by the future tense, whereas the past tense is maintained by VAN DER PLOEG. In connection with participle Qal of *hyh*, the participle Niphal may be an insignificant modification due to style (thus also xi 4, 9). BARDTKE's rendering: 'alles Sein und Geschehen' is perhaps preferable because it avoids any specific time-aspect read into the text.—Our passage is closely related to CD ii 9 f, where we read: *wprwsh qṣyhm lkl hwy ʿwlmym wnhyyt ʿd mh ybw' bqṣyhm lkl shny ʿwlm*. RABIN has seen that the periphrastic genitive construction occurs in *qṣyhm lkl hwy ʿwlmym* and in *bqṣyhm lkl shny ʿwlm*; this clarifies the meaning of the passage considerably. In two respects, however, his translation can be corrected on the basis of the parallel in our passage: (a) *hwy* should not be taken as referring to persons; (b) *nhyyt* should not be corrected to *nhywt* (SCHECHTER suggested this emendation, and it has been adopted by all scholars); it is a most interesting orthographical point that in both our passage and in CD ii 10 the word is spelt with two *Yods*, whereby the consonantal *Yod* is distinguished from the vowel letter (see SEGAL's *Mishnaic Grammar*, § 57); the retention of the text as it stands makes perfect sense, *nhyyt* being the construct form of

nhyyh governed by the following *'d*, which should not, as it has been done by all scholars, be taken as an adverb ('until'), but as a noun ('eternity'), and the translation runs: 'and the exact statement of the periods of everything which is happening for ever (*kl hwy 'wlmym*), and which happens for ever (*nhyyt 'd*), what is going to happen in all the years of eternity'.

[49]) For the idiom, cf. Prov. xvi 3, xx 18. The word *mḥshbh* is taken in the meaning 'thought' by MILIK, and the suffix is taken by him as referring to conscious beings; the sense of the passage then is: 'before they (i.e. the human beings) come into existence He has fixed all their thoughts', in other words: the predestination goes as far as determining not only actions, but even thoughts, beforehand. As we have seen above (cf. note 48) the assumption of reference to conscious beings only is not likely in view of the contexts in which *hwh* and *nhyh* are used in 1QS and CD; besides, the following *bhywtm* in l. 16 appears to correspond logically to *lpny hywtm* ('*before* they exist ... and *when* they come into existence'), in which case it makes better sense to take *mḥshbh* in the meaning 'plan', 'design' (cf. VAN DER PLOEG).

[50]) Hebr. *wbhywtm lt'wdwtm*. The construction is periphrastic, and the phrase is equal to *wbhywt t'wdwtm*, and it means: 'when their *t'wdwt* happen', i.e. when they are revealed and come into existence; but the use of *t'wdh* is strange.

[51]) Hebr. *l'yn lhshnwt*. The form of the verb appears to be Niphal, in which case, however, the meaning of the phrase would be: 'and nothing could be repeated' (cf. DEL MEDICO). There can be little doubt that the verb is used in the meaning 'to change'; this meaning is in keeping with the context, and may also be supported by reference to passages in Pseudepigraphal literature, such as Enoch ii 2, v 2; Test. Napht. iii 2. We may, then, have here a Hitpael form with assimilation of *Taw*.

[52]) Hebr. *bydw mshpṭy kwl*, cf. also x 16 f. For the meaning of *mshpṭ* here, cf. 2 Kings i 7; Judges xiii 12. The sense of our passage seems to be that all beings act, and all things happen, according to qualities which have been instilled in them beforehand by God. The phrase *mshpṭy kwl* does not occur in the Old Testament, but the expression underlies the Ethiopic text of Enoch xxii 8; one Greek manuscript reads κριμάτων, which is regarded as corrupt by CHARLES; but the phrase has been preserved in the Ethiopic version (*kᵘennānē kᵘellū*) and now turns up in 1QS in its pure, Hebrew form—another interesting link between our manuscript and Pseudepigraphal literature.

[53]) Hebr. *whw'h*. The form of the pronoun is the one frequently used in the Scrolls, see the Introduction.

[54]) Cf. Ps. cxii 5. Note the pun on *kwl* ... *yklklm* ... *bkwl*.

[55]) Cf. Ps. viii 7. For *mmshlt tbl*, cf. Ecclus. x 4.

[56]) We have mentioned above (see note 43) the peculiar usage of *rwḥ* in the present essay, as designating a metaphysical, transcendental principle, as well as a psychological inclination in the individual man. As a parallel to our passage Dupont-Sommer refers to Yasna xlv 2 and xxx 3, both passages suggesting a metaphysical interpretation of the term *rwḥ* in our passage; on the other hand, Test. Judah xx 1, which provides us with a very close parallel to our context, appears to recommend the taking of *rwḥ* as a psychological term, cf. especially Otzen who refers to Test. Asher i 3 ff. It is a question, however, whether a reference to the obviously psychological implication of the word 'spirit' in the Testaments is really relevant here; it cannot be denied that in 1QS iii the two spirits are something outside man, something which forms an integral part of a metaphysical pattern; this is in accordance with Zoroastrian usage of the term, but different from the Testaments and the New Testament where the terminology is taken over, but interpreted psychologically (cf. 1 John iv 6), all traces of a metaphysical frame-work having been abolished. It appears, therefore, that the original Zoroastrian thought has influenced both the Testaments, the New Testament, and 1QS, but whereas in the case of the two former the mythological speculation, in which the idea of the two spirits was incorporated, has been dropped, the latter has preserved a reminiscence of the original metaphysical conception. One reason for the purely psychological application of the idea in the Testaments and the New Testament, may be found in the desire to get rid of the strictly dualistic pattern in the Zoroastrian speculation; it is to be noted, however, that even in 1QS, where the conception still bears the imprint of Zoroastrian, metaphysical speculation, our author found no difficulty in maintaining traditional Jewish monotheism.

[57]) Hebr. *mw'd pqwdtw*, cf. CD xix 10. The suffix probably refers to God (cf. Brownlee).

[58]) The parallelism with *mmqwr ḥwshk* in the following recommends the emendation proposed, cf. x 12. The use of the preposition *b* is no objection to this interpretation, for it is used in Ugaritic, and in the Old Testament (cf. Gen. xliv 5) in the meaning 'from'.

[59]) Cf. Test. Asher v 3 (πᾶσα ἀλήθεια ὑπὸ τοῦ φωτός ἐστίν) and Enoch cviii 11 ff.

[60]) Hebr. *śr 'wrym*, cf. CD v 18. In that passage HVIDBERG takes the designation as referring to God. We can now see, however, that the expression refers to an angel, perhaps Uriel (GINZBERG). For the idea of angels set over mankind, see Enoch xx 5.

[61]) Hebr. *bny ṣdq*. The designation 'sons of righteousness' is common in Pseudepigraphal literature, cf. Enoch xci 3, xciii 2; Jub. x 6 (man. A). In fact, this designation provides us with one of the most important links between 1QS and Pseudepigraphal literature: the pious circles behind Enoch called themselves by this name, as did the circles behind 1QS. The relationship between the expressions *bny ṣdq* and *bny ṣdwq* in 1QS v is not clear, because in pl. v *bny ṣdwq* seems to refer to a particular leading group within the community, whereas *bny ṣdq* in our passage is clearly used of the community as a whole; on the other hand, the exposition of Ezek. xliv 15 in CD iii 21 ff suggests that *bny ṣdwq* of that biblical passage was taken as referring to the actually existing pious community as a whole, no doubt, because *bny ṣdwq* was taken as alluding to *bny ṣdq*, the community. Cf. note on v 2.

[62]) The doctrine of the two ways is to be found in Pseudepigraphal and early Christian literature (cf. Test. Asher i 3-v 2; Barn. Did.), see especially AUDET. For 'walking in light and darkness', cf. 1 John i 6 f, ii 11; John viii 12, xi 10, xii 35 (BROWNLEE).

[63]) DUPONT-SOMMER equates this expression with 'Belial' in i 18, 24 etc. It is to be noted that the angel concerned is inferior to God, not His equal counterpart, cf. MICHAUD.

[64]) Hebr. *bny 'wl*, cf. *bny 'wlh* in 2 Sam. iii 34, vii 10; Hos. x 9; Ecclus. xvi 1 (xli 8: *'nšhy 'wl*), and *mwldy 'wlh* in 1Q27 i 5.

[65]) Cf. Prov. ii 13.

[66]) This is perhaps an echo of Ezek. xliv 15. The biblical phrase suggests that *t'wt* of our passage is simply to be taken as a construct infinitive.—For the idea that the pious are lead astray and afflicted by satanic powers, see Test. Dan v 6; Test. Benj. iii 3. CD ii 17, and no doubt also 1QpHab x 9, allude to people outside the community.

[67]) Cf. 1 Cor. iv 1 (BROWNLEE).

[68]) Hebr. *'d qṣw*. All scholars take *'d* in the meaning 'until'; if, however, we are right in assuming that *qṣ* is used in 1QS only in the meaning 'time', 'period' (see note on i 14), it seems a little difficult to maintain the preposition in that meaning. The translation is based on the assumption that *'d* here means 'during', 'as long as', a meaning which is traceable in the Old Testament. DRIVER, in a letter to me, draws my attention to a number of passages where *'d*, used as a con-

junction, means 'while', e.g. 1 Sam. xiv 19; in this meaning the word is derived from the root *'dd*, whereas in the meaning 'until', it is from the root *'dh*. Attention may also be drawn to the distinction in Syriac between ܥܕ 'while' and ܥܕ 'until'. The suffix in *qṣw* is *genitivus auctoris*, going back to God, cf. DUPONT-SOMMER.

69) Cf. CD iv 5.

70) Hebr. *mśṭmtw*. The suffix suggests that the word be taken as a noun, as in Hos. ix 7, 8, rather than as a name, cf. CARMIGNAC; on the other hand, it is reasonable to assume that some pun is intended; that the community, from which 1QS originates, was fully familiar with Mastema as a name may be regarded as certain, in view of the many points of contact between 1QS and Jub., cf. DELCOR.

71) Hebr. *wkwl rwḥy gwrlw*, cf. Jub. xix 28: 'Mastema and his spirits', 'spirits' being used in the meaning 'angels', as already in the Old Testament (Ezek.), and very frequently in Pseudepigraphal literature. The idea of the angel of darkness ruling over a host of angels is in line with the mention of Satan and his angels in e.g. Test. Dan vi 1; Test. Asher vi 4; Matt. xxv 41. *Rwḥ* is normally feminine and takes feminine ending in the plural, but in several passages in the Scrolls the word is constructed with masculine ending (CARMIGNAC). For the use of *rwḥ* as a masculine noun, see also ALBRECHT, in *ZAW*, xvi (1996), p. 42 f.

72) Hebr. *lhkshyl* = a finite form, as in Mishnaic Hebrew, cf. SEGAL's *Mishnaic Grammar*, p. 166 f.

73) Cf. Gen. xxxiii 20; Ps. lxviii 36.

74) For 'God's angel', cf. Gen. xxiv 7; Test. Sim. ii 8; Acts xii 11.

75) Hebr. *'ẓr*. The use of singular here, after a composite subject, is irregular; besides, we might have expected imperfect instead of perfect. The word might perhaps be read as a noun (DUPONT-SOMMER); another way out of the difficulty would be to emend *wml'k* to *bml'k*, in view of the possible confusion of *Bet* and *Waw*, due to the fricative pronunciation of the former.

76) I.e. the two spirits of light and darkness, identical with the two spirits of truth and deceit in l. 18 f.

77) Whether we should read this word as *'lyhwn* (Aramaic suffix, cf. BURROWS), or as *'lyhyn* (an unusual application of *plene* writing, DUPONT-SOMMER) is impossible to decide; the disputed letter appears to be different from the preceding *Yod* and may therefore have been meant as a *Waw*; but this is uncertain. In the Samaritan Pentateuch and in the *Ketib* of MT there are cases of *Yod* being used for *Segol*, see SPERBER, in *HUCA*, xiv (1939), p. 178.

[78]) Cf. CD ii 7.

[79]) The bottom line is damaged by worm eating. BROWNLEE reconstructs the line on the assumption of dittography in the following way: [*w'l drky*]*hn kwl 'bwdh w'l drkyhn* [*kn*]*l* [*'bw*]*dh*. DUPONT-SOMMER suggests the reading: [*'l swdy*]*hn kwl 'bwdh w'l drkyhn* [*kw*]*l* [*pqw*]*dh*.

Pl. iv

[1]) Hebr. *'dy 'wlmym*. The use of *'d* in the plural does not occur in the Old Testament.

[2]) This phrase has an interesting parallel in CD ii 8 which we are now able to translate correctly: *wyt'b 't dwrwt mdm* should be emended to *wyt'b 't dwrwt sdm*: 'and He abhorred the generations of their congregation', the present text being due to confusion of *Samek* and *Mem*, to which the copyist could easily fall victim, because the two letters are closely similar. For the use of *sōd* here, cf. 1QS xi 9, 10.

[3]) Hebr. *drkyhn*. The suffix goes back to the two spirits (*rwḥwt* in iii 25); having described in iii 13 ff the metaphysical foundation for the state of mankind, the author now proceeds in ll. 2-8 to give an account of the 'spirit of truth' in man and the subsequent blissful state in the hereafter, and—as a negative counterpart—a description of the vicious corruption of the 'spirit of deceit' in man, and the subsequent painful state in the hereafter (ll. 9-14); accordingly, it is clear that something is missing in the headline in iv 2; the phraseology of l. 9 suggests that we should supply *lrwḥ 'mt*, cf. DUPONT-SOMMER.

[4]) Hebr. *lh'yr blbb 'ysh* (for the verb, cf. also 1QSb iv 25), translated according to DUPONT-SOMMER.—Cf. ii 3, xi 3, 5; Eph. i 18.

[5]) The phraseology here is an echo of Isa. xl 3, xlv 13; Ps. v 9; cf. Ps. of Sol. x 3. The expression 'ways of righteousness' does not occur in the Old Testament, but cf. Jub. i 20; Enoch xci 18, 19, xciv 1; CD i 16.

[6]) Hebr. *'mt*, a gloss originally perhaps written in the margin and later incorporated in the text. The combination of the two, apparently quite synonymous, expressions is frequent, see l. 24, v 3 f, viii 2, xi 14; CD iii 15, xx 29 f; cf. Enoch xxxix 6.

[7]) It is not quite clear whether *mshpṭ* should be taken in the meaning '(punishing) judgment' (DUPONT-SOMMER), or in the meaning 'law', 'commandment' (MILIK). The phrase is an allusion to Ps. cxix 161, and it appears that our author, relying on his memory, unconsciously

substituted *mshpṭ* for *dbr* of the biblical phrase; consequently the latter interpretation is to be preferred. It also appears that the parallelism with the preceding *drky ṣdq* supports this.

[8]) For the combination of 'humility' and 'patience', see CD ii 4. Our passage has a striking parallel in Enoch lxi 11, from which passage it appears that *rwḥ* should be taken as a *nomen regens*, not only of *'nwh*, but also of the subsequent *'wrk 'pym*, *rwb rḥmym* etc. (cf. VAN DER PLOEG).

[9]) For the combination of *rḥmym* and *ṭwb*, cf. especially Enoch xcii 3 where the expressions *hirut* and *sahl* describe the ideal demeanour of the pious, in exactly the same way as *rḥmym* and *ṭwb* in our passage. Furthermore, in both passages the virtues are 'eternal'.

[10]) Hebr. *wḥkmt gbwrh*. All scholars take *gbwrh* in the meaning 'might'. It is to be noted, however, that our phrase is dependent on Job xii 13, where *gbwrh* is used in connection with *ḥkmh*, *'ṣh*, and *tbwnh*, cf. Prov. viii 14. In these passages *gbwrh* appears to be used in the meaning 'wondrous, mysterious wisdom'. In this connection it may be relevant to draw attention to the fact that Sept. uses σύνεσις in its rendering of *gbr* in Job xxii 2, and the same Greek word is used also in Theod. in Dan. ii 20 as a translation of *gbwrt'*. Closely connected with this meaning of *gbwrh* is the meaning 'wonder', 'mystery', in which the word is used in CD xiii 8 (the parallel passage in 1QS ix 18 has *rzy pl'*); Ecclus. xxxviii 6, xlii 17 (gloss), 21, xliii 25, see SMEND. This meaning is also the foundation for our translation of i 21.

[11]) Hebr. *m'mnt bkwl m'śy 'l*. YALON rightly stresses that there can be no question of translating *m'mnt* by 'believing in': that interpretation fits neither the context, nor the following *nsh'nt*; so, the root *'mn* should here be taken in its original meaning 'be firm', cf. BURROWS. Accordingly, there is no foundation for the assumption here of the combination of 'faith' and 'wisdom' (against DUPONT-SOMMER). As for *m'śy 'l* (cf. i 19, 21, x 17; CD i 1, ii 14) BROWNLEE refers to CD xiii 7 f; in that passage there is reason to believe that the expression means 'the *secrets* of God', not 'the *works* of God'. The text is generally read: *yśkyl 't hrbym bm'śy 'l wybynm bgbwrwt pl'w wyspr lpnyhm nhywt 'wlm bprtyh*, and translated: 'He shall instruct the Many in the *works* of God and make them understand His wonderful *mighty deeds*, and he shall recount before them the *events* of eternity' (cf. RABIN), and HVIDBERG, referring to CD ii 14, takes the text as referring to the inspector's teaching of God's mighty deeds in the

past. But in other passages dealing with the teaching activity of the inspector in the community, the subject taught is 'the laws' (CD xv 10 f, verb: *hwdy'*), or 'all the laws of the community' (1QS vi 15, verb: *hbyn*), or 'the exact meaning of the Law' (CD xiii 5 f, verb: *hbyn*), and the inspector alone had power to do so (CD xv 10 f). As has been noticed by RABIN, CD xiii 7 f is parallelled by 1QS ix 18, where we read: *wkn lhśkylm brz y pl' w'mt* ('and thus instructing them in the secrets of wonder and truth'). What in CD xiii 8 is called *gbwrwt pl'w* is in 1QS ix 18 called *rz y pl'*, and it appears natural to assume that the two expressions are synonymous, in other words: *gbwrh* is used in the meaning 'mystery', 'wonder'. It seems right, therefore, to translate *wybynm bgbwrwt pl'w* by: 'and he shall make them understand His wonderful mysteries'. CD xiii 7 f consists of three phrases, each of them, so it seems, conveying the same meaning by way of variation; we are therefore confronted with the task of establishing the meaning of *m'śy 'l* as 'the *secrets* of God', and of reading the last three words of CD xiii 8 in a way which not only suits the context and yields a satisfactory sense, but also is warranted by the shape of the letters in the manuscript. As for *m'śy 'l* it may be pertinent to draw attention to the occurrence of the same expression of Ecclus. xi 4, where the Syriac version renders: 'Wondrous are the *secrets* of God'. It is quite possible that the Syriac translator, by translating *m'śy* by 'secrets', has struck the right meaning, cf. Arab. غَشِيَ 'to cover'. The assumption of a Hebrew root *'śh*, going back to Arab. غَشِيَ and meaning 'to cover', throws interesting light on Prov. xi 16, where the meaning may be: 'Every prudent man *covereth up* knowledge, but the fool layeth open his stupidity' (as for the root *'śh* 'to cover', see EITAN, *A Contribution to Hebrew Lexicography*, p. 57 f, and DRIVER, in *VT*, iv (1954), p. 243). As for the last three words in CD xiii 8 it should be noted that, in spite of the reading *nhywt* by all scholars, the manuscript clearly reads *nhyyt*, a form which is not to be emended to *nhywt*: as in CD ii 10 (*nhyyt 'd*, see note on iii 15) the form is participle fem. Niphal, and it is to this word that the suffix for 3rd fem. sing. of the last word refers. The word concerned is read by all as *bprtyh* and has been emended in various ways. It has not occurred to scholars that what appears to be a *Resh* may in fact be taken as the lower part of a *Lamed*, the upper part of which has disappeared. On this assumption we read *bpltyh*, which is to be understood as the preposition *b* + *pl'* in the

plural (= *pl'wt*) + suffix, and we can translate the word 'with its wonders'. In support of this interpretation one might refer to 1QS xi 3 f where *brzy nhyh whww' 'wlm* is parallel to the preceding *bnpl'wtyw*, cf. l. 5: *mrzy pl'w bhww' 'wlm*. The translation of the three parallel and synonymous phrases in CD xiii 7 f then runs:
'He shall instruct the Many in the *secrets* of God,
'He shall make them understand *His wonderful mysteries*,
'He shall recount before them *what is for ever*, *with its wonders*'
and the context may be taken as dealing with the inspector's imparting of secret knowledge to the members of the community. The context of 1QS iv 3-4, with its strong intellectualistic flavour, makes it reasonable to assume that *m'śy 'l* there is meant in the same way as in CD xiii 7 f; we are lead in the same direction when we consider that legal knowledge is alluded to in l. 2, as well as in l. 4, cf. l. 6, which deals with the duty of the members to conceal such secret legal knowledge.

[12]) That *ḥsdw* should be read as plural (cf. HABERMANN) is suggested not only by the parallel phrase in x 16, but also by the expression *rb ḥsdyw* in Ps. cvi 45.

[13]) Hebr. *wrwḥ d't bkwl mḥshbt m'śh*. VAN DER PLOEG regards the preposition as introducing the object. Taken thus the phrase is to the effect that the pious man has a knowledge of the plan, or structure, of every action, and accordingly he knows how to perform it: *mḥshbh* is taken in its objective sense, referring to something outside the agent. Another interpretation is, however, equally possible: *mḥshbh* may be taken in the meaning 'thought', referring to the thinking capacity of the agent; in which case the phrase is to the effect that the pious man possesses a spirit of knowledge, or discerning capacity, when reflecting what to do: *mḥshbh* then refers to the reflection which precedes the action (DUPONT-SOMMER), or to the thought which is turned into action (SCHUBERT). For *rwḥ d't* BROWNLEE refers to Isa. xi 2 from where *rwḥ 'ṣh* in iii 6 was taken. The expression recurs in Wisdom literature (Ecclus. xxxix 6: πνεύματι συνέσεως) and in Pseudepigraphal literature (Enoch lxi 11: *manfasa ṭebbab*).

[14]) Cf. iii 1.

[15]) Hebr. *wmḥshbt qwdsh byṣr smwk*. There can be little doubt that *mḥshbh* here means 'thought', 'intention', and our phrase appears to support the subjective interpretation of the word in the preceding expression. For *yṣr smwk* (also viii 3), cf. Isa. xxvi 3. ORIGEN, in his *Hexapla*, states the Hebrew text to have been *yṣrw* which is also the

text upon which Sept. is based. So, we have here an interesting example of our author's being acquainted with a text which is identical with MT and different from the Hebrew on which Sept. is based.

[16]) Cf. 'men of truth' in Exod. xviii 21 and the Syriac version in Ecclus. i 15, and 'sons of truth' in Test. Jud. xxiv 3 and Test. Levi xviii 8.

[17]) The text reads *wṭhrt kbwd*, which most scholars translate: 'purity of glory', i.e. 'glorious purity'. The translation given is based on the assumption that the word intended is *'bwd(h)*. The interchange of *Kaph* and *Ayin* occurs also in viii 9, and is frequent in Ecclus. (cf. Greek and Hebrew at vii 13, xxxii 2, and the marginal gloss at xli 23). Our passage is the antithesis of *'bwdt ṭm'h* in l. 10, and the interpretation given has the great advantage of suiting the context exactly: if the disputed word alludes to *worship* the continuation becomes perfectly understandable, *glwlym* being used in its general sense 'idols', and not in the sense 'impure thoughts'; cf. note on ii 11, a passage whose contents are closely related to those of iv 5. As for the omission of the feminine ending, one of the characteristic features of the orthography of CD, see note on v 14.

[18]) Hebr. *mt'b*. The word is most naturally taken as participle Piel, and the apparent masculine form here may be explained either as a *constructio ad sensum*, the virtual subject being the pious man, or as a feminine form with the ending left out.

[19]) Hebr. *whṣn' lkt*, cf. Mic. vi 8, from where *'hbt ḥsd* was quoted in ii 24. As in that passage *'hbt* is to be taken as a substantive, not as an infinitive, thus also in our passage *hṣn'* is to be translated as a substantive (cf. Dupont-Sommer); the expression is parallel to the preceding *ṭhrt*. The root *ṣn'* has been examined by Thomas, in *JJS*, i (1948-49), pp. 182 ff, who reaches the conclusion that the basic meaning of the root is that of *guarding* and *strengthening*; derived from this basic meaning is the sense 'humble' in which the root is used in Mic. vi 8, 'for a man who is guarded, careful, in walking with his God ... is humble, or pious.' The passages, in which Mic. vi 8 is alluded to in 1QS, have been examined by Hyatt, in *ATR*, xxxiv (1952), pp. 235 ff. Examining the meaning of the root *ṣn'* in the Old Testament, and in later Hebrew and Syriac literature, he finds that it implies the following shades of meaning: (a) humility, modesty; (b) purity, chastity; (c) secrecy, privacy; (d) wisdom, skilfulness. The idea of secrecy he rules out, as far as 1QS is concerned, because the phrase there refers to walking with man, and by a process of elimination

he finds that in all passages concerned the meaning 'walking wisely' fits the context best. This rendering he finds particularly apt in our passage, because of the following *'rmt kwl*. It may be objected that by this way of reasoning the idea of secrecy is not ruled out in viii 2 where the context deals with social behaviour, because it may be argued that the meaning is that the secrets of the society should be safely guarded among the brethren within the community, cf. our passage where the phrase is followed by the verb *ḥb'*; besides, it should be noted that Isa. xxvi is alluded to in l. 5, and that the same biblical text is used in x 25 in a highly secretive context. The translation given, then, is based on the assumption that the root *ṣn'* is used in our passage in the Aramaic sense 'to conceal' (see JASTROW's *Dictionary*, II, p. 1292 f). The continuation in l. 6 suggests this interpretation; the same meaning may be intended in viii 2 f, although this is less certain, and it should be admitted that there is nothing in v 4 which suggests the meaning we are dealing with here. On the other hand, it should be remembered that the mother tongue of the author was Aramaic, and that he consequently must have been aware of the meaning 'to conceal' and could read that meaning into the biblical passage when the context required it—but I must refer the reader to the following note.

[20]) Hebr. *b'rmt kwl yḥb' l'mt rẓy d't*. This difficult passage has been interpreted in a variety of ways, and this is not only due to the difficulty of reading the third word correctly, but also due to the fact that scholars have not been aware of the biblical background of the whole phrase. All scholars take *b'rmt kwl* in connection with the previous *whṣn' lkt*, and this interpretation is, of course, obvious with those who read the third word of the line as *wḥb'* which is the reading of BURROWS, in his edition. There are, however, two passages in 1QS which show that this interpretation, with or without the reading *wḥb'*, is wrong. In l. 11, which represents an exact antithesis of our line, the phrase *w'rmt rw'* is parallel, not to the previous *ḥwshk*, but to the preceding *kybwd lb* which is explained by the following *llkt bkwl drky ḥwshk*; but better still is a reference to x 25 where the phrase *wb'rmt d't* indicates the means by which the pious hedges the truth; in the same way the phrase *b'rmt kwl* in our passage indicates the means by which the pious conceals 'the mysteries of knowledge'. Thus we are lead to reject the reading *wḥb'*, and we are left with the reading *yḥb'*, which suggests the taking of the whole sentence as a circumstantial clause which explains, or develops further, what was indicated

by the previous phrase *wḥṣnʿ lkt* (cf. preceding note). That this reading is right is confirmed by the apparent dependence of *yḥbʾ lʾmt* on Isa. xlii 3. The biblical context deals with the Servant of the Lord who 'shall not quench the dimly burning wick, and shall faithfully bring forth true religion'. Our author has applied the passage to the pious (cf. the application of Isa. xlii 1 in viii 6), and has connected *ykbnh* with what follows. By pronouncing the *Kaph* fricatively he has derived the verb from *ḥbʾ* and has seen in the passage an allusion to the mission of the pious in the world. This interpretation is an interesting example of our author's exegetical abilities: the Servant of the Lord has been taken collectively as alluding to the pious community, and whereas the mission of the Servant according to Isa. xlii 3 is to *reveal* and *make known*, the mission of the pious, according to our author's particular interpretation, is to *cover up* and *conceal*. The dependence of our phrase on Isa. xlii 3 also clarifies the problem of the syntactical position of *lʾmt*. As in the biblical passage it means 'faithfully' (cf. MILIK). For 'mysteries of knowledge', cf. Enoch li 3.

[21]) For the meaning of *yswd* here, cf. CD iv 21, x 6.—*ʾlh*, of course, is retrospective.

[22]) Hebr. *lmrpʾ*. It appears natural to regard the enumeration of the blissful goods in store for the pious as starting here, and to take the previous *pqwdt* as pointing forwards (cf. e.g. BROWNLEE). The word *mrpʾ* is used in the Old Testament as referring to eschatological salvation, visualized as 'healing' (cf. Jer. viii 15, xiv 19; Mal. iii 20). The conception is common in Pseudepigraphal literature, see e.g. Enoch x 7, xcv 4, xcvi 3; Jub. i 29 (combined with 'peace' and 'blessing' as in our passage), xxiii 29.

[23]) Hebr. *prwt zrʿ*, to be taken in a figurative sense (BARTHÉLEMY). The idea of plenty of progeny is so common in Jewish eschatological speculations (cf. e.g. Enoch x 17) that it is reasonable to believe that our community took over this idea, quite irrespective of whether they practiced marriage or not. The idea goes back to the Old Testament (Isa. xlix 20, liii 10).

[24]) Hebr. *wśmḥt ʿwlmym*, cf. Isa. xxxv 10, li 11, lxi 7 (BROWNLEE).

[25]) Hebr. *wklyl kbwd*. Many scholars (e.g. MILIK) prefer the taking of *klyl* in the Hebrew meaning of 'fullness' (cf. *mklwl hdr* in 1QSb iii 25). For the meaning 'crown' (Aramaic), DUPONT-SOMMER refers to Test. Benj. iv 1; 1 Pet. v 4.

[26]) Hebr. *mdt hdr*. The word *mdh* may be translated either 'measure' (VAN DER PLOEG), or 'attire' (BROWNLEE), or 'reward' (DELCOR, cf.

JASTROW's *Dictionary*, II, p. 732).—Cf. 'garments of glory' in Enoch lxii 15 (*lebsa sebhat*).

[27]) Cf. Isa. lx 19; Enoch xlv 4. For the entire enumeration of the blissful goods, cf. Ps. xxi, whose phraseology has much in common with that of ll. 6-8.

[28]) All scholars rightly translate *rḥwb* and the following *shpwl* as nouns, and not as infinitives. Forms of other roots, similar to those which Tiberian *rōḥab* and *shēphel* assume here, occur in both 1QS (see the Introduction) and 1QIsa[a]. YALON ascribes this feature to Aramaic influence and draws attention to the occurrence of Segolates with *Waw* instead of *Segol* in the old *Piyyūṭīm*; it should be noted that lines of connection may also be drawn to the Samaritan dialect, in which e.g. the word *'ōhel* assumes the form *'ahōl* (cf. DIENING, *Das Hebräische bei den Samaritanern*, p. 54); on the other hand, in both 1QS and 1QIsa[a] there are a great many cases of segolates where the Tiberian pronunciation is clearly presupposed, and no uniformity exists.—For the idiom *rḥwb npsh*, cf. Prov. xxviii 25 (REICKE). The phrase refers to greediness, not to pride (against SCHUBERT).

[29]) Cf. Eccles. x 18 (HABERMANN).

[30]) Cf. Isa. xxxii 17.

[31]) Cf. Jer. xlviii 29; 1QpHab viii 10.

[32]) Hebr. *'kzry* which belongs to both *wrmyh* and the preceding *kḥsh*, cf. HABERMANN. VAN DER PLOEG refers it to *wrmyh* only, DUPONT-SOMMER, taking it as a substantive, to neither.

[33]) Hebr. *ḥnp*; the defective spelling is worthy of note. All translators take the word as 'impiety', the meaning in which it is used in Isa. xxxii 6; for the meaning 'hypocrisy', see JASTROW's *Dictionary*, I, p. 484 f. Ὑποκρίτης is used for *ḥānēph* in Job xv 34 (Aqu., Symm.), xx 5 (Aqu.), xxxvi 13 (Theod.), xxxiv 30, xxxvi 13 (Sept.); Prov. xi 9 (Aqu., Symm., Theod.); Isa. xxxiii 14 (Aqu., Symm., Theod.). Ὑπόκρισις is used for *ḥōneph* in Isa. xxxii 6 (Aqu., Symm.)

[34]) Cf. Prov. xiv 29 according to Sept. 'Stupidity', 'folly' is not the meaning of *'wlt* here, where it indicates indecency, cf. the use of *nbl* in vii 9, and the Greek version at Ecclus. xxx 13 which renders *b'wltw* by ἐν τῇ ἀσχημοσύνῃ αὐτοῦ.

[35]) Cf. 1QpHab xii 8. For the translation, which is based on the assumption that *m'śy tw'bh* belongs to what precedes (cf. DEL MEDICO), cf. the contrast which appears to be intended between 'inertia in righteous activity' of the previous line, and 'shameless zeal for abominable doings' of our line.

[36]) Cf. Hos. iv 12; Test. Reub. iii 3; Test. Jud. xiii 3, xiv 2; Test. Levi ix 9.

[37]) Hebr. *wdrky ndh bʿbwdt ṭmʾh.* For the translation of *ʿbwdh* as 'worship', cf. Ezek. xxxvi 17 f which deals with the polution of the land due to worship of idols. *ʿbwdt ṭmʾh* in our passage forms the negative counterpart of *ṭhrt* (*ʿ*)*bwd* in l. 5.—Cf. CD ii 1, iii 17, xii 1f; Jub. xxi 21, xxii 16, xxiii 14.

[38]) Cf. CD v 11 f (Brownlee).

[39]) Cf. CD i 9, xvi 2.

[40]) Hebr. *kbwd* = Tiberian *kōbed.*

[41]) Hebr. *qwshy* = Tiberian *qᵉshī* (Deut. ix 27).

[42]) Hebr. *wkybwd.* This form is orthographically interesting because *Yod* is used in front of *Dagesh forte* (see the Introduction). Yalon, denying that *Yod* is used in the Scrolls in this way, suggests the reading *wkwbwd.*

[43]) Cf. Prov. ii 13.

[44]) Lit.: 'wicked wisdom'.

[45]) Hebr. *mlʾky ḥbl,* cf. CD ii 6 and *mlʾky ḥblh* in rabbinic literature (e.g. Sabbat 55a, cf. Weber, *Jüdische Theologie,* p. 172). Perhaps we have here a case of omission of the feminine ending. Cf. Enoch lxiii 1, lxvi 1 (Brownlee), liii 3, lvi 1, lxii 11 (Delcor).

[46]) Hebr. *lshḥt ʿwlmym. Shḥt* is in Sept. occasionally rendered by ἀπώλεια, the translators obviously having connected it with the root *shḥt,* and not with *shwḥ.* It therefore appears that the expression *shḥt ʿwlmym* means exactly the same as *klt ʿwlmym* in ii 15.—Cf. Ps. of Sol. ii 35; 2 Thess. i 9.

[47]) Hebr. *bʾp ʿbrt ʾl nqmt.* For the expression *ʾl nqmwt,* cf. Ps. xciv 1; by the correction the phrase was broken up: the word is no longer plural of *nqmh* belonging to *ʾl,* but participle Qal going back to *ʿbrt.*

[48]) For this enumeration, cf. biblical passages like Ps. lxxi 13, lxxviii 66; Jer. xxiii 40.

[49]) Hebr. *mḥshkym,* used in the Old Testament (Ps. lxxxviii 7) as referring to Sheol. For the combination of darkness and fire, see note on ii 8.

[50]) The translation given presupposes the assumption of a periphrastic genitive construction in *wkwl qṣyhm ldwrwtm*; furthermore, it seems clear that *qṣ* is used here in the meaning 'period' (for which, see note on i 14), and not in the meaning 'end' (against Lambert). The phrase has an exact parallel in Enoch x 14 (Greek: μέχρι τελειώσεως γενεᾶς αὐτῶν; Ethiopic: *eska tafsāmēta tewwelda tewweld*), *qṣ* in the

Hebrew original having been taken erroneously by the translators as 'end'.

51) Hebr. *b'bl ygwn*. The meaning 'sorrow' of *'bl*, which is presupposed here by all translators, may not be the meaning intended by the author: the parallelism with the following *r't mrwrym* appears to favour the translation given; there seems to be some evidence for the view that *'bl*, at a later stage, besides the meaning 'sorrow' in classical Hebrew, assumed the meaning with which we are dealing here. Greek λύπη covers both meanings and is used accordingly in Sept., expressing 'sorrow' as well as 'pain', 'distress' (as for Ecclus., see SMEND's *Index*, p. 149), and it is very tempting to assume that in the Hebrew original of Enoch cii 7 and cviii 5 the word was used in the meaning 'suffering', 'affliction', rather than in the meaning 'sorrow'; the context appears to recommend this interpretation.

52) The reading *bhwwwt* is presupposed in the translations of many scholars who connect the word with biblical *hawwāh* 'disaster' (DUPONT-SOMMER, BROWNLEE etc.). The combination in our passage with 'darkness' appears, however, to suggest that it is used as indicating the locality where the suffering of the impious takes place, cf. *hawwōth* in Ps. v 10; the word there is generally taken in its usual sense 'calamity', but the preceding *qrbm*, and especially the following *qbr ptwḥ* seems to show that the word is used in the meaning 'depths', cf. Syriac ܗܘܬܐ (the same consideration has no doubt guided REICKE in his translation 'i mörka djup'); the word taken in this meaning makes excellent sense here, and the idea of hell as a deep, dark gulf is in perfect accordance with the notion in the Pseudepigrapha (see e.g. Enoch xxii 2; Jub. vii 29), and in the New Testament (2 Pet. ii 4). The translation of VAN DER PLOEG presupposes the reading *bhwywt*, plural of *hwyh* 'existence', cf. also YALON.

53) Cf. Jer. xliv 27; Enoch xix 1.

54) Cf. Ezra ix 14; CD ii 6 f (BROWNLEE); Enoch lii 7; Jub. xxiv 30. As for *shryt*, cf. 1 Chron. xii 38.

55) Hebr. *b'lh twldwt*. The two words have been written with a different hand. Cf. Gen. ii 4, another indication of the fact that the whole of the present essay (pl. iii-iv) is based on the initial chapters of Genesis, dealing with the Creation and Fall. For the phrase *twldwt kwl bny 'ysh*, cf. iii 13; there the wise man was instructed to teach the 'children of light concerning the genealogies of all mankind with respect to both sorts of their spirits with the (different) characters of their actions'. This teaching has now been given, and the section ll. 15-26 is nothing

but a variation of the same theme: the two spirits governing the two sections of mankind, the final elimination of all wickedness and the angelic existence of the pious in the world to come. BROWNLEE finds allusions to a Messiah, especially in ll. 20 ff; as the following commentary will show, there is no foundation for this interpretation: the section deals with no particular individual, but continues the description of the two opposite sections of mankind.

[56]) Hebr. *wbmplgyhn*. The word is undoubtedly the biblical *mplgh* (2 Chron. xxxv 12), cf. DUPONT-SOMMER who correctly refers the suffix to the two spirits. In our passage the word has masculine ending in plural, but the regular form occurs in l. 17. For the idea of the two parties or divisions KUHN refers to parallels from the Gathas (Yasna xxxi 2, 3, xliii 12, xliv 15) where the conception is fundamental.— The preposition is taken rightly by BARDTKE in the sense 'within', the meaning being that every human being throughout the ages belongs to one or the other of the two divisions. The author has not yet turned his mind towards the future angelic inheritance of the pious: he deals with this prospect in l. 22, and BROWNLEE's suggestion that *mplgyhn* alludes to the angelic companies of the spirits, in which 'all the human hosts will receive their inheritance according to their respective societies ', reads too much into the text: (a) the use of the verb *nḥl* does not necessarily allude to inheritance in the hereafter; (b) the use of *mplgh* in the context of l. 17 f clearly shows that we are dealing with the two divisions of the spirits as materialized in humanity; (c) the interpretation of *dwr* as 'society' is, as we have already seen (see note on iii 14), unwarranted in pl. iii-iv: the word means 'generation' and cannot be taken as alluding to the 'respective societies' in the hereafter.

[57]) Periphrastic genitive, equal to *ṣb'wt dwrwtm*. The use of *ṣb'wt* is another reminiscence of Genesis (ii 1), the word having been taken as alluding to mankind exclusively; in 1QSa i 6 the word refers to the community. *Ṣb'wtm ldwrwtm* is most naturally taken as the subject of the previous *ynḥlw*, the verb, which anticipates the allusion to Num. xxvi 56 in the next line, being used absolutely.

[58]) Hebr. *p'wlt m'śyhm*, cf. l. 25. In our passage the compound expression seems to be a stilted phrase meaning 'activity', with no view to 'reward', good or bad; the context is to the effect that all activity is done within the two classes; a similar translation of the same expression appears preferable in l. 25: that God knows the *result* or *reward* of human activity does not seem to contain a very profound

thought, as He Himself is the judge who measures out reward or punishment; the phrase is more suitably taken to mean that God knows beforehand everything concerning human activity (cf. BURROWS' translation).

[59]) Cf. Num. xxvi 56, where *byn rb lm'ṭ* means 'either many or few'. In our passage, however, the expression is applied to the individual *'ysh*, the idea being that every man has his share of one of the two spirits, and some have a larger or smaller share than others. DUPONT-SOMMER explains the expression as being to the effect that every human soul is a mixture of *both* spirits, the individuality being due to individual 'mixtures'. In view of the context, however, which deals with the two distinctly separate classes into which mankind is divided, that interpretation does not appear right; the meaning seems rather to be that the human individual has a share in either the good or the evil spirit, and his individuality depends on the quantity of his share. For *mw'ṭ*, see RABIN, in note on CD xiii 1. —For our phrase, cf. also 1QSa i 18.

[60]) Hebr. *bd bbd*. That this idiom is biblical (Exod. xxx 34) and in its biblical context means 'in equal parts' is, so it appears from the translations, realized by all scholars. DUPONT-SOMMER interprets it as being to the effect that although the two spirits are distributed unequally in the isolated individuals, they are found 'dans l'ensemble à égalité'; VAN DER PLOEG takes the passage to indicate numerical equality of the two divisions. In either case we seem to be faced with logical difficulties, and there are good reasons for believing that our author took the phrase to mean 'separately'; that this rendering suits the context which deals with the irreconcilability of the two spirits and their classes far better, is obvious; it is difficult to see how the fact that God has set the two classes in equal parts can be an explanation (*ky'*) of the actual existence of the two sharply distinguished groups, whereas, with the translation of *bd bbd* as 'separately', the general trend of the author's argument becomes quite clear: the two groups are irreconcilably contrary to one another simply because God has put them down as such ;that is also the reason for the 'eternal hatred' between them (l. 17) and for the fact that 'they do not walk together' (l. 18); cf. REICKE's translation 'side by side'.

[61]) Cf. 1QpHab vii 7, 12.

[62]) The phrase is taken from Ezek. xxv 15, xxxv 5. Considering the close affinity of the whole essay to Gen. i ff, it is reasonable to assume that our author, by using this phrase, also alludes to Gen.

iii 15, in which passage he appears to have seen an allusion to the irreconcilability of the two opposite classes of mankind. DUPONT-SOMMER refers to Yasna xliii 8, 15, xlvi 6.

[63]) In the use here of the word *tw'bh* there is an interesting, and no doubt intended, pun on the previous *'ybt*; this pun becomes particularly clear if we may venture to suppose that the pronunciation of the former was *tō'ēbat*. Cf. Prov. xxix 27.

[64]) For *mshpṭ* in this meaning, see note on iii 17.

[65]) Lit.: 'in the mysteries of His wisdom'; a similar expression in 1QpHab vii 14, cf. Enoch li 3, lxix 8 (*hebbu'āta tebbab*).

[66]) Hebr. *qṣ*, see note on i 14.

[67]) See the close parallel in Enoch x 16. For the idiom *yṣ' lnṣḥ*, cf. Hab. i 4; in 1Q27 i 6, a passage closely related to ours, the verb *glh* is used.

[68]) The verb *htgwllh* is translated by many as 'wallow' (DUPONT-SOMMER and others); for this interpretation one might refer to the following *bdrky rsh'* (cf. Prov. xv 9) which seems to suggest that the verb implies a motion; on the other hand, the meaning 'wallow' seems very harsh with 'truth' as the subject, and the same objection applies to CD iii 17 where the verb is used with the members of the community as subject; RABIN, in his note on that passage, takes the verb as derived from *glwlym* 'defilement', regarding the meaning 'wallow' out of the question on the strength of the phraseology in 1QS iv 21; in Ecclus. xii 14 the Hitpael of *gll* is used in the meaning 'pollute oneself' (SMEND).

[69]) Lit.: 'the fixed time of judgment of something decided'.—For *nḥrṣh*, cf. Isa. x 23, xxviii 22; Dan. ix 27; in all these passages it is used in connection with *klh* 'destruction'.

[70]) The latter part of the passage is an allusion to Mal. iii 3 (BROWNLEE) which provides us with the key to the right interpretation of our line: it is to be noted that in that biblical passage the object of the cleaning is 'the sons of Levi', whereas in our passage all that is left of this original object is the insignificant *dativus ethicus lw*. We have already seen that our author in iii 11 f, in quoting Num. xxv 13, replaced *khnt* by *yḥd*, and we have in our passage another example of avoiding any exclusive reference to priesthood: 'the sons of Levi' was replaced by *mbny 'ysh*: 'a part of mankind', this expression of course alluding to the pious community; for the preposition *mn* used in this way, cf. Isa. lviii 12. The translation given, presupposing the taking of *mbny 'ysh* as the object of *zqq*, follows VAN DER PLOEG. Also BROWN-

LEE originally understood the passage thus, but has later suggested a quite different interpretation, according to which the text deals with the Messiah as expected by the community. Both DEL MEDICO and REICKE see in *gbr* one man alluded to, and it is this view which BROWNLEE develops; for the view that *gbr* alludes to Messiah he refers to 2 Sam. xxiii 1; Zech. xiii 7, and it is maintained that the generic use of the word is doubtful (this last mentioned point, however, is obviously wrong, see e.g. 1QS x 18). Furthermore, in *mbny 'ysh* the preposition is taken comparatively ('more than'), the whole phrase being understood as referring to the Servant's suffering. This interpretation is based on a number of dubious assumptions of liguistic nature (such as the exclusively individualistic interpretation of *gbr*, and the taking of *lw* as the object of *zqq*), and the context strongly speaks against it: the previous, as well as the following, lines deal with collective groups, and not with individuals; besides, the community probably expected two Messiahs, cf. ix 11; it is true that our passage, and in parts the context, echoes the Servant motif, but far from suggesting an individualistic interpretation, this fact on the contrary supports the collectivistic interpretation of the passage as referring to the community as a whole: we have already seen (cf. note 20 above) that Isa. xlii 3, dealing with the Servant of the Lord, was interpreted collectively as alluding to the special mission of the community in the world; it is also worthy of note that in viii 6 the members of the community call themselves 'those chosen by divine pleasure', a designation which is dependent on Isa. xlii 1 which was interpreted collectively; it may also be relevant to draw attention to the interesting fact that one of the most important messianological passages in the Old Testament, Isa. xxviii 16, in viii 7 f is interpreted as referring to the community.

[71]) Hebr. *mtkmw*, elongated form of the suffix, corresponding to *lmw* for *lhm* (BROWNLEE). YADIN reads *mtkmy* and connects the word with Arab. تَخِمَ 'suffer from indigestion'; he then translates: 'the inward parts of the flesh'.

[72]) Lit.: 'his flesh and to clean it'. For the emphatic position of the object, cf. ix 14; for the (superfluous) *Waw*, see ix 7. The use of the root *ṭhr* here is due to the fact that the author still has Mal. iii 3 in mind (cf. BROWNLEE).

[73]) Cf. Ps. cxli 4 according to Pesh.

[74]) Cf. iii 9; Num. xix 21. That the text alludes to spiritual baptism

seems clear; BROWNLEE aptly refers to Isa. xliv 3 and Joel iii 1 f.

[75]) The verbal form is best taken as a construct infinitive governed by an understood *mn*, parallel with the previous *mkwl tw'bwt shqr* (cf. DUPONT-SOMMER). This interpretation seems to suggest itself, because the verb must have the same meaning in which it was used in l. 19 ('to pollute oneself', see note 68 above).

[76]) Cf. Num. xxiv 16.

[77]) The expression corresponds to *wellūda samāyat* or *wellūda samāy* in Enoch vi 2, xiii 8, xiv 3, where these designations, as *bny shmym* in our passage, refer to angels. In Enoch ci 1 the expression is used of the pious, and VERMÈS and AUDET think that it is used in the same way in our passage.

[78]) Cf. Ps. cxix 1; Prov. xi 20; 1QSa i 28.

[79]) The verb 'to choose' is a favourite with the authors of 1QS and CD, cf. the designation 'the chosen ones' applied to the community in 1QS viii 6, ix 14 (cf. xi 7 and 1QSb i 2); CD iv 3 f (also 1QpHab x 13, v 4).

[80]) This phrase occurs also in CD iii 20 in a slightly different form. *'dm* is by many scholars translated as 'man' (e.g. VAN DER PLOEG). Others translate by 'Adam' (e.g. DUPONT-SOMMER). Ecclus. xlix 16 may give some clue to the interpretation of our phrase. That the Hebrew text of that passage is slightly corrupt becomes clear by comparison with the Greek: *npqdw* is an error for *nkbdw*, caused by the use of the verb in the previous line (SMEND), and the translation is as follows: 'Shem and Set and Enoch are honoured, but the glory of Adam surpasses that of any living being'. This appears to suggest that we should understand *'dm* in CD iii 20 and in our passage as alluding to Adam, the conception being that the glory in store for the pious is identical with, or of similar grandeur to, the glory of Adam in Paradise before the Fall.

[81]) Hebr. *w'yn 'wlh*, also viii 10 and 1Q27 i 6. These parallels suggest that the expression be taken by itself, unconnected with the following verb which is *masculine* (cf. VAN DER PLOEG).

[82]) Cf. CD ii 17; Matt. xi 12, apparently an apocalyptic term marking the transition to the messianic era.

[83]) The doctrine of the two spirits appears to be applied psychologically here, and KUHN refers to Rom. vii 23 and Gal. v 17 as parallels.

[84]) Hebr. *wkpy nḥlt 'ysh b'mt*, cf. Num. xxxv 8. This phrase enables us to reconstruct CD xiii 12 where the text is read by RABIN as *kpy hywtw bgwrl h'*[*mt*]. The text is blurred, but the parallel in our passage

suggests that the second word should be read as *nḥlt*, which is also supported by the shape of the letters in the facsimile edition by ZEITLIN: we can now see that the first letter of the word is the upper part of a *Nun*, that the second letter is a *Ḥet*, not a *He*, and that the third is the lower part of a *Lamed*, not a *Waw*; furthermore, our passage suggests that we should reconstruct *h*'[*mt*] with RABIN.

[85]) Cf. Isa. xliii 19.

[86]) See note 58 above.

[87]) The suffix refers to the spirits.

[88]) The restoration may be regarded as certain, in view of the general dependence of this whole essay on Gen. i ff; cf. Gen. ii 9. The application of this scriptural passage is a very interesting example of our author's dualistic way of interpretation: he took *ṭwb wr*ʿ as referring to the two main groups of mankind of which one knows good, the other evil.

[89]) Lit.: 'casting lots'.

[90]) In front of *pqwdh* ca. nine letters are lost.

Pl. v

[1]) Hebr. *wzh hsrk l*, cf. CD x 4, xii 22, xiii 7 (BROWNLEE); 1QSa i 1; for the meaning of *srk*, cf. note on i 1. DUPONT-SOMMER takes the following section to deal with the obligations under which the more advanced members of the society are put, and he finds in the expression *hmtndbym* the designation applied to this particular group of the community; linked up with this view is his interpretation of pl. i as dealing with the novices and their reception into the society. As we have already seen, however, (cf. note 47 on pl. ii) that interpretation is untenable: the first two plates of our manuscript deal with the annual ceremony in which the whole community took part; *hndbym* in pl. i and *hmtndbym* in pl. v are slightly varied forms of designations which the members of the community applied to themselves.

[2]) Hebr. *'nshy hyḥd*, cf. v 2 f, vi 21, vii 24, viii 16, ix 5 f; CD xx 32 (BROWNLEE).

[3]) VERMÈS compares Greek ἑκουσιαζόμενοι, applied to the Hasidaeans in 1 Macc. ii 42. It is not quite clear whether, as we have presupposed it in the translation, the enumeration of the pledges starts with *lhbdyl* at the end of the line (cf. VAN DER PLOEG), or whether *hmtndbym* should be taken absolutely, in which case the enumeration of the pledges starts with the immediately following *lshwb* (cf. DUPONT-SOMMER); for the latter interpretation speaks the absolute use of

hmtndbym in l. 8; against it speaks the phraseology in l. 22 where the expression, as in our passage, is followed by *lshwb*, and where the infinitive is obviously closely connected with the preceding participle.

4) Cf. e.g. Jer. xliv 5.

5) The root *ḥzq* is a favourite with the authors of 1QS and CD, cf. 1QS v 3, ix 14; CD iii 12, 20, vii 13, xix 14, xx 27 (Brownlee).

6) The word *rṣwn* is in 1QS used exclusively of God's will or pleasure; in CD it is used of man's will as well (ii 21, iii 3, 11, 12, xi 4).

7) Cf. Num. xvi 21 (Brownlee, who suggests that the word *'dh* is used here as alluding to the Sanhedrin; this view is based on the use of *'dh* in Sifra 19a and Sifre 41, and stems from the conception that our community is anti-pharisaic; *'dh* occurs *in malam partem* also in CD i 12 and viii 13, alluding to the adversaries of the community, and there is nothing in the contexts of these passages which might support Brownlee's interpretation of the word in our passage).—For *lhbdl* (cf. also 1QSb v 2; 1Q34bis ii 6), Rabin, in note on CD vi 14, refers to Jub. xxii 16 and Ps. of Sol. ii 38.

8) Cf. note on iii 21.

9) *hyh l* may mean 'to belong to' (Dupont-Sommer), or 'to become' (Lambert). The former translation is unfortunate in view of the headline which suggests that the following section applies to the members of the community; the phrase, therefore, should rather be taken as describing the way in which the full members are supposed to live within the community. The usage of *hyh l* in the meaning 'to show oneself as', or simply 'to be' is biblical, cf. e.g. 1 Sam. iv 9. Cf. 1QS ii 24.

10) *Twrh* here, as in vi 22, means 'study of the Torah' and alludes to the main activity of the society. It cannot be stressed too much that we are here dealing with a Jewish, Torah-studying society.

11) Cf. the parallel phrase in l. 15 f. The verb refers to answering of questions concerning the Torah, put to the members (Delcor). Dupont-Sommer emends *mshwbym* to *mwshbym* which he then takes in the meaning of Greek οἴκησις; for this interpretation he refers to CD xii 19, 22, xiii 20, xiv 3. In all these passages, however, the word *mwshb* is traditionally taken in the meaning 'session', 'habitation'. For the meaning 'to answer' of *shwb* in Hiphil, cf. e.g. Job xiii 22.

12) Cf. also 1QSa i 2. The prepositional expression *'l py* has been taken in the meaning 'on the demand of' (van der Ploeg), in which case the sentence is to the effect that the members were supposed to submit their response when they were called upon to do so; this would

agree with the strict rules in pl. vi securing order at the sessions. The translation given follows DUPONT-SOMMER; the sentence is then to the effect that individual members' disagreement with the view of the priests and the community as a whole could not be tolerated: legal and exegetical questions should be decided upon in accordance with the rules in general use; this interpretation is in agreement with the regulation in vi 11, that no one must say anything at the sessions which is contrary to the 'pleasure' of the community, and is recommended by the fact that *ʿl py* occurs in the following line in connection with *gwrl*, echoing the usage in Num. xxvi 56,where the prepositional expression is used in the meaning 'according to'.—The designation 'sons of Zadok' appears to be used here as referring to the priests of the society exclusively, as different from the rest of the community; there seems to be a difference in this respect from CD iv 2-7 in which the designation, taken from Ezek. xliv 15, refers to the community as a whole; in 1QS ix 14 BURROWS, in his edition, reads *bny hṣdwq*, and this passage plays the greatest rôle for the understanding of the application of 'sons of Zadok' amongst the pious groups behind 1QS and CD. VAN DER PLOEG suggests the reading, either *bny hṣdq* or *bny ṣdwq*. BROWNLEE rightly observes that an expression descriptive of the community as a whole instead of the priesthood alone suits the context best. However, an emendation is hardly necessary when the transcription is corrected to *bny hṣdyq*. In Sept., in some passages, *ṣdyq* has been taken as the equivalent of *ṣdq* (see HATCH and REDPATH, *Concordance*, s.v. δικαιοσύνη), and this is due to a pronunciation of the segolates, differing from that of the Massoretes (cf. notes on iii 14 and i 26). The Samaritan Pentateuch and the transliterations of Hebrew words in JEROME's works show numerous examples of dissylables with *a* or *i* in the second syllable which are identical with the nouns called 'segolates' according to the Tiberian grammarians, see DIENING, *Das Hebräische bei den Samaritanern*, p. 54 ff, and SPERBER, in *HUCA*, xiv (1939), p. 206 f, and xii-xiii (1937-38), p. 185. In this connection it may be regarded as especially significant that the equivalent in the Samaritan Pentateuch of *ṣdqh* in Gen. xv 6 is *ṣadíqah* (DIENING, *op. cit.*, p. 65), this form presupposing masc. *ṣadíq* (= Mass. *ṣédeq*) which occurs in the Venice Bible of 1515 as a marginal note on Jer. xi 20 (see SPERBER, *op. cit.*, xiv (1939), p. 206). Thus no correction of 1QS ix 14 is necessary, the text bearing the impress of the Samaritan dialect, and the expression *bny hṣdyq* may be taken as a designation of the community as a whole, equal to *bny ṣdq* in iii 20, 22. The reason why ix 14 presents an orthographically noticeable form of the current *bny ṣdq* is not difficult to detect; the continuation runs: *wbbḥyry hʿt lhḥzyq*, cf. CD iv 3 f: *wbny ṣdwq hm bḥyry yśrʾl*: 'and the sons of Zadok are the chosen of Israel'. From the close affinity between the two passages we may conclude that Ezek. xliv 15 was interpreted in the same way by the authors of 1QS and CD. GINZBERG and LÉVI have suggested that the occurrence of *bny ṣdwq* in CD iv 3 does not bear testimony to the sect's name as being 'sons of Zadok'; Ezek. xliv 15 played an important part for the religious circles from which 1QS and CD originate, not because it contains the name of Zadok, but because it was possible, by means of the Midrashic canon of interpretation, to read the meaning 'sons of righteousness' into it. 1QS ix 14 emphasizes this by using the article. In fact, this way of interpretation possesses closely related parallels within rabbinic literature; thus GINZBERG points out that in Lev. Rabbah, ch. i, the name *ṣdwq* is interpreted as the highpriest Aaron, *ṣdwq* having been equated with *ṣdyq*; a similar case exists in CD iv 3; 1QS ix 14, *ṣdwq* having been taken as equal to *ṣdyq* which was, for reasons mentioned above, read as 'righteousness'. The question now is how the designation should be understood in our passage, 1QS v 2 (and 9). In this connection it is important to draw attention to the fact, not only that the whole section v 1-10 reminds us of Ezek. xliv 15 by the mention of *bny ṣdwq*, but also that the passage is an unmistakable echo of CD iii 18-iv 7. This close relationship appears from: (a) *mḥzqym* in 1QS v 3, cf. CD iii 20; (b) *qwdsh* in 1QS v 6, cf. CD iv 6 where *hqwdsh shwnym* undoubtedly is a corruption of *hqwdsh hm*, the proper translation being: 'and the sanctuary (i.e. the one mentioned in Ezek. xliv 15) (refers to) those whom God forgave', which in a most excellent way alludes to CD iii 18 f: 'and He forgave their sin and built for them an immovable house in Israel'—the passage which caused the quotation of the following scriptural proof; (c) *byt hʾmt byśrʾl* in 1QS v 6, cf. CD iii 19: *b- nʾmn byś-*; (d) *nlwym* in 1QS v 6, cf. CD iv 3 where the word is an interpretation of *hlwym* in the Ezekiel passage; (e) *kpr* in 1QS v 6, cf. CD iii 18 and iv 6. Considering this close relationship and paying full attention to the fact that *bny ṣdwq* in the Midrashic interpretation of Ezek. xliv 15 in CD iv 2-7 was expounded in reference to the messianic community as a whole (without using the expression concerned about the priesthood exclusively), it would be natural to expect that *bny ṣdwq* in 1QS v 2, 9 is used in the same way: It was, as we saw, the case in ix 14, as *bḥyry h'ʿt* there does not refer to a group different from *bny hṣdyq*, but is a variation of this expression. It is, however, difficult to carry this point in v 2, 9, 'the sons of Zadok'—partly by the addition *hkwhnym* and partly by the coordination of the expression with *rwb 'nshy brytm* (l. 9)—apparently being conceived as a part of the community, different from the laity; on the other hand, the parallel expressions in v 2 f (*shwmry hbryt* parallel with *hmḥzqym bbryt*) and in l. 9 f (*dwrshy rṣwnw* parallel with *hmtndbym yḥd l'mt*, both phrases expressing dedication to the study of the Torah) are worthy of note, suggesting that the apparent reference to two different groups of the community is merely rhetorical, both expressions alluding to the community as a whole; in this way, pl. v would in no way differ from ix 14 and CD iii-iv. If this view is not accepted, the recognition of a discrepancy here between 1QS v on one hand and CD iii-iv on the other becomes the only alternative; but it should be noted that whatever view is adopted, the designation *bny ṣdwq* is not to be taken, either in CD or in any of the passages concerned in 1QS, as the actual name of the society.

[13]) Hebr. *rwb*. Some scholars (e.g. DEL MEDICO) take the word to mean 'majority' (see JASTROW's *Dictionary*, II, p. 1454 f). The word also occurs in l. 9 and vi 19, and in the former passage the meaning 'majority' is out of the question; besides, it appears that *rwb* is the Hebrew equivalent of Greek πλῆθος, as this word is used in Ecclus. vii 7, 14; Acts vi 5 (in the sense of 'congregation'), cf. VAN DER PLOEG.

[14]) Cf. Isa. lvi 4 (BROWNLEE). Similar phraseology in 1QSa i 3; 1QSb i 2.

[15]) Lit.: 'the fixed measure of the lot shall go out'. For *yṣ' hgwrl*, cf. Joshua xix 1; 1QSa i 16. YALON connects *tkwn* with the noun *tōken* in Exod. v 18; in that case the word is to be classified as a segolate with the stress on the second syllable. MILIK explains the word as a noun of the *kittūb* type; the noun is then to be taken in the meaning 'assigned place, position, or time' (BROWNLEE), or in the sense 'fixed rule' (MILIK).—Our phrase is taken literally as referring to real casting of lots by BURROWS and others. A couple of features may, however, be taken to point towards a figurative interpretation of the expression: (a) the combination of the phrase with *ʿl py* which, as we have seen (note 12 above), should be taken in the meaning 'in accordance with'—in which case a literal interpretation of *yṣ' hgwrl* is impossible; (b) in vi 16 ff, where the expression also occurs, the case of the novice is clearly decided upon by the members' discussion, not

by an automatic casting of lots; (c) in CD xiii 2 ff a skilled, learned levite is said to be the one, for whom it is fitting to 'cast the lot', to the exclusion of an uneducated priest; the reason for this appears to be that the phrase is used figuratively of the making of decisions on the basis of halakic knowledge for which purpose, of course, an uneducated priest was worse than useless.

[16]) Hebr. *mshpṭ*. For this meaning, see SMEND on Ecclus. xxv 4.

[17]) For the asyndetic juxtaposition of *'nwh* and *ṣdqh*, cf. Ps. xlv 5.

[18]) Cf. Matt. xxiii 23; Acts xxiv 25.

[19]) Hebr. *'shr lw'*, cf. l. 10, 14, 15, 16. In late Hebrew the use of *'shr* was expanded, cf. BROCKELMANN, *Vergleichende Grammatik*, II, p. 614. The word is best left untranslated, cf. MILIK.

[20]) Cf. Ps. xcv 10.

[21]) Hebr. *w'ynyhw*. For the form of the suffix, cf. *GK* § 91 l, and S. R. DRIVER, *Notes on the Hebrew Text of the Books of Samuel*, p. 120.

[22]) Cf. CD ii 16.

[23]) Cf. Deut. x 16, the second half of which ('and be no more stiff-necked') accounts for the following *w'wrp qshh* in our passage. The dependence on Deut. x 16 suggests that the members of the community are meant to be the agents of *lmwl*—and of the following infinitives.

[24]) Cf. Isa. xxviii 16, quoted explicitly in 1QS viii 7 ff. The application of the biblical phrase in our line is an interesting example of our author's disregard of a natural stop in the ground text: he took the words *h'myn l' yḥysh* in close connection with what precedes, seeing in *h'myn* an allusion to *'mt* and taking *yḥysh* as suggestive of *yḥd* and *yśr'l*. *L'* could easily be replaced by *l*, as the latter in ancient manuscripts is sometimes used for *l'* (thus e.g. CD vi 16; 1QIsa[a] xxix 9; 1QpHab v 13). The allusion in our passage to Isa. xxviii 16 presupposes the Masoretic interpretation of *mwsd mwsd*.

[25]) For 'Israel' used in the meaning 'the true Israel', cf. Gal. vi 16; Rom. ix 6. The translation follows BROWNLEE.

[26]) In all passages in CD, which deal with forgiveness (ii 4 f, iii 8, iv 6 f, 9 f, xiv 19, xx 34) God is mentioned as the one who absolves; this is also the case in some passages in 1QS (e.g. ii 8, xi 14), while other passages appear to express the idea that the pious atone for their sins by living their lives in ethical integrity (v 6, viii 6, iii 6 ff).

[27]) The parallelism of *qwdsh* with *byt* in the following suggests

that the former should be taken as 'sanctuary' (cf. MILIK), and not as 'holiness' (against DUPONT-SOMMER). The idea is that of the pious forming a spiritual temple, cf. 1 Cor. iii 16; 2 Cor. vi 16; Eph. ii 21; 1 Pet. ii 5. It is very interesting that this idea is shared by Christians and the pious circles behind our manuscript; as we have seen (cf. note 12 above) the conception is found also in CD iv 6 where the text is slightly corrupt, but easily restored.

[28]) 'Aaron' and 'Israel' are used here in parallelism, designating the two constituent parties of the community: priests and laity, cf. CD i 7, vi 2 f, xix 10, xx 1. For 'Aaron' used as a collective proper name, cf. 1 Chron. xii 28. The expression *byt n'mn* in CD iii 19 can only mean 'a solid house' (cf. 1 Sam. ii 35); the particular use of *'mt* in 1QS suggests that the meaning of 'solidity' is not intended either in *byt h'mt* of our line, or in *mwsd 'mt* of the previous line; in the same direction we are lead by viii 9: 'a house of integrity and truth'.

[29]) Cf. Isa. lvi 6, *ʿl YHWH* of the biblical phrase having been replaced by *ʿlyhm*; for a similar case of a slight change of the consonants of the Tetragrammaton, see i 18. The translation follows DUPONT-SOMMER in understanding the preposition *l* in front of *hnlwym*.

[30]) Cf. 2 Sam. xv 4; CD xiv 12; 1QSa i 13 f. Both *ryb*, *mshpṭ*, and *lhrshyʿ* are terms belonging to the sphere of jurisprudence; cf. CD i 19 f (alluding to Prov. xvii 15) which speaks of transgression of the covenant (for the interpretation of *wyʿbyrw* as Qal, see note on i 16); it seems therefore natural to understand *ḥwq* in our passage as 'covenant', and not, as it is generally interpreted, as 'statute'.

[31]) Cf. ix 21.

[32]) LIEBERMAN draws attention to the fact that the same verb as the one used here (*bw'*) is applied in rabbinical literature as a technical term for both the application for *ḥaverut*, and particularly for conversion. Our passage has a close parallel in CD xv 5 f (DELCOR); in fact, it is possible that the two passages refer to the same situation, viz. that of a man entering the society; consequently there is no reference in CD xv to the 'sons' of the man who joins the community. On the assumption of the passage being an anacoluthon, we may translate it in the following way: 'And the one, who enters into the covenant—for all Israel an eternal covenant—their children (*'t bnyhm*, the suffix constructed *ad sensum*, going back to Israel) who enter in order to pass over to those who are numbered (*hpqwdym* = the full members) shall give an undertaking by the oath of the covenant'.

[33]) Cf. CD v 12, vii 5, xiv 2, xx 17; 1QpHab ii 4.

[34]) Cf. Num. xxx (3, 5, 11, 14, 15). The orthography suggests that the form is meant to be Hiphil, cf. Num. xxx 15, but the meaning is clearly not that of 'to keep', 'to establish' (as in the biblical passage), but that of 'to swear', cf. Ecclus. xliv 21 (see SMEND).

[35]) 2 Kings xxiii 25 is the nearest scriptural parallel, but nowhere in the Old Testament occurs the phrase: 'to return to the Law'; for this, cf. e.g. Targ. at Exod. xxxiv 7. Cf. CD xv 11 ff (BROWNLEE).

[36]) Reference is made to the particular interpretations, 'revealed' to the members of the community by study; the Torah was the given material on the basis of which the *halaka* of the society was built up. Consequently, the prepositional expression *mmnh* should be rendered as in the translation given (cf. DUPONT-SOMMER).

[37]) Cf. Ecclus. ii 16: ζητήσουσιν εὐδοκίαν αὐτοῦ.

[38]) Reference is made here to the whole community, consisting of priests and laity; the phrasing of l. 9 f, however, suggests that this distinction is more rhetorical than real: both *dwrshy rṣwnw*, applied to the priests, and *hmtndbym l'mtw*, applied to the multitude, allude to Torah studying activity; for the suffix in *brytm* (also 1QSa i 2), which goes back to the priests (VAN DER PLOEG), cf. Neh. xiii 29. See Ezek. xxx 5, according to Sept.

[39]) Cf. i 11; it is clear from the context of our passage that the expression alludes to dedication to the study of the Torah, and it appears that this interpretation makes excellent sense also in i 11; it is also to be noted that both in pl. i and pl. v the reference to the *study* of the Torah is followed by the distinct reference to the holy lives of the members of the society in accordance with the *halaka* gained by study. The word 'all' in the translation is our rendering of *yḥd* in the text (cf. YALON).

[40]) Hebr. *wlhtlk* = *wlhthlk*.

[41]) Hebr. *bbryt*. YALON draws attention to Ps. cv 8 f where *bryt* is used in this meaning.

[42]) Cf. iv 19; CD ii 2 f, viii 9; Enoch xciv 1.

[43]) Cf. l. 18 which suggests that *hḥshbw* in our passage cannot be meant as an active form. BROWNLEE suggests the form be taken either as Hophal or as Hitpael with *Taw* left out.

[44]) Cf. Zeph. i 6 b which our author, according to his usual way of interpretation (see note on i 2), took as referring to the searching of the Lord in the Bible; in order to make this clear he added *bḥwqyhw* (for the form of the suffix, see note 21 above).

[45]) Hebr. *hnstrwt*, cf. Deut. xxix 28; the combination with *d't*

in our passage suggests that our author uses the word in the meaning 'hidden things', thus alluding to the 'secrets' of the Torah, 'found' by the members of the society by study. BROWNLEE suggests *hnstrwt* be taken in accordance with the usage in Ps. xix 13, as referring to unconscious sins; correspondingly he takes *hnglwt* as referring to conscious sins; the latter interpretation would fit the following *byd rmh* well, but we have no evidence that *hnglwt* can refer to conscious sins. Cf. CD iii 14.

46) Cf. Num. xv 30 (VAN DER PLOEG); CD viii 8, x 3.

47) Cf. Ezek. xxiv 8 (BROWNLEE) which suggests that *lʿlwt* should be taken as Hiphil (VAN DER PLOEG); it also suggests that *wlnqwm* should be taken as parallel of *lmshpṭ* (MILIK), and not of *lʿlwt*.

48) Cf. Deut. xxix 20; CD i 17, xv 2.

49) Cf. Exod. vi 6, vii 4. VAN DER PLOEG refers the suffix in *bm* to the preceding *b'lwt*, but see Ezek. v 15.

50) Cf. ii 15, iv 14.

51) The text reads *ybw'*, and the singular is kept by VAN DER PLOEG who points to the abrupt transition as a sign of compilation from different sources. The fact that the scribe has left a space in front of *'l ybw'* supports the assumption that an entirely new section starts here, containing a warning to the members against having anything to do with those outside the society, with particular reference to purification rites in which non-sectarians were forbidden to take part (BAUMGARTEN). REICKE finds in the section a polemical attitude against water rites altogether, presupposing that the society did not practise them; this view might find some slight support in the spiritualistic interpretation of water rites in iv 21 ff; on the other hand, the archaeological evidence points the other way: at Khirbet Qumran a large room has been found, next to the principal building, which is believed to have been used for ritual baths (cf. DUPONT-SOMMER). The author is not consistent in the following: *ybw'* is singular, the next two verbs are plural, but the suffixes in l. 14 are singular, whereas in l. 16 they are plural; the attempt to distinguish the singular forms from the plural forms as referring to two different groups appears futile.

52) Hebr. *lgʿt bṭhrt*, referring to participation in the lustrations which gave admission to touching certain ritually clean articles. The use here of the verb 'to touch' suggests that *ṭhrh* alludes to something palpable, and LIEBERMAN has pointed to the use of the word in rabbinic literature as denoting the ritually clean articles of the *ḥaverim*.

[53]) Cf. Exod. xxii 30.

[54]) Cf. Jer. xviii 8, xxiii 14, xliv 5.

[55]) Hebr. *ṭm'* (*bkwl ʿwbry dbrw*). If taken as an adjective, the best translation of *ṭm'* is that of GINSBERG: 'something unclean'. There is reason to believe, however, that the word intended is *ṭum'āh* 'impurity' cf. VAN DER PLOEG. The spelling of the word is either due to omission of the feminine ending (cf. CD ii 6; 1QIsa[a] viii 3, xxiv 20, xxvii 12), or it is due to the pronunciation of the word as *ṭumāh* with complete muteness of *Aleph*; this would be in keeping with the general weakness of the gutturals in all the Scrolls, cf. e.g. 1QIsa[a] xl 2 where *mālᵉ'āh* of MT is spelt *ml'*, due to muteness of the *Aleph* (pronunciation: *mālā* for *mālᵉ'āh*).

[56]) The verb is Qal, cf. Gen. xlix 6 (note in that passage the use of *sōd* and *kābōd*, and in our passage *ʿabōdāh*; this cannot be accidental). For the application of *Yod* as indicating long *ē*, see the Introduction.

[57]) Cf. CD xx 7. The suffixes of *ʿbwdtw* and *bhwnw* are best taken as referring to the impious man.

[58]) Cf. Lev. xxii 16. The subject of this sentence is the 'unclean' person, and the object the 'holy' man; in the previous sentence it was the other way round.

[59]) Cf. viii 14. RABIN, in note on CD xi 18, draws attention to the occurrence of the Aramaic equivalent *shkn ktyb* in the late *Midrashim*.

[60]) Exod. xxiii 7 according to Sept. (GOTTSTEIN).

[61]) For the juxtaposition of *twrh* and *mshpṭ*, cf. Num. xv 16.

[62]) Hebr. *ywkl*, with *Aleph* left out, cf. vi 13. BROWNLEE compares the oaths of the Essenes which prevented them from eating non-sectarian food (*Jewish War*, II, 143).

[63]) Cf. 1 Sam. xii 4.

[64]) Lit.: 'without a price', cf. Isa. xlv 13; Jer. xv 13. *'shr lw' b* is equal to Mishnaic *shl' b* 'without' (RABIN), cf. SEGAL, *Mishnaic Grammar*, p. 206. The usage is much older than Mishnaic times: *'shr l' brʿ* in Ps. x 6 is rendered in Sept. ἄνευ κακοῦ.—The wording of the present prohibition appears to exclude the idea of a consistently communistic society; for the principle, cf. CD xiii 15, where the expression *kp lkp* probably alludes to the same practice.

[65]) Cf. Isa. ii 22 (MILIK). Our author has had a text similar to that of MT in front of him; for *bmh* Targ. and Pesh. read *kmh*; the verse is not in Sept. REICKE, in his translation of the biblical passage, renders it as he thinks the author has interpreted it; thus, instead of 'whose

breath is in his nostrils', he translates: 'whose breath is under His wrath'. This ingenious suggestion would be in accordance with what we otherwise know from our manuscript of our author's extraordinary exegetical powers.

[66]) Cf. ἀνὴρ ὅσιος Test. Gad v 4; Test. Joseph iv 1; Test. Benj. v 4.

[67]) Hebr. *hbl*, no doubt used by the author because of *nshmh* in the quotation of Isa. ii 22 in l. 17: both words mean 'breath'; accordingly, our phrase is a part of the exposition of the scriptural passage.

[68]) Cf. Ps. xxxix 6; that *kl hbl* of that passage is corrupt for *ky hbl* is suggested both by Pesh. and our passage.

[69]) Cf. Jer. xxiii 17 according to Sept.

[70]) Cf. CD ii 1. RABIN refers to Ezek. xxxvi 17; Jub. xxiii 17.

[71]) Hebr. *ṭm'*, cf. note 55 above.

[72]) For the form of the suffix in the original text, see l. 21, ix 14, and cf. *bw'wm* in 1QSa i 4. The only analogy which the present writer has been able to find in the Old Testament is Judges xx 45 where we may now be able to see why the Massoretes offer the reading *gidʿōm*; it seems clear that the rendering in Pesh. ('until Gibeon') is secondary; on the other hand, the verb *gdʿ* is used in xxi 6, in a context which obviously alludes to the previous narrative by way of a pun on that root. It is very tempting to presume that the Massoretes, by pointing the word in xx 45 as *gidʿōm*, have preserved an old, perhaps dialectal, form of the suffix for 3rd person plural which is not otherwise recorded in the Old Testament; the biblical phrase *ʿd gdʿm* is then to be translated: 'until they had hewn them down'; no emendation, not even of the vowels, is needed.

[73]) The verb is singular, but the suffix in *rwḥwm* is plural. It seems that we have here the same careless style as in ll. 13 ff, cf. the singular suffixes in l. 21. A literal translation must preserve this inconsistency.

[74]) Cf. ii 22; 1QSa i 9. The construction is periphrastic (*lyḥd lʿdt qwdsh* = *lyḥd ʿdt qwdsh*); see note on i 8. Our phrase offers the only case in 1QS in which *ʿdh* is used as a designation of the community (BARTHÉLEMY); the word is used constantly with reference to the community in 1QSa. BROWNLEE refers to CD vii 20 and x 4.—Our context is another description of the annual ceremony by which all the members of the community entered into the covenant, as described in pl. i-ii; that this is the case appears from: (a) *ybw' bbryt* (l. 20, cf. ii 18); (b) *bsrk* (l. 23, cf. ii 20); (c) *shnh bshnh* (l. 24, cf. ii 19); (d) the expression *mʿśyw btwrh* (l. 21) could only be used with reference to members, not to strangers.

[75]) Cf. l. 23, vi 14, 18. RABIN, in note on CD xiii 11, draws attention to the rabbinic contrast of *limmud* and *ma'aśeh* (Abot i 17, v 17). An exact equivalent to our phrase may be found in the Latin version of Ecclus. xvi 4 (which is quite different from the Hebrew): 'omnis misericordia faciet locum unicuique *secundum meritum operum suorum et secundum intellectum ... ipsius*'.—Cf. 1QSa i 17.

[76]) Cf. Deut. viii 18 (with God as subject).

[77]) Hebr. *wlpqwd*; the translation follows LAMBERT.

[78]) There is some evidence that two dots were used as indicating *separation*, see xi 15 and 21, and there is therefore reason to believe that they are used in the same way in our passage. The translation follows DUPONT-SOMMER who takes *r:b* as equal to *rwb bny*, cf. the similar expression in l. 2, 9, vi 19. For the 'sons of Aaron', cf. ix 7.

[79]) Hebr. *wktbm*. BROWNLEE, translating the verb impersonally, draws attention to vi 22 where the enrolling appears to be the responsibility of the Supervisor; on the other hand the verb *ktb*, referring to the same practice, is used in the plural in CD xiii 12, and GINSBERG may be right in assuming that the form *wktbm* is plural written defectively, cf. also RABIN, in notes on CD viii 19 and xiii 12, and MILIK's translation.

[80]) The verb (also vi 2) is Niphal. For *hkwl* used collectively, see note on ii 24. SCHUBERT takes the verb as Hiphil and regards *hkwl* as a neuter object ('to tell each other everything'), but the similarity of phraseology in vi 2 makes that interpretation improbable.

[81]) Lit.: 'the little the great'. BURROWS suggests that the adjectives allude to difference in age, but our context appears to favour the taking of the words as alluding to differences in position within the society: the preceding sentence alludes to rank and position within the society, based on spiritual values, and our phrase is taken as alluding to rank by most scholars.

[82]) Hebr. *pwqdm*, spelt defectively.

[83]) Hebr. *drkw*, spelt defectively, cf. the plural in i 13, ii 2.

[84]) Hebr. *l'ḥrw*. Most scholars (e.g. VAN DER PLOEG) take the verb to mean 'to set back'; as, however, the proper counterpart of 'elevating' would be 'lowering', BROWNLEE's suggestion that the verb here means 'to retard', may be right, cf. the practice of the *Ḥaverim* (Yoma 12b): 'they elevate in holiness, and do not debase' (*m'lyn bqwdsh w'yn mwrydym*).

[85]) Hebr. *kn'wytw* or *kn'wwtw*; the word is unknown, but the meaning is clear.

[86]) The following is an interpretation of Lev. xix 17, closely related to that of the same biblical passage in CD ix 2 ff (cf. CD vii 2 f). In both contexts the admonition (a) must not be launched in anger, (b) must not be delayed, and (c) must be made in front of witnesses. The practice of admonishing each other was an important feature in Jewish, as well as in Christian religious circles, see Ecclus. xix 13 ff; Sabbat 119b; Test. Gad vi 3, 6; Matt. xviii 15; Luke xvii 3; Rom. xv 14; Hebr. x 25.

[87]) As in CD ix 8 our text has *r'* instead of *'myt* of Lev. xix 17. Does it not indicate some literary relationship between 1QS and CD?

[88]) The combination of *'nwh* and *'hbt ḥsd* in ii 24, v 3 f, 25 suggests that CD xiii 18 should be read *b'nwh w'hbt ḥsd*; the first letters are not quite distinct though; RABIN's reading of a *Waw* as the last letter of the first word is a mere conjecture: there is no trace of that letter in the facsimile edition by ZEITLIN.—It appears that the scribe doubted the correctness of the text and stopped after *l'ysh*, leaving a gap between this word and the next sentence. VAN DER PLOEG takes the word mutually, apparently regarding the text as short for *l'ysh 't r'hw*.

[89]) Hebr. *'lwhyhw*, a, possibly dialectal, form of the preposition *'l* + suffix for 3rd masc. sing. For the form of the suffix, see note 21 above. MILIK assumes dittography here.

[90]) Hebr. *btlwnh*, in the Old Testament used only in the plural.

[91]) The text had here an expression, enlarging on *blbbk* of Lev. xix 17. The top of a *Lamed* is visible, and BROWNLEE's reconstruction may be right.

[92]) The translation may be supported by reference to the parallel text in CD ix 6 ff which inculcates that admonition must be done as soon as possible and not be kept overnight, cf. BROWNLEE. YALON reads the original text as *bywmyw* (cf. BURROWS: 'in his days') which he takes as the equivalent of *bywmw*, referring to cases of the suffix *-yw* being used as equal to *-w* in 1QIsa[a]; but a reference to 'his day' or 'his days' is strange in the context. A closer examination of the facsimile edition suggests that the original text was *bywmwr*, a phrase whose obscurity is due to the dropping out of *Aleph* (= *bywm 'wr*, cf. Amos viii 9): anger must not be kept overnight, cf. Eph. iv 26. This attitude throws a most interesting light on the application of Ps. xcv 7 in Heb. iii 13.

Pl. vi

[1]) Our passage employs *'wwn* for 'sin' whereas the parallel passage in CD ix 8 uses *ḥṭ'* of MT in Lev. xix 17.

[2]) Hebr. *hrbym* which is best taken as alluding to the community, or the lay members thereof, cf. *rbym* in rabbinic literature (LIEBERMAN) and ὁι πολλοί in the New Testament.—While the previous instructions dealt with more 'private' cases, in which only two members of the community were involved, the present passage deals with 'public' cases, in which apparently the community formed the judiciary.

[3]) Hebr. *twkḥt* which refers to the proof which the accuser is supposed to produce (IWRY); the parallel passage in CD ix 3 uses *hwkḥ*. Our passage is to the effect that no case should be brought before the Many unless the accusation could be proved by reliable witnesses.

[4]) Hebr. *mgwryhm* which does not necessarily imply exile. The root *gwr* may simply mean 'to dwell', and the word in our passage is taken accordingly as 'dwellings' by MILIK and others. It is not impossible, however, that the original connotation of the root is intended here: our pious felt themselves as strangers in the land. It is curious to note that in Jer. xxxv 7, dealing with the Rechabites, the same verb is used with the implication of 'exile', and it is equally remarkable that 1QS vi 14 in using the phrase *yśyg mwsr* echoes Jer. xxxv 13 (an even closer parallel is 1QSa i 7 f: *lqḥ mwsr*). Is this due to accident? Should we not rather assume that our sectarians have felt themselves as spiritually akin to the Rechabites?

[5]) Hebr. *kwl hnmṣ'*. BROWNLEE and others take *kwl* personally; following up this interpretation GINSBERG paraphrases: 'whenever they happen to be together'. The application of the same expression in ix 20 speaks against this interpretation and suggests that *kwl* should be taken impersonally. The phrase alludes to the present amount of legal knowledge available to the me mbers of the society; the conception of the gradual revelation of *halaka*, as this is expressed in viii 4, ix 13, 14, 23 is one of the distinct characteristics of our community.

[6]) Cf. note on v 23.

[7]) Both *ml'kh* and *mmwn* are 'ordinary Mishnaic terms for property', cf. RABIN, in note on CD xx 7.

[8]) Cf. CD xiii 1 f (BURROWS). The insistence that at least ten persons must be present in order to constitute a community, is well known

in Jewish circles (see e.g. Sanhedrin i 6; Abot iii 6; Megillah 23b; Berakot 6ab).

[9]) The parallel passage in CD xiii 2 insists on the erudition of the priest, whereas there is no mention of this in 1QS vi 4, probably because in the latter manuscript the education of the priest is taken as a matter of course, cf. v 9, 22.

[10]) The sentences form an anacoluthon.—The verb is jussive (RABIN, in note on CD xiii 2).

[11]) For *tkwn*, see note on v 3. That each member had his definite seat according to his rank is known also from rabbinic circles, cf. Sanhedrin iv 4 and Baba Mezia 86a.

[12]) Hebr. *wkn*, translated according to MILIK.

[13]) Hebr. *ysh'lw*. Scholars are divided on the question whether this form should be read as Qal or as Niphal. LAMBERT interprets the form as Qal, whereas BROWNLEE reads it as Niphal. As we have seen, the members 'answered' at the sessions (cf. v 2); it seems natural, therefore, to take the forms of *sh'l*, wherever they occur with the community as subject, as passive forms; in vi 11, 15 there is no doubt as to the reading of the verb as Niphal, and on the basis of these clear cases it seems justifiable to read the verb as Niphal also in our passage and in l. 9. The logical consequence of this interpretation of the verb, when applied to the members of the community, is that *h'ysh hshw'l* in l. 12 designates the person who put the questions to the members; he was, so to speak, the president of the session and not, as it is generally supposed, some member of the society.

[14]) Cf. CD xiv 6.

[15]) Hebr. *htyrwsh*.—The following description is interpreted sacramentally by DUPONT-SOMMER and others; for this interpretation cf. 1QSa ii 11 ff. LAMBERT and others maintain that we have here a description of an ordinary communal meal.—A close comparison of our passage with CD xiii 2 f yields most interesting results. HVIDBERG has seen that the author of CD in the word *'l pyhw yshqw kwlm* is dependent on Gen. xli 40; although the meaning of the biblical phrase is not quite clear, there can be little doubt that the author took it to mean 'obey', 'comply with an order', which is the meaning given to the phrase by modern scholars. The biblical context, dealing with the leading position of Joseph in Egypt, favours this interpretation, and the same consideration applies to the context in CD which deals with the leading position of the priest in the community. Now, in the parallel text in 1QS, in spite of the almost word by word

similarity to CD, we note the following differences: (a) in 1QS there is no explicit quotation of Gen. xli 40; (b) in 1QS the leading position held by the priest at the meal is described, not the leading part played by him in the daily life of the community by virtue of his legal knowledge. Keeping in mind that the word *mshqh* 'drink' is used twice in 1QS (vi 20, vii 20) there can be little doubt that the author of 1QS has understood Gen. xli 40 as follows: 'on his command they shall all be given to drink', and consequently went on to describe the leadership of the priest on such occasions on which drinking played a part, in other words: CD and 1QS here represent two different interpretations of an obscure biblical passage. Incidentally, it is interesting to notice that RABIN, in note on CD xiii 2 f, draws attention to Targ. in which Gen. xli 40 is taken as alluding to 'eating', and suggests that 'this might well be an allusion to the priest's precedence in eating and drinking, 1QS vi 4-5'.

[16]) Hebr. *lhbrk br'shyt hlḥm*. The close similarity of this phrase to Gittin v 8, and especially Gittin 59 b (JASTROW's *Dictionary*, II, p. 1437) suggests that the priest, mentioned in the preceding clause, should be taken as the subject of *lhbrk* (cf. BURROWS), and that *br'shyt* should be taken as disconnected with *hlḥm* (cf. KUHN). The apparent Hiphil of *brk* is unprecedented. For grace at meals BROWNLEE refers to the practice of the Essenes (*Jewish War*, II, 131), of the Pharisees (Berakot vii 3), and of the Christians (Matt. xiv 19).

[17]) That we have here a case of dittography is a view held by all scholars except LAMBERT.

[18]) The construction would be easier if we presuppose confusion of *Bet* and *Mem* in *bmqwm* and emend it to *mmqwm*; on the other hand, the similar phraseology in l. 3 suggests that our author is just being careless.

[19]) Hebr. *dwrsh btwrh*, cf. *dwrsh htwrh* in CD vi 7, vii 18; Ezra vii 10. If we are right in our assumption that *'l ypwt* in the following line alludes to the perpetual study of the Torah as carried out by the relief of one member on duty by another member, it appears that the use of singular here cannot be taken to refer to a man holding a particular office, in which case there is a difference in usage between 1QS and CD. According to the former manuscript every member of the society was a Torah student (BROWNLEE).

[20]) Cf. Ps. i 2 (LAMBERT).

[21]) The context is to the effect that there was always one member of the society studying the Torah; in this way the community lived up to the ideal expressed in Ps. i 2.

[22]) The translation follows VERMÈS: the text refers to vigils in the third part of the night, i.e. the members were to get up at two o'clock in the morning in order to recite and expound Scripture and say benedictions. In Midrash Rabbah, on Eccles. ix 9, we hear that a certain Jewish community, called 'the holy congregation' (*'dh qdwshh*), 'divided the day into three parts—a third for Torah study, a third for prayer, and a third for work', but our passage has nothing to do with this.—It should be mentioned that RABINOWITZ finds in the allusion to the old three-fold division of the watches of the night contained in our passage, an indication that 1QS was written before 70 A.D.; the fourfold division was introduced by the Romans, and is presupposed in the Gospels and Talmud.

[23]) Hebr. *lqrw' bspr*. For *qr' b* in this meaning, see Jer. xxxvi 6. *Spr* here = the Bible or the Torah.

[24]) Cf. Isa. i 17 (BROWNLEE), probably taken by the author as alluding to the exegetical activity of the society. Cf. viii 24.

[25]) Hebr. *mwshb* which seems to be used everywhere in 1QS in the meaning 'session', 'Sitzung', 'séance'. BROWNLEE would translate the word in the same way in CD xii 19, 22, xiv 3 (cf. RABIN), see however note on v 2.

[26]) The verb is taken in the meaning 'sit down' by BROWNLEE, and *lrshwnh* is accordingly understood chronologically. Most scholars take *yshb* in the meaning 'to sit', and *lrshwnh* as indicating rank.

[27]) Cf. CD ix 4. For the discrepancy between our passage and ii 19 ff, see note on ii 19: in the latter passage the group after the priests is said to be the levites, not the elders as in our passage, but in both passages reference is probably made to the same group, i.e. we have here a difference in nomenclature only (REICKE). YALON suggests the reading *whlwym* in our passage.

[28]) For the reading of the verb as Niphal, see note 13 above. In favour of this interpretation speaks the use of the verb in connection with *mshpṭ* and *'ṣh* which, as is clear from the use of the singular suffixes in l. 22 f, alludes to answers and advice given by the members at the sessions; this usage has an interesting parallel in Ecclus. xxv 4 where κρίσις and βουλή no doubt presuppose *mshpṭ* and *'ṣh* in the Hebrew original, and where *mshpṭ* was used in the meaning of 'correct answering to a question' (SMEND).

[29]) Hebr. *lhshyb 'ysh 't md'w*. The infinitive with preceding *l* is best taken as explaining and developing the implication of the previous main verb (cf. MILIK), in which case, of course, an active interpreta-

tion of *ysh'lw* is out of the question. The noun *md'* is taken in the meaning 'intimate' by GINSBERG, but this interpretation is only possible if the following *l'ṣt hyḥd* is taken as 'concerning the *counsel* of the community' (cf. LAMBERT); as, however, *'ṣt hyḥd* is otherwise used in 1QS as a designation of the community, it is also here best taken in that way, and the sentence is to the effect that each member should, on request, present his 'knowledge' to the other members taking a part in the sessions, cf. DAVIES who suggests that *md'* in our passage does not just mean 'opinion', but the knowledge which each member discovered, and was supposed to contribute to the common store of secret knowledge.

30) Lit.: 'No one must speak in the middle of the words of his friend before his brother has finished talking', cf. Ecclus. xi 8, and especially Abot v 7. BROWNLEE refers to 1 Cor. xiv 31 f, 40.

31) Hebr. *lpny tkwnw hktwb lpnyw*. The translation follows BARDTKE in referring *hktwb* to the suffix in *tkwnw*. The sentence is simply to the effect that a member must not speak before the one who is enrolled in front of him; for the construction, cf. Ezek. xlii 14, x 3; Ezra viii 1; Neh. vii 64 (I am indebted to Prof. DRIVER for these references).

32) Hebr. *btrw*, cf. CD xiv 11. The occurrence of this expression suggests that the verb *ybw'* in CD xiv 10 is a scribal error for *ydbr*, due to the following *b'y*; accordingly, the CD passage originally ran: 'At his (i.e. the inspector's) request the members of the community shall speak, each in his turn'. So, according to both CD and 1QS (cf. vi 12) the inspector was the chairman of the sessions.—The defective writing of *btrw* is remarkable, and YALON suggests that the spelling may be due to a different pronunciation of the word.

33) Cf. Acts vi 5.

34) Hebr. *wky'*, used for emphasis, cf. 1 Sam. xxiv 20; Isa. xxxvi 19; Job xxxix 27. The translations of MILIK and LAMBERT are nearest to the one given; our interpretation has the following advantages: (a) it keeps the text unemended; (b) it agrees with classical usage; (c) it stresses the powerful position of the *Mevaqqer* when acting as the leader of the sessions.

35) Hebr. *hmbqr 'l hrbym*, cf. CD xv 8. From our passage, and possibly also from CD xiv 10 (cf. note 32 above) it appears that he was the chairman at the sessions, and from other passages in CD (ix 18 ff, xiii 7 ff, 13) we get additional information about his functions in the society. REICKE, in his examination of the position of the *Mevaq-*

qer in CD and in 1QS, reaches the conclusion that he plays a far more powerful part in the life of the community according to CD than he does according to 1QS and this, to REICKE's mind, points towards the assumption of CD being later than 1QS. The argument hinges on the fact that the *Mevaqqer* is more frequently referred to in CD in various functions than he is in 1QS, and is a typical *argumentum e silentio.*— For literature about the *Mevaqqer*, see ROWLEY, *The Zadokite Fragments and the Dead Sea Scrolls*, p. 36, n. 5.

[36]) Hebr. *'shr lw' bm'md h'ysh hshw'l 't 'ṣt hyḥd. M'md* is taken as 'office' by BROWNLEE, and as 'rank' by LAMBERT, but the difficulties are: (a) if the person concerned was in no position to ask, then it is unlikely that he should ever, in any circumstances, obtain permission to speak; (b) the members did not ask, but were asked; it was their responsibility to answer questions put to them, cf. note 13 above; consequently, *h'ysh hshw'l* denotes the person who put the questions to the members of the session; (c) *'shr* is not a relative particle in our passage, *'shr lw' b* meaning 'without', see note on v 17. The translation given is based on the assumption of confusion of *Ayin* and *Ḥet*; the meaning, then, is that a man who wanted the assembly to discuss a problem, the consideration of which seemed undesirable and irrelevant to the president, had a right to appeal directly to the members of the session, whose responsibility it then was to decide whether the question concerned should be dealt with or not. The interchange of *Ayin* and *Ḥet* in this particular word may be the explanation of the difference between the Greek and Syriac versions of Ecclus. xxxix 11 of which, unfortunately, the original Hebrew has not been preserved; the Greek version reads ἐὰν ἐμμείνῃ, and the Syriac: 'if he will (√ ܪܓܐ); these variants can be explained on the assumption that the Hebrew original had *y'md* which by the Syriac translator was taken as the equivalent of *yḥmd.*—For the procedure, see Sanhedrin v 4.— Cf. 1QSa ii 9.

[37]) For this idiom, cf. Sanhedrin vii 5.

[38]) Hebr. *ywmrw*, with omission of *Aleph*, see S. R. DRIVER, *Notes on the Hebrew Text of the Books of Samuel*, p. 122. Notice the close similarity of phraseology to 1 Sam. xv 16.

[39]) The section vi 13-23 gives the regulations for admission of new members to the society.

[40]) 'Israel', i.e. the Jews, cf. CD iv 2, 4, v 19. The phraseology appears to suggest that non-Jews could not be admitted to the community.

[41]) Hebr. *lhwsyp*. The form is Niphal, cf. viii 19; CD xiii 11 (BROWN-

LEE); 1QSa i 1. In Acts v 14, xi 24 προστίθεσθαι is used in a similar way (KUHN).

[42]) Hebr. *hpqyd*. ROWLEY, *The Zadokite Fragments and the Dead Sea Scrolls*, p. 37, n. 1, cautiously suggests that this officer may be identical with the *Mevaqqer*; there are in fact weighty reasons for assuming that this is so (cf. BROWNLEE and others): both 1QS vi 15 and CD xv 10 f deal with the exposition of the rules of the society to the newcomer; in 1QS this is said to be done by the *Paqid*, and in CD by the *Mevaqqer* (DELCOR); the impression that the two designations refer to one and the same officer may also be supported by reference to the fact that the parallel text in CD xiii 11 f uses the verb *pqd* for describing the activity of the *Mevaqqer*.

[43]) Hebr. *brw'sh hrbym* which should be taken in connection with the previous title (cf. MILIK) and not in connection with the following verb (against VAN DER PLOEG), cf. l. 12 where *'l hrbym* corresponds to *brw'sh hrbym* of our passage, and CD xiv 7 as restored by RABIN.

[44]) As for the form of the verb, cf. *GK* § 60b.

[45]) Hebr. *yśyg mwsr*. We have already (see note 4 above) drawn attention to the link with Jer. xxxv 13 in the use of *mwsr*. The word is one of the key-words of the Wisdom literature and occurs 27 times in Prov. alone; in Ecclus. xxxii 14, l 27 it is best translated 'ethics' (after the late Prof. DANBY, orally), and BROWNLEE's translation: 'if he attains to a disciplined life' is excellent; the intellectualistic ring of the phrase *yśyg mwsr* should not be overlooked, however, and RABIN's translation of CD vi 10 (restored after the phraseology of our passage): 'grasp instruction', is equally justifiable: knowledge and perfect living went hand in hand in our community.

[46]) Cf. CD xiii 13, and see note on i 7.

[47]) Cf. ix 20 f; Ecclus. xxxviii 10.

[48]) Cf. CD xiii 5; for the suffix, cf. *GK* § 59f.—Cf. 1QSa i 5.

[49]) In CD xv 11 nothing is said of the community's part in the decisions reached concerning the novices: the inspector alone could decide on the question of admission or rejection. We may here see an indication of some development of the organization within the religious circles behind 1QS and CD, but in what direction did the development go? Did the power gradually slide from the hands of the inspector into the hands of the community (i.e. did the development go from CD to 1QS), or did the office of the inspector become more and more significant in the course of time, until at last there was no room for the views of the community (i.e. did the

development go from 1QS to CD)? LIEBERMAN draws attention to the interesting parallel to our context in rabbinic writings, according to which the potential candidate for membership of a *Ḥavurah* assumes his obligations in the presence of the members of the society. The terms used are *bpny ḥbwrh* and *brbym*.

50) Viz. whether he can be accepted (HABERMANN).

51) Lit.: 'and as the lot comes forth on the counsel of the Many'; the allusion to the casting of lots here is clearly meant figuratively (cf. BROWNLEE), see note on v 3.

52) The verb used is *qrb*, also used of admission to the *Ḥavurah* (LIEBERMAN).

53) See note on v 13.

54) Or: 'they'. VAN DER PLOEG translates by singular, and MILIK by plural. For the reading as singular speaks *ydwrshhw* in l. 14 and *ypqwdhw* in l. 21; against it speaks the immediately preceding clauses, in which the community as a whole was alluded to. We are confronted with the same problem in l. 25 where the reading of *wybdylhw* as plural cannot be supported with absolute certainty by reference to *yshpṭw* in the previous line, as the latter form may be taken as Niphal, and not as Qal.

55) Defective spelling, see note on i 17.

56) Cf. Lev. xxv 29 f where we read: 'And if a man sell a dwelling house in a walled city, then he may redeem it within a whole year after it is sold; for a full year he shall have the right of redemption. And if it be not redeemed *within the space of a full year*, then the house, which is in the walled city, shall be assured for ever to him that bought it, throughout his generations, it shall not go out in the Jubilee'. The word by word quotation of the biblical phrase suggests that our author found a scriptural foundation for the rules followed by admission of novices to the community, by interpreting Lev. xxv 29 f allegorically: 'the walled city' stands for the community, and 'the dwelling house' for the novice; as in a walled city a house, which has been sold, may be redeemed within a year, but after that should be regarded as belonging to the buyer for ever, thus a novice is, during his first year, only to be regarded as loosely connected with the community, and not as a full member; during that period he is free to leave the order, and should therefore not be initiated in anything. Our text cannot be interpreted in any other way than as to the effect that the potential new member should be a constant object for examination throughout a full year. As for the spelling *myl't* (also 1QSa i

10), it may be that we have here a case of *Yod* being used for *Shwa*, cf. rabbinic custom (see also CD viii 5 and RABIN's note on that passage), or perhaps the pronunciation *millēt* is intended (cf. BROWNLEE).

57) Cf. l. 22 below and viii 23. The use of the root *'rb* is to DUPONT-SOMMER an indication of complete communistic organization of the society, but vii 5 ff appears to speak against this assumption; on the other hand, the phraseology of our passage does suggest that there was a common fund, in which the full members of the community had a share, and from which communal expenses were paid.

58) For the reading of the verb as Niphal, see note 13 above.

59) Cf. v 9, and note on that passage.

60) Hebr. *swd* = *'ṣh* (GINSBERG, YALON), cf. the two words in parallelism in ii 25.

61) The original text was corrected because Hiphil of *qrb* is used in 1QS in the meaning 'sacrifice' (viii 9), whereas Piel is constantly used for 'bringing near' new members to the society (vii 21, viii 18, ix 15).

62) Presupposing BURROWS' reading scholars find in this phrase an allusion to an official, distinct from the *Mevaqqer*, whose particular responsibility it was to look after the 'work' or 'property' of the community. That the title of *Mevaqqer* should be used of more than one official is an unlikely assumption, and there is in fact nothing in our passage which might support it. With the correct reading the phrase *'l ml'kt hrbym* is best taken as a gloss of the previous *'l yd h'ysh hmbqr*, added in order to prevent any misunderstanding.

63) The parallel phrase in CD ix 18 shows that the agent is the *Mevaqqer*. The following *bydw* is, in connection with *ktb*, without particular emphasis (cf. SCHUBERT); the idiom 'to write with one's hand' does not occur in MT, but it is interesting to notice that in Sept. of Jer. xxxvi 18 the last word (*bdyw*) is not translated, which may be due to the fact that the translator read the word as *bydw* ('with his hand') and consequently regarded it as superfluous. Our passage shows that the novice was treated fairly: what he brought into the society was put down in writing by the leader, so that if he left the society before his possessions were 'pooled' he would get them all back *in toto*. It appears that our author has borrowed his phraseology from 2 Kings xii 10 ff, xxii 4 ff.

64) For the idiom *hwṣy' 'l*, cf. 2 Kings xv 20. The sentence is to be taken in close connection with the preceding one: the money of the novice must not be touched before he is a full member, because he

can claim the whole of his property back if he leaves the society before being acknowledged as such. There can be little doubt that this regulation stems from considerations of a practical, business-like kind, rather than from a feeling that the property of the novice was unclean.

[65]) Hebr. *mshqh* (also vii 20). LIEBERMAN draws attention to the use of *mshqyn* in rabbinical literature as denoting liquid food from which the novice was still excluded, because *mshqyn* could never be immunized against ritual uncleanness.

[66]) The meaning is clear: 'he shall examine him, and the decision concerning him shall be made according to the Many'. REICKE has noticed that the community is mentioned only in connection with the second examination, from which circumstance he draws the conclusion that the first examination was done by the *Mevaqqer* alone whereas the presence of the whole community was required at the final and most important examination.

[67]) The context suggests that *yktwbhw* should be read as singular and taken as referring to the *Mevaqqer* (cf. VAN DER PLOEG). In the parallel passage in 1QSa i 21 the verb is Niphal.

[68]) Hebr. *bsrk tkwnw*. The parallel phrase in v 23 suggests that *tkwnw* should be taken as *nomen rectus* of *srk*. For the following *btwk 'ḥyw*, cf. 1QSa i 18.

[69]) For the meaning of *ṭhrh*, see note on v 13.

[70]) Hebr. *hwn*. The word is clearly used here in its Hebrew sense of 'property', cf. note on i 12.

[71]) Hebr. *wmshpṭw*; for the meaning, see note on v 3.

[72]) Hebr. *w'lh hmshpṭym 'shr yshpṭw bm* which might also be translated: 'these are the punishments by which they shall be punished'. For *'lh hmshpṭym* (also viii 20), cf. Exod. xxi 1.

[73]) Hebr. *bmdrsh yḥd*. The translation follows BROWNLEE; the object of study is naturally the Torah, from which the various punishments were derived, and our phrase appears to indicate that the community as a whole had a say in the matter; on the other hand, ix 7 tells us that only the priests should have control over 'Torah and law' which seems to leave no power to the community. The question has been treated by DELCOR who draws a distinction between the study of the community, through which the members were able to express an opinion when they were called upon to do so, and the actual legislative power as concentrated in the priests who settled legal questions and meted out the punishments. If this dis-

tinction is to be upheld in our passage it seems impossible to translate *mdrsh yḥd* as we have done above, and the expression should be taken in some other way, e.g. as the title of a book (cf. SCHUBERT who suggests that the designation refers to the following code), or as referring to a locality where the punishments were meted out, the 'school' of the society (MILIK). Both interpretations, however, are unsatisfactory in view of the references to the Torah studying activity in vi 7 and viii 24 where the same roots are used as in our passage, and it seems impossible to find an alternative translation to the one given. The discrepancy with ix 7, then, may be explained as due to the literary character of 1QS: it represents a compilation of fragments which reflect some development within the society in the course of time. At the time when vi 1, 24 was written the community as a whole possessed both judicial and legislative power. At some other stage in the history of the community the judiciary was formed by a particular body of professional judges (cf. CD ix 10, x 1, 4 ff, xv 4), whereas the legislative power was formed by the priests who alone could interpret the Torah properly (ix 7).

74) For *dbr* as a judicial term (also vi 1), cf. Exod. xviii 16, 22, xxii 8 (DELCOR). VAN DER PLOEG, referring to Gen. xliii 7 whose phraseology is closely related to that of our passage, takes the word as alluding to the *facts* on which the evidence is based.

75) Cf. CD ix 12 and especially xiv 20 which we may now, on the evidence of our passage, reconstruct as follows: '[*sh*]*r* [*sh*]*q*[*r*] *bmmwn whw' ywd*'. Both passages are dependent on Lev. v 1 which deals with deliberate suppression of knowledge, and they both deal with the case of a man who, testifying in money-matters, suppresses his knowledge and commits perjury. Acts v 1 ff is no parallel (against JOHNSON).

76) Cf. note 54 above.

77) Cf. CD ix 21, 23, constituting only partial excommunication (BROWNLEE).

78) CD xiv 21: 'six days' which seems mild, compared to one year in 1QS; in 1QS vii 8 it is the other way round: CD presents the stricter punishment.

79) Hebr. *wn'nshw*. The form cannot be taken as plural; the final *Waw* must be taken as a suffix and we are obliged to take the form as Niphal + suffix which seems strange; the same construction, however, occurs in viii 11 (*wnmṣ'w*). This is not according to classical usage as we know it, but it may perhaps be explained as due to an expanded usage of Niphal + '*t*.

[80]) Hebr. *rby'yt lḥmw*. Whether the privation of food is understood in the ensuing punishments, is not clear.

[81]) Hebr. *yshyb*. The parallel passage in CD xiv 21 reads *ydb*[*r*].

[82]) Cf. Prov. viii 33, xiii 18, xv 32 (Brownlee).

[83]) Hebr. *b'mrwt*. Our context is closely related to CD ix 9 f: *'ysh 'shr yshby' 'l pny hśdh 'shr l' lpnym hshpṭym 'w m'mrm hwshy' ydw lw*. That in that passage *lpnym* should be emended to *lpny* seems obvious and was suggested already by Schechter. The real problem, however, lies in the word *m'mrm*. On the face of it, it looks as if the word is to be connected with *'mr* 'to say', and both Hvidberg and Rabin read the word *mē'omrām*. Thanks to the parallel in our passage we are now able to see that the word should be derived from quite a different root. It is to be noted that in both passages the biblical idiom *hwshy' ydw lw* (cf. Judges vii 2; 1 Sam. xxv 33) is employed; we may therefore assume that in *m'mrm* of CD and *b'mrwt* of our passage we have one and the same verb. The meaning in our passage is clear, *b'mrwt* being the equivalent of *bhmrwt* (van der Ploeg and others). The same meaning is intended in CD where *m'mrm* should be read as participle Hiphil of *mrh* + suffix, the translation being: 'The man, who swears (*yshby'* being Niphal) in the open field, and not before the judges, or (in any other way) *rebels* against them (i.e. the judges)—his hand has saved him'. In both CD and 1QS the context deals with disobedience (in CD against the judges; in 1QS against a member of higher rank), and in both CD and 1QS we find Hiphil of *mrh* spelt with an *Aleph*.

[84]) Hebr. *lpnyhw*; for the suffix, see note on v 25.

[85]) Cf. note 83 above. The preposition *l* + suffix for 3rd masc. sing. is here spelt with an *Aleph*, as sometimes in MT (e.g. Lev. xi 21).

[86]) Hebr. *yzkyr dbr*; for this meaning of the verb, see Isa. xlviii 1 where it is used in parallelism with *nshb'*. Cf. CD xv 2, where Hvidberg translates by 'mention', but makes it clear in his commentary (p. 181) that the word refers to swearing.

[87]) Cf. Deut. xxviii 58; Ecclus. xlvii 18 (Lambert). The end of the line is lost.

Pl. vii

[1]) The parallel text in CD xv 3 reads *ḥll*, cf. Lev. xix 12 which deals with swearing and profanation of the Name (cf. also Abot v 9); is the present difference between 1QS and CD due to

confusion of *Qoph* and *Ḥet* (cf. note on viii 10)? Our author seems to be alluding to Exod. xxii 27; 1 Sam. iii 13 etc. There can be no doubt that our passage virtually alludes to the special case of a man who curses *God*, and not just to the general case of a man who uses bad language (VAN DER PLOEG), or blasphemes (BROWNLEE), or in some other way commits a profanation (LAMBERT). In 1 Sam. iii 13 we read: *mqllym lhm bnyw*. That the biblical passage originally read *'lhym* (cf. Exod. xxii 27) may be seen from Sept. At an early stage, however, the blasphemous expression of 'cursing God' was avoided by reading *lhm* for *'lhym*, although the syntactical position of the word is difficult (see S. R. DRIVER, *Notes on the Hebrew Text of the Books of Samuel*, p. 43 f). In Job i 5, 11, ii 5, 9 the original text may also have read the verb *qll* instead of *brk* of MT (see BEER, *Der Text des Buches Hiob untersucht*, p. 5). Our author knew the original reading in either 1 Sam. iii 13 or Job i 5 etc., but avoided the blasphemy in a most ingenious way: he followed the consonants of the idiom concerned as far as *qll 'lh*, and divided *'lh* into *'w lh(b't)*.

[2]) Hebr. *lhb't mṣrh*. Job xv 24, on which our passage appears to be dependent, shows that *lhb't* should be derived from *b't* (Niphal: 'to be horrified'), cf. VAN DER PLOEG. The biblical passage also shows that *ṣrh* is not necessarily to be taken as alluding to persecutions under Antiochus Epiphanes in 1 and 2 Macc. as BROWNLEE thinks, referring for this interpretation to Dan. xii 1.—Cf. 1QSb v 23.

[3]) Hebr. *'w lkwl dbr 'shr lw*, written by another scribe; cf. Lev. v 24 according to Sept. The biblical passage deals with swearing, as does our context.

[4]) For this meaning of *qr' bspr*, cf. note on vi 7. Reference is made to a blasphemous act perpetrated during the recitation of the Torah at divine service; that this could apply to any member of the community, and not only to the priests, let alone to one particular person whose office it was to 'read aloud from the Book' (against BROWNLEE), is in accordance with Jewish tradition, according to which any full-grown person of integrity may recite the Torah in the synagogue.

[5]) As the previous expression, this phrase alludes to a function at the communal worship, cf. vi 3.

[6]) Hebr. *whbdylhw* which may be read either as singular or as plural, see note on vi 22.

[7]) This strict practice agrees with Rabbi Meir (Abodah Zarah 7a; Bekorot 31a), but is contrary to rabbinic Judaism (LIEBERMAN).

[8]) The emphatic position of the priest should be noticed; it is

due to the fact that what follows is closely connected with what precedes: the author is still dealing with a case of 'cursing', in other words: *qll* in l. 1 with God as understood object, is parallel with *dbr bḥmh* with 'one of the priests' as explicit object; the two verbs are in fact identical, and the different punishments are due to the different objects. *Spr* can hardly mean 'Torah' here.

[9]) For solitary confinement, see also CD xii 3 ff, xiii 6. We have followed BROWNLEE's interpretation of *'l npshw*, but the expression may also mean 'for the sake of his life', cf. REICKE, referring to 1 Kings xix 3; 2 Kings vii 7.

[10]) Hebr. *bshggh* (also viii 24; cf. Lev. iv 2, 22, etc.) put with emphasis in front of the sentence, introducing a modification of the previous regulation.

[11]) Cf. Lev. v 21. The apparent confusion of *Samek* and *Shin* is striking; the translation of *md'* as 'knowledge' is suggested by the fact that the use of the word here reflects our author's interpretation of *b'mytw* of Lev. v 21: it is difficult to see why he should shift the consonants of the word in the biblical passage, if the word constructed by him conveyed the same idea as the word in the biblical original. The translation follows VAN DER PLOEG and others. BROWNLEE takes *bmd'w* as the object of *ykḥs* ('denies his knowledge', viz. of having so spoken), but the present regulation has nothing to do with the previous one. When our author introduces a modification of a preceding regulation, he uses *w'm*, cf. l. 3, 5, 8 etc. So, it appears that *w'shr* introduces an entirely new regulation, parallel with *h'ysh 'shr* in l. 4 and *w'shr* in l. 5.

[12]) Hebr. *yṣḥh*, cf. Syriac ܨܚܐ (MILIK).

[13]) Hebr. *blw mshpṭ*; the phrase is used idiomatically in order to stress the atrocity of the action *in any case*, cf. the use of *l' bmshpṭ* in Jer. xvii 11; Ezek. xxii 29, and the very frequent usage of the Arabic equivalent بغير حق or بغير الحق in the Quran (e.g. Sura iii 20, 108, 177, iv 154 where Muhammad speaks about those who killed the prophets 'without right'—not suggesting, of course, that the killing might have been justifiable, cf. also Sura xxii 41, xlii 40, xlvi 19, vi 93, vii 143 etc.)

[14]) Hebr. *bmrym*. BROWNLEE points to the following verb as suggesting that our phrase implies some deceitful action, fraud being the subject-matter of ll. 5-8. In view of this we seem justified in equating *mrym* with Tib. *mirmāh*; for a similar shift of the tone, cf. 1QIsa[a] ix 5: *mśyrh* for Tib. *miśrāh*.—For the phrase, cf. Gen. xxxiv 13 according to Pesh.

[15]) Cf. note 11 above. The present regulation makes it clear that the word cannot be taken in the meaning 'friend' here: the friend (*r'h*) is introduced with emphasis in the ensuing regulation which is to be regarded as a modification of the present main rule, introduced by *w'm*. For the interpretation of ll. 5-8 this construction is important to have in mind. In l. 5 is put down the rule that a case of fraud should be punished with six months; in ll. 6-8a two modifications are given: (a) in certain circumstances the punishment should not exceed three months; (b) if the culprit by his fraudulent act wastes communal property and is unable to make it up, he is to be punished only sixty days.

[16]) Hebr. *ytrmh*, translated according to MILIK. For Hitpael of *rmh*, which is otherwise unknown, cf. the equally unparalleled Hitpolel of *ryb* in ix 16. The text, of which 1QS is a copy, had the verb in front of *br'hw*; the scribe was obviously struck by the discrepancy of syntax between this and the following sentence, suspected the correctness of the text, and left a space open for potential later completion; afterwards the verb was written above the line to the left of *br'hw*, whereby complete syntactical similarity was restored between l. 6a and 6b. The preposition in *br'hw* is not necessarily to be taken in the same meaning as in the word *bhwn* in the following, cf. the use of *kḥsh b* in Lev. v 21 f in two different meanings; in fact, the biblical parallel suggests the translation given of *br'hw* in our passage.

[17]) Cf. Lev. v 24 (BROWNLEE) which suggests that the text be transcribed according to BURROWS, in his edition.

[18]) For the idiom, see Lev. xiv 22 (BROWNLEE), xxv 26.

[19]) Cf. Lev. xix 18; as for the prepositional expression *'shr lw' b*, see note on v 17; the phrase *'shr lw' bmshpṭ* is equal to *blw mshpṭ* in l. 4 and is used in the same way (see note 13 above). Cf. Matt. v 22.

[20]) The two words are written above the line; they are a variant with which the scribe was aquainted from CD xiv 22, cf. RABIN's reconstruction of, and note on, that passage. We have here one detail which points towards the assumption that there is some sort of literary connection between CD and 1QS; other facts, which appear to point in the same direction, are that the participle Niphal of *hyh* is spelt with two *Yods* both in CD ii 10 and in the parallel passage 1QS iii 15, and that in CD ix 10, as well as in 1QS vi 26, the Hiphil of *mrh* is spelt with an *Aleph*, see notes on iii 15 and on vi 26.

[21]) Hebr. *lnwqm lnpshw*. VAN DER PLOEG translates: 'the one who avenges himself'; against this interpretation speaks, however, the

normal usage, according to which the verb alone would have been enough (cf. e.g. Lev. xix 18 which our author still has in mind). The translation given follows MILIK; the author, by adding *lnpshw*, may have wanted to give the biblical passage a turn towards the idea of vi 26 f and CD ix 4 f.

[22]) Hebr. *dbr nbl*. For the meaning 'improper' of *nbl*, cf. RABIN, in his note on CD x 18.

[23]) Lit.: 'and for the one who speaks in the middle of the words of his neighbour', cf. vi 10.

[24]) Hebr. *yshkwb* = *yishkab* of classical Hebrew. 1QIsa[a] provides us with several examples of this kind, cf. also Ecclus. vi 35, xliii 10 (var.). The phraseology of our passage is modelled on Ps. iii 6, iv 9; in both passages the verbs are used as expressing the complete trust of the pious in God. The situation presupposed in our passage is not identical with the one in vi 7; the latter passage dealt with nightly vigils, whereas the regulation in our passage stems from the practical need of discipline at the sessions (KUHN). The text does not, as EDELKOORT thinks, deal with a man who goes away in order to lie down and sleep, but with a man who stretches himself during the actual session and falls asleep. This seems to imply that the members sat on benches, and also that the membership was relatively large.

[25]) This translation of ll. 10-12, a section which has caused the greatest difficulties, is based on the following considerations: (a) *wkn* in l. 10 introduces a regulation concerning a case similar to the preceding one and metes out the same punishment; in this way *wkn* is used also in l. 9. The point is of fundamental importance because the great variety of suggestions as to the interpretation of this section is partly due to the fact that scholars have not realized that the preceding regulation, as well as the following one, deal with the case of a man who lies down during a session; (b) *hnpṭr* should be taken in the meaning 'the one who goes away'; the root *pṭr* is very common in Aramaic and in Mishnaic Hebrew in this meaning, and there is no compelling reason why the use of the verb here should denote some improper act, as VAN DER PLOEG suggests ('yawn' or 'break a wind'); (c) *'shr lw' bʿṣh wḥnm* should be taken as consisting of two, roughly synonymous expressions of which the former is identical with *bl' ʿṣh* in Ecclus. xxxii (xxxv) 19, and the opposite of *bʿṣh* in Prov. xx 18, and the latter is used in the same way as in 1 Sam. xix 5; Job ii 3.—The translation reflects the view that the text refers to the case of a man who leaves the meeting without valid

reason, for which misdemeanour our context puts down the punishment of ten days, provided that he does not do it more than three times; what exactly our author understood by 'valid' reason we do not know; compliance with a call of nature may have been regarded as such (DRIVER); in any case, the present regulation shows indirectly that the sessions of the society were long, and the two sorts of misdemeanour which naturally had to be punished were sleep and departure. The meaning of ll. 10-12 is quite clear: a man who lies down and falls asleep is liable to a punishment of 30 days; that is the fundamental rule. Therefore, if he has been sleeping, and then gets up and walks away, his punishment is naturally that of one who has fallen asleep, and not that of one who has walked away; so, he is liable to the punishment of 30 days and not of 10 days, which is the punishment for walking away; (d) *yzqpw* is generally taken as a verb in the plural, somehow describing what the other members of the session are doing at the time of perpetration of the offence, thus VAN DER PLOEG: 'stand erect' which is by RABIN, in his note on CD xii 19, taken as alluding to *voting*; another suggestion is that of LAMBERT, that the verb indicates *protest* from the fellow members, an interpretation which the present author earlier adopted and expanded. The root *zqp* may mean 'to stand erect' or 'to erect', but in view of the context which deals with a man who is lying down, it is better to take it in the meaning 'to assume a straight position', viz. after lying down (cf. JASTROW's *Dictionary*, I, p. 410); furthermore, the verb describes what the culprit does, and not what the fellow members do, and it is to be taken as singular; the final *Waw*, then, may be taken as the suffix used reflexively (cf. SEGAL's *Mishnaic Grammar*, p. 206), and the verb in our phrase means: 'if he raises himself up', viz. from his prone position.

[26]) Lit.: 'walks in front of his brother'. HABERMANN points the verb as Piel which is probably right, cf. the similar idiom in Yeb. 63b (see JASTROW's *Dictionary*, II, p. 1115).

[27]) Hebr. *'rwm*. The usage of the idiom *hlk 'rwm* in rabbinical literature (cf. previous note) appears to suggest that *'rwm* should not be taken in its literal meaning, but rather in the meaning 'insufficiently clad'—a usage which is already classical and which has close parallels in Arabic (See *GB*, s.v.).

[28]) Hebr. *'nwsh*. GINSBERG suggests the translation 'compelled', on the assumption of confusion of *Sin* and *Samek*. Another suggestion is that of IWRY that the word means 'ill'. A third suggestion is that the word means 'man', so that the sentence means 'with nobody

else there' (VAN DER PLOEG). None of these suggestions is satisfactory. The translation given is based on Ecclus. xi 12, where *ywtr 'wnsh* is translated by the grandson of the author as πτωχείᾳ περισσεύει, which is the meaning required by the context.—The text as translated is to the effect that if a man was clad in rags because of poverty he should not be punished.

[29]) The prohibition is known from the Essenes (see *Jewish War*, II, 147) and from the Falashas (see LESLAU, *Falashic Anthology*, p. 21).

[30]) The word *yd* here is taken to mean '*membrum virile*' by MARCUS. DRIVER, in a letter to me, associates himself with this. There does not seem, however, to be any compelling reason for this interpretation; in l. 13 f are mentioned three misdemeanours for all of which the punishment is 30 days: (a) spitting, (b) stretching out of the hand in an improper way, and (c) guffawing; and it appears that we are here dealing with regulations which should secure good table manners at the communal meal. Our passage, then, alludes to the reaching out for food, cf. Ecclus. xxxi (xxxiv), 14, 18.

[31]) Hebr. *pwḥ*. The translation given follows the suggestion of BROWNLEE that *pwḥ* be equated with *pwḥḥ*. Other scholars connect the word with *pyḥ* 'to blow', thus, with minor differences, VAN DER PLOEG, MILIK, LAMBERT and others.

[32]) With our interpretation of the context as dealing with good table manners it is clear that *'rwtw* is not to be taken as referring to the *pudenda* (against VAN DER PLOEG, MILIK).

[33]) Lit.: 'laughs in stupidity, making his voice heard'. For the phraseology, cf. Isa. lviii 4; 2 Chron. v 13; Ecclus. xlv 9. The condemnation of noisy laughter may be taken to indicate that the meal was, or should be, consumed in silence, cf. Taanit 5b.

[34]) In other words: they should sit up when eating, and not indulge in lying down. This interpretation suggests itself by the mention of the left hand only, and by the character of the context which deals with table manners. The verb, then, is to be connected with *shḥḥ* 'to crouch', 'to bow down' (in Ecclus. xliii 10 simply 'to lie down'). This seems a better suggestion than that of VAN DER PLOEG and others, that the verb refers to 'speaking' (cf. *śyḥ*); the left hand, then, is assumed to denote that the speaking was accompanied by gesticulations (for the condemnation of which, cf. Prov. vi 13), but why, then, only the left hand?—Cf. Gen. xxiv 63.

[35]) Cf. Lev. xix 16 (BROWNLEE). The following regulation is derived from this scriptural passage (our author having translated it as follows:

'do not walk round as a tale-bearer *about* thy people') and has been taken absolutely, i.e. as entailing the severest possible punishment: excommunication; v. 16b suggested to our author that a milder punishment should be applied if the object of slander was a single person.

36) The error is due to *h'ysh 'shr* in the preceding line; the emendation proposed is more in keeping with the phraseology of this plate (cf. l. 1, 2, 3, 5, 6, 17), than the restoration *w'ysh* <*'shr*> *brbym*, suggested by RABIN, in his note on CD x 13.

37) The modification, which applies to a case of slander, also applies to a case of grumbling: if it is directed against the community it entails irrevocable excommunication; if, however, it is directed against a single person it entails only a temporary punishment. The verb may be read either as *yillōn* or as *yālīn*; palaeography appears to recommend the former reading. The formal similarity of the present regulation with the preceding one, recommends the emendation of *yswd* to *swd* (for the expression *swd hyḥd*, cf. vi 19). *'shr lw' bmshpṭ* is to be taken as in l. 8, see note 20 above. As in that passage, the idiom is applied here in connection with a case of misdemeanour towards the neighbour; it should be noticed, also, that in both cases the punishment is six months. The variant 'one year' was, however, only added in l. 8, and not in l. 18.

38) The translation is based on the combination of the verb with Arab. زاغ 'to deviate' which is often used in the Quran (e.g. Sura iii 5: فأما الذين في قلوبهم زيغ 'concerning those in whose hearts there is deviation').

39) Hebr. *myswd hyḥd*; for our interpretation of this expression, see note 38 above. The phraseology of ll. 18 ff suggests that the context deals with a case of apostasy, and the whole passage is remarkable because it presupposes the possibility of readmission: the repentant may, if he so desires, obtain his former status in the community in the course of two years, i.e. he must go through the initial stages of a novice once more. The discrepancy between our passage and viii 22 ff (the latter passage putting down irrevocable excommunication for a wilful transgression of the Torah, as understood by the society) should not be smoothed over, cf. RABIN's observations in his note on CD xii 6. The possibility of readmission appears to be presupposed also in CD xx 4 f. We have here an indication that our community in the course of time relaxed their strict regulations concerning the possibility of readmission of fallen members.

[40]) The root *bgd* is used also in CD i 12, viii 5, xix 17, 34; 1QpHab viii 10.

[41]) The following lines with erasions and empty spaces suggest that the text before the scribe was illegible in parts.

[42]) For the meaning of *mshqh*, cf. note on vi 20. The word has been written above the line. The photograph shows that an original word, viz. *bb'yr*, has been erased; as for the *plene* spelling, cf. forms like *yyḥd* in v 14 and *sh'yryt* in CD ii 6. The text, then, originally alluded to the well from where the drinking water of the society was drawn, and by the correction it was made clear that the drinking water, and not the well itself, was meant. As for the phrase 'the well of the Many' we have a similar expression in CD iii 16: *wyḥprw b'r lmym rbym* 'and they dug a well with much water' where, however, the 'digging of the well' is to be taken symbolically as alluding to the Torah study of the community. The expression 'much water' occurs in Song of Sol. viii 7 (Rabin) and should not be corrected to 'living water' (against Ginzberg and Hvidberg), but the closely related phrase in our (original) text appears to suggest that *rbym* by the author of CD was taken as alluding to the community. The difference in usage between 1QS and CD stands: *b'r* is in CD interpreted midrashically as alluding to Torah study (cf. apart from iii 16 also vi 3 f), whereas in 1QS vii 20 it is used literally as alluding to the well from where the members drew their drinking water.

[43]) Cf. vi 17, 18, 21.

[44]) See note on vi 4. Brownlee translates correctly here.

[45]) Cf. vi 22.

[46]) Hebr. *w'ḥr ysh'l 'l hmshpṭ*. The translation follows Brownlee who refers to vi 22 f. As there, thus also in our passage, *hmshpṭ* alludes to the common store of halakic knowledge of the community; so, the word should not be taken as 'this matter' (against Milik who regards the following *kwl 'ysh 'shr yhyh b'ṣt hyḥd* as subject of *ysh'l*).

[47]) The adding of *Waw* should secure against the drawing of the following words to what precedes. The parallel passage in vi 22 f also suggests that the sentence *w'ḥr ysh'l 'l hmshpṭ* is to be regarded as the end of the section, l. 22 dealing with an entirely different case, viz. that of a man who, in spite of membership of ten years' standing, deserts the society.

[48]) Hebr. *'l ml't*. The phrase is identical with *'d ml't* (vi 17, 20 f, viii 26); for the interchange of the two prepositions, cf. Ps. xix 7, xlviii 11; Job xxxvii 3. As for the ten years, cf. 1QSa i 8.

[49]) Hebr. *wshbh rwḥw lbgwd*. As we have seen (cf. note 48 above) the present regulation is not to be regarded as a continuation of what precedes; it is, therefore, impossible to take *shwb* as a complementary verb in the meaning 'to do again' (against MILIK); it must mean 'to turn away' (cf. BROWNLEE). Cf. CD xix 34.

[50]) For the idiom, see Gen. iv 16; Lev. ix 24, x 2: our author used the biblical idiom, replacing the Tetragrammaton by *hrbym*.

[51]) The case of apostasy dealt with in ll. 22-24 (which entails irrevocable excommunication) appears to be different from the case dealt with in ll. 18-20 (according to which readmission is possible) only with respect to the mention of the ten years' membership. The phraseology of the two regulations is very much the same, and they seem to lay down different rules for the same group of people: the apostates. In ll. 22 ff the meaning seems to be: re-admission is possible, except in cases where the apostate has belonged to the community for ten years or more. In ll. 18 ff the meaning appears to be: readmission is possible in any case, provided of course that the apostate cares to come back (*'m yshwb*). Cf. note 40 above.

[52]) Cf. vi 17, 22, viii 23, ix 8. The verb also occurs in CD xi 4, but is emended by LÉVI to *ytr'b*.

[53]) The use of *ṭhrh* with singular suffix supports the view of LIEBERMAN (see note on v 13) that *ṭhrh* refers to ritually clean articles, particularly food.

[54]) BARDTKE propounds a particular interpretation of l. 24 f: according to him our passage is to be taken in close connection with what precedes, the meaning being: if a man deals treacherously with the community, neither the fact that he has belonged to the community ten years, nor the fact that his property has been pooled with that of the other members, can make readmission possible. That interpretation is ingenious, but unlikely because: (a) it is based on a mistranslation of l. 24 f ('Wenn es sich handelt um einen Mann aus den Männern der Gemeinde, mit welchem sie Anteil gehabt hat an seiner Reinheit und an seinem Vermögen, das er unter das Vermögen der Vielen hingegeben hat, so soll sein Urteilsspruch wie über ihn (i.e. the one mentioned in the preceding clause) sein, ihn zu entlassen'): the phraseology of vi 17 shows that *'ysh*, and not the community, is the subject of *yt'rb*; (b) if l. 24 were intended as a special case under what precedes, it would, according to the structure of the present code, no doubt be introduced by *w'm*, see note 11 above; (c) the ten years mentioned in l. 22 should not be taken as an extenuat-

ing circumstance which might justify readmission of the lapsed person; on the contrary, it is mentioned as an aggravating circumstance which gives the reason for irrevocable exclusion. The two cases recorded in ll. 22 ff are, therefore, entirely different, the meaning being: the person, who deals treacherously with the community after a membership of ten years' standing, is to be expelled from the society; and the same punishment applies to any member of the community who has anything to do with him, socially or commercially.

Pl. viii

[1]) The following section (to l. 16) is of great importance for the understanding of our community, but there is some disagreement among scholars as to whether we have here a description of the functions of an 'inner council' within the community or whether the society as a whole is alluded to. We are confronted with this problem at the very beginning of this plate, because the designation *'ṣt hyḥd* appears to be used here of a separate body of prominent members forming a special council (cf. 1QSa i 26, according to the context), and the phrase is in fact taken thus by DEL MEDICO and others. The same designation is quite frequent in 1QS as referring to the community as a whole (see note on iii 2), and BROWNLEE compares the beginning of our passage with viii 11 (*btwk 'ṣt 'nshy hyḥd*) with which our phrase appears to be identical. So, *'ṣt hyḥd* should probably also in our line be taken as alluding to the community as a whole, and the meaning is: 'within the community there must be twelve men and three priests' (cf. LAMBERT). Therefore, what is said in the following applies to the community, and not to the twelve or fifteen men exclusively. viii 1 is the only passage in 1QS, in which a special body of members is mentioned; the context seems to favour the view that it was their particular responsibility to guide the other members in their actions; whether they formed a judiciary is uncertain; they were not mentioned in vi 1, and it seems natural to assume that their function was limited to that of guidance and instruction. On the other hand, the mention here of a particular body within the community has a parallel in CD x 4 ff where reference is made to a tribunal in front of which lawsuits were to be tried. If an allusion to a similar body is made in 1QS viii 1, we shall have to assume that vi 1 and viii 1 reflect different stages in the organization of the society in the course of time: at one time the judiciary was in the hands of a particular body of men, and at some other time it was conferred on the community

as a whole.—Another problem is whether the text refers to twelve or fifteen persons; the latter assumption is the most common among scholars (thus VAN DER PLOEG and others). On the other hand, DUPONT-SOMMER argues that if the priests were meant to be distinct from the twelve, the former would probably have been mentioned first (this might be supported by reference to CD x 5 f), and REICKE draws parallels between the purported mention of 'twelve' in our passage and the 'twelve' in the Primitive Church.

[2]) Hebr. *tmymym*, here alluding to perfect *knowledge* (cf. MILIK). The word is best taken as referring to the whole body, and not only to the priests, cf. CD x 6 according to which erudition in the *Book of Hagu* is required of the entire council, and not only of its clerical members. In fact, the two parallel phrases in 1QS (*tmymym bkwl hnglh mkwl htwrh*) and in CD (*mbwnym bspr hhgw*) are complementary: the 'revelations', mentioned here and elsewhere in 1QS (i 9, v 9, viii 15, ix 13, 19) were contained in a particular book, called the *Book of Hagu*, and this book was a halakic handbook in which were recorded the regulations of the society. As for the meaning of the preposition *mn*, cf. note on v 9.

[3]) I.e. the community as a whole, cf. note 1 above, and MILIK's translation. The construction is somewhat loose, the virtual subject of the infinitive being *'ṣt hyḥd* in the beginning of l. 1; this and the following infinitives are thus without difficulty taken as referring to the activity of the community as a whole. This interpretation is also in accordance with the fact that the whole of l. 2 is made up of phrases which are in other passages of 1QS applied to all members of the community (see e.g. i 5, ii 24, v 4).

[4]) Hebr. *hṣn' lkt*, see note on iv 5.

[5]) Cf. Isa. xxvi 2 f (*b'rṣ* is from Isa. xxvi 1).

[6]) Also xi 1, cf. Ps. li 19 (BROWNLEE).

[7]) Hebr. *wlrṣt*, cf. Lev. xxvi 43 (quoted more fully in ii 26, iii 1).

[8]) Hebr. *b'wśy mshpṭ wsrt mṣrp*. Our phrase appears to indicate the means by which sin is 'paid off', and the two expressions *b'wśy mshpṭ* and *ṣrt mṣrp* seem to be parallel. For the form of the abstract noun *'wśy* (= *'ōsē*, cf. ix 1), see Isa. xxxviii 15 (*ḥōzēh*) and Num. xxiv 20, 24 (*'ōbēd*). As for the meaning of *mṣrp*, see note on i 17.

[9]) Hebr. *'m kwl* = *'m kwl ḥy* in ix 12.

[10]) The original text read 'on the foundation of truth', cf. v 5. The parallelism with *tkwn* suggests that the corrected text is preferable, but the original text is an interesting example of an alternative

reading, due to the almost identical forms of *Mem* and *Samek*. An exact parallel to this may be found in Enoch xcix 12, where one group of Ethiopic manuscripts reads: 'woe to you who make deceitful and false *measure*', and another: 'woe to you who lay down a deceitful ... *foundation*'.

[11]) Cf. ix 12, 18. The thought behind the expression in our passage may be that the fulfilment of a commandment must happen in the particular time in which the action concerned is required, cf. note on i 15.

[12]) Hebr. *bhywt 'lh*. All scholars translate 'when these things come to pass in Israel': *'lh* is taken impersonally. The phrase occurs also in l. 12 and ix 3 where *'lh* most naturally is taken as referring to the members of the community; the pronoun is also used in this way in l. 12 in the phrase *'l ystrhw m'lh* 'let him not conceal it from these'. The realization of *'lh* as referring to the members of the community also in our passage, is of paramount importance for the right understanding of the conception governing the following lines where the community is described as the true spiritual temple; according to KUHN this conception is known from the New Testament (1 Cor. iii 16; 2 Cor. vi 16) and nowhere else. The following lines, syntactically somewhat clumsy, may be a hymn, or fragments of one.

[13]) For the description of the community as a plant, cf. xi 8; CD i 7; Jub. xvi 26, xxi 24 (DELCOR). The combination of 'plant' with 'house' in our passage is interesting and may be due to the insight that the two words were closely related in meaning. In this connection it may perhaps be pertinent to draw attention to the fact that *nṭ'* in Ecclus. iii 9 is rendered in the Greek version by οἶκος, and that the corresponding verb in Ecclus. iii 14 is translated by προσανοικοδομεῖν, the root *nṭ'* apparently conveying to the grandson of the author the idea of housebuilding (SMEND).

[14]) I.e. a temple.—The preposition *l* in the following expression is used in order to avoid a row of construct states, 'Israel' and 'Aaron' indicating the constituent parts (priests and laity) which make up the 'temple'. Almost all scholars translate the preposition by 'for', but by that rendering an important point is obscured, if not, indeed, missed.

[15]) In spite of the translation it is to be noted that *qwdsh qwdshym* no doubt alludes to the 'Saint of Saints' of the Temple, and it is not due to accident that 'Israel' (i.e. the laity) is mentioned in connection with the 'holy house' and 'Aaron' (i.e. the priests) in connection with the

'Saint of Saints" into which the laity were not allowed to enter; the phraseology of our passage suggests, therefore, that the priestly element had supreme dignity in the community (BAUMGARTEN).—Cf. 1 Chron. xxiii 13.

[16]) For 'true witness', cf. Prov. xiv 25, 5; Jer. xlii 5. BROWNLEE translates: 'true witnesses with regard to religion', referring for this meaning to ROWLEY, *The Servant of the Lord*, p. 14. His translation is due to the fact that he finds an echo of the Servant motif (Isa. xlii 3, xliii 10-12) here. For the assumption that our author has the 'Servant of the Lord' in mind, speaks the fact that the following *bḥyry rṣwn* (= the pious community, cf. ἐκλογὴ χάριτος in Rom. xi 5) appears to be an allusion to *bḥyry rṣth npshy* in Isa. xlii 1: our author interpreted the Servant song concerned collectively (cf. Sept.), finding in it an allusion to the privileged position and the high vocation of the members of the society, and we have already seen, how in iv 6 the community was invested with a particular function of the Servant of the Lord as evinced in Isa. xlii 3 by a peculiar interpretation of that passage. Whether, however, our author by *lmshpṭ* here alludes to the same scriptural passage is at least questionable—and even if he did so, there is no telling that he understood *mshpṭ* in the same way as modern scholars do.

[17]) For the active participle of the original text, cf. CD ii 15.

[18]) Cf. Num. xxxv 33 which suggests that the phrase should be taken in close connection with the following *wlhshyb rsh'ym gmwlm*: the atonement for the earth is effected through the shedding of the blood of the impious, cf. Prov. xxi 18 which displays a closely related notion.—Cf. 1QSa i 3, as restored by BARTHÉLEMY, and 1Q22 iv 1.

[19]) Cf. Ps. xciv 2, also quoted CD vii 9. RABIN has noticed that both in 1QS and CD we have the same difference from MT, namely *rsh'ym* for *g'ym*. From this observation he draws the conclusion that our two passages contain 'a real variant reading'. But is the fact that 1QS and CD, in quoting a biblical passage, show the same deviation from MT, due to dependence on a biblical text which is different from MT? Would it not be possible to assume that one of our texts, in alluding to Ps. xciv 2, quotes the passage freely, and that the other text, in alluding to the same passage, is literally dependent on that free rendering? If that could be shown to be the case, we would have an interesting indication of a direct literary relationship between the two texts—whichever way the influence is thought to go. There can be little doubt that *rsh'ym* in CD vii 9 and in our passage has come

in from Ps. xciv 3 where it occurs twice with great emphasis. Besides, there is another case where CD and 1QS, in quoting a biblical passage, display the same deviation from MT, and where the assumption of dependence on a biblical text, different from MT, is most unlikely, see note on v 25.

[20]) BURROWS transcribes the text as *hy'h*; for this reading speaks the immediately following *ḥwmt hbḥn* and the preceding *ʿṣt hyḥd* in l. 5; on the other hand, the masculine suffix in the inserted word *yswdwtyhw* in l. 8 suggests that we should read *hw'h*; both *byt* and *swd* in the preceding line are masculine words; it appears natural to assume that the pronoun in any case refers to the community. For the idea of the community as a walled city, see note on vi 17.

[21]) Cf. Isa. xxviii 16, the biblical *'bn* having been replaced by *ḥwmh*. The replacement is due to the fact that our author interpreted the biblical passage as alluding to the community (cf. the plural forms in the following, referring to the members) and naturally wanted a word for something consisting of more than one stone. Having quoted Isa. xxvi 1 in l. 3 he had no difficulty in drawing from that passage the word *ḥwmh* which to him, as well as to the audience, was taken figuratively as alluding to the community. By thus changing the biblical wording for this purpose he destroyed the parallelism with *pnh*. Targ. interprets Isa. xxviii 16 about Messiah. The defective writing *hbḥn* is against the usual practice of the scribe, but cf. in the present plate *wlrṣt* in l. 3 and *yʿbr* in l. 22. The use of the article in *hbḥn* (not in MT) is due to the audience's acquaintance with the scriptural allusion ('that is the *well known* tested wall'). For *yqrt* of MT our text has *yqr*.

[22]) Hebr. *yšwdwtyhw* (for the suffix form, see note on v 25). The suffix, according to BARDTKE, alludes to God, but the assumption of a reference to *hw'h* in the previous line seems equally possible. The construction is admittedly strange.

[23]) Same verb in Targ.

[24]) Hebr. *wbl yḥyshw mmqwmm*. The context makes it clear that our author has understood the verb *ḥwsh* in the meaning 'to be dislodged' (cf. MILIK). The usual meaning in classical Hebrew of *ḥwsh* is 'to hurry'. In Arab. حَثّ means 'to make haste', and عَشّ 'to dislodge'; is it possible that in Isa. xxviii 16 we have the Hebrew equivalent of the latter, and not of the former? If so, all emendations of the text are superfluous, and once more the Scrolls help us to understand a difficult biblical passage better.

[25]) For *m'wn* used of the Temple, cf. Ps. xxvi 8; 2 Chron. xxxvi 15. In 1QS x 12 the context requires the reading *m'yn qwdsh*.

[26]) For the emended text, cf. ii 3; for the interchange of *Kaph* and *Ayin*, see note on iv 5.

[27]) Cf. v 19. The parallel construction of the next phrase suggests the emendation proposed. In terms taken from Deut. xxxiii 8 ff and Ezek. xliv 15 (both passages alluding to the particular and privileged position of the priests in the cult), our author describes the high vocation of the priestly element in the community, but the context, as well as the atmosphere permeating the whole of 1QS, suggests that the allusions to sacrificial cult here should be taken as highfaluting expressions in a poetical context, and not as an indication of sacrificial practice.

[28]) Num. xv 13, with *'shh* left out. In the Old Testament *nyḥwḥ* is always used in connection with *ryḥ*; the original wording of our passage was *lqryb nyḥwḥ* (*ryḥ*, written above the line, was added later); for this biblical usage, cf. also iii 11, ix 5, the two other passages in which the word occurs in 1QS.

[29]) Cf. v 6. For the combination of *tmym* and *'mt*, cf. Joshua xxiv 14; Judges ix 16, 19.

[30]) In l. 5 f the sequence was 'Israel-Aaron' (cf. CD i 7); in l. 9, however, 'Aaron-Israel', as is always the case when the text deals with the Messiah (see ix 11; CD xii 23 f, xiv 19, xix 10 f, xx 1).—For *b* (in front of *yśr'l*) used as introducing the material of which something is made up, cf. *GB*, s.v. (section B, 3, c); the parallel phraseology in l. 5 f suggests that we must take the preposition thus, and not locally.

[31]) See note on v 22.

[32]) Hebr. *lḥwqwt 'wlm* (also 1Q22 iv 4), cf. Ezek. xlvi 14. The parallel phrases in CD v 12 and xx 29 suggest that the preposition is used here in order to discontinue the sequence of construct states. The spelling in the original text is due to confusion of *Ḥet* and *Qoph*, see note on vii 1. BROWNLEE's reading of the original text as *lḥwmt 'wlm* is not supported by the photography.—A long passage, a variation of l. 6 f, has been written above the line. The place of the inserted passage is not quite clear and scholars vary in their views. They all appear to agree that the beginning of the insertion is to be translated immediately after *'wlm*, but the real problem is whether *w'yn 'wlh* at the end of the inserted line is to be taken as continuing *mshpṭ rsh'h* (MILIK), or is to be translated after *btmym drk* in the original text (VAN DER PLOEG). The manuscript shows two dots after *mshpṭ rsh'h*, which

may indicate that the insertion to be read after *'wlm* is brought to an end with those words; the dots may, however, also draw attention to some scribal error in the insertion: a few words have in fact been erased in front of *w'yn 'wlh*. The question is very difficult to decide, also because the position of *ybdlw*, inserted in the next line, is problematic. Does it belong to *btmym drk* or to *w'yn 'wlh*, or does it introduce the apodosis after the sentence beginning with *lhkyn*? The translations of the passage vary very much; in the translation given we have tentatively presupposed that the entire insertion, *ybdlw* included, is one coherent passage which is to be translated after *'wlm*; being short of space the scribe continued his insertion on the next line.

[33]) The sacrificial terminology here is taken from passages like Lev. i 3, xix 5 etc., the sacrifice being the subject in the biblical passages; thus also here, reflecting our community's conscience of being themselves the sacrifice.

[34]) Cf. 1QpHab ix 1; Enoch xcvii 1: 'the day of unrighteousness'.

[35]) Same phrase in iv 23.

[36]) For the reading of the verb as Niphal, cf. l. 5.

[37]) Cf. vii 17 and 18, and notes.

[38]) As for the form *wnmṣ'w*, see note on vi 25. Our passage throws an interesting light on the meaning of *mṣ't* in CD vi 19.

[39]) Cf. vi 6, and note. No particular man, holding a special office, is alluded to here (against DELCOR): the use of the definite article is due to the particular case with which the context deals, see *GK* § 126q and t. The parallel phrase in vi 6 appears to indicate that the following *'l* should not be taken as 'God' (against MILIK), but as the negative particle. We also know from Pseudepigraphal literature (e.g. Test. Reuben iii 5) that it was considered a sin to conceal anything from 'friends' (i.e. members of one's community); cf. the correction of *'str* into *'spr* in x 24.

[40]) For *(rwḥ) nswgh*, cf. Prov. xiv 14; CD vii 21.

[41]) *lyḥd btkwnym h'lh* has been added later above the line. Whereas it is clear that *lyḥd* is to be taken immediately after *'lh* and before *byśr'l* (against VAN DER PLOEG), the syntactical position of *btkwnym h'lh* is not quite clear. VAN DER PLOEG takes the expression after the verb *ybdlw*, whereas MILIK takes it after *byśr'l*. The translation given is based on the suggestion that *btkwnym h'lh* be taken as a continuation of *lyḥd* in the preceding line: as was the case in l. 10 f the corrector found that there was not sufficient space for the addition in one line and continued in the next. The parallel phrase in ix 3 reads the preposition *k* instead of *b*.

[42]) Cf. Num. xvi 21.

[43]) Cf. v 2. For the interchange of *Aleph* and *He*, see note on vi 26, and cf. *hnshym* in 1QSa i 27.

[44]) Allusion to Isa. xl 3 which is quoted in the next line. *'t drk hw'h'* corresponds to *drk YHWH* of MT. It is well known that in the pious circles behind both CD and 1QS any writing down of the divine name in square script in a non-biblical text was avoided (see note on i 2), and BROWNLEE assumes that in our passage the Tetragrammaton is replaced by HUHA, taken as a proper name. Other scholars (e.g. DEL MEDICO) regards *hw'h'* as an elongated form of the personal pronoun which often in the Scrolls assumes the form *hw'h*, and we have adopted that view in our translation. YALON suggests that the scribe may have wanted to indicate that the personal pronoun here refers to God, and therefore added an *Aleph*; for the use of the personal pronoun as a substitute for God he refers to GINZBERG, *Eine unbekannte jüdische Sekte*, p. 57, and he thinks that what has hitherto been written on this matter has been verified through our passage.

[45]) Cf. Isa. xl 3. Our author follows MT by regarding *bmdbr* as parallel to *b'rbh*, cf. also 1QIsa[a]; in Sept., Vulg., Targ. and Pesh. *bmdbr* is taken as belonging to *qwl qwr'*. In reading *yshrw* our text agrees with MT, and not with 1QIsa[a] which has *wyshrw*. For the replacement of the Tetragrammaton by four dots, cf. 1QIsa[a] xl 7 and xlii 6. The practice has been explained in two ways :(a) as a practical device to indicate the empty space with a view to later completion (LIEBERMAN); (b) as due to fear of the Tetragrammaton (EISSFELDT).—BROWNLEE compares John the Baptist and his message, and BURROWS and others are in favour of a literal interpretation of the reference to the withdrawal into the desert. DELCOR suggests that the first part of the verse, dealing with retirement into the desert, is to be taken literally, whereas the second part, dealing with preparation of the way, is to be understood figuratively as alluding to the study of the Torah.

[46]) Hebr. *mdrsh htwrh*, cf. CD xx 6. BROWNLEE refers to Ezra vii 10.

[47]) The relative particle is by REICKE taken as going back to *mdrsh*, not to *htwrh*, but this interpretation presupposes the taking of *l'śwt* as referring to the study and runs counter to the usage of that verb elsewhere in 1QS; especially i 2 f shows that the verb alludes to the *doing* of the Law, and that Moses and the prophets are mentioned as authors, and not as ideal interpreters, of the Law. Cf. also the closely similar phrase *mṣwt 'l byd mwshh* in CD v 21.

[48]) Cf. ix 13. For the use of the preposition, cf. *shnh bshnh* 'year by year', *p'm bp'm* 'time and again' etc.

[49]) Cf. Eph. iii 5. Our passage enables us to understand the phrase in CD vi 1 which forms the parallel to 1QS viii 16, as CD v 21 does to 1QS viii 15. CD vi 1 is generally translated: 'and also by the holy anointed ones'. We can now see that the word *rwḥ* has dropped out, the proper translation being: 'and also by those who were anointed with the holy spirit' (i.e. the prophets), the phraseology being closely related to that of CD ii 12 f, for the interpretation of which, see note on iii 7. *Rwḥ qwdsh(w)* is the expression used in the Old Testament (Isa. lxiii 10; Ps. li 13). It may not be irrelevant to draw attention to the fact that the 'holy spirit' mentioned in Isa. lxiii 10 f and Ps. li 13, is in Targ. interpreted of the prophetic spirit.

[50]) An obvious case of a variant reading incorporated in the text, cf. VAN DER PLOEG.

[51]) Cf. Joshua xi 15. For the usage of *mṣwh* in the sense of the entire set of regulations, cf. Jer. xxxv 14. RABIN, in his note on CD x 3, has noticed the difference between the regulation in our passage, and that in l. 22, and suggests that *hmṣwh* in our passage alludes to the sect's oral law which would explain the two different punishments meted out in l. 17 and l. 22.

[52]) Hebr. *'d 'shr yzkw m'śyw mkwl h'wl*. This sentence is closely related to v 13 f: *ky' lw' yṭhrw ky 'm shbw mr'tm*, and these two passages held together enable us to realize the correct meaning of CD x 3: *'d zkw lshwb*, the interpretation of which has always been a crux to scholars. 1QS viii 18 suggests that in CD x 3 *zkw* should not be emended to *hzkw* (construct infinitive Niphal), but the use of the plural may simply be due to erroneous omission of *m'śyw*; again, 1QS v 14 furnishes us with the interpretation of *lshwb* in the CD passage, of which the meaning is: 'until their actions have been purified *by turning* (from sin)'.

[53]) Cf. Ps. ci 2: *bdrk tmym 'thlk ... bqrb byty*, which our author translated: 'on the way of perfection ... I will walk ... *when I am admitted to my house*'—seeing in 'house' an allusion to the community.

[54]) As for the fricative pronunciation of *Bet*, which is the reason for the original spelling, Prof. DRIVER draws my attention to ORIGEN's transcriptions ιεσχαυ (= *yishkab*) and Ραυ (= *rᵉhōb*).

[55]) Hebr. *wkmshpṭ hzh*. For a similar phrase, cf. CD xvi 12, xix 13, 29.

[56]) See note on vi 24. The formula *'lh hmshptym* is used in both vi 24 and here as introducing a penal code (DELCOR).

[57]) For the emended text, cf. CD xx 2, 7. The designation is applied to the community as a whole, and not to a particular body within it (against HVIDBERG).

[58]) Cf. ii 25. The phrase is here governed by what follows (cf. REICKE). The construction is admittedly unusual, but similar cases may be found in the Old Testament, cf. *GK* § 128c.

[59]) Hebr. *mhmh*, the only occurrence in 1QS of this form of the suffix; very common in 1QIsa[a].

[60]) Hebr. *y'br*. The unusual, defective spelling makes it difficult to decide whether the verb is meant to be Qal, or perhaps Piel. The former alternative, which may be supported by reference to the closely similar phrase in CD x 3 where the reading of the root as Qal is certain, is adopted by VAN DER PLOEG and others; the latter alternative, which may be supported by reference to the related passage in l. 17 (where the verb, as we have seen, should be read as Hiphil, and not as Qal), is preferred by YALON who takes it to mean 'remove'.

[61]) Hebr. *byd rmh wbrmyh*, which stands for *byd rmh wbyd rmyh*. As for the compound expression continued by simple preposition (cf. CD vi 1) Prof. DRIVER draws my attention to Ezek. vii 28.

[62]) Cf. vii 2, 17, 24, ix 1—from Jer. xxii 10.

[63]) For the combination of *hwn* and *'ṣh*, cf. vi 22. The use here of both *b* and *'m* is peculiar, although the verb may be constructed with either.

[64]) See note on vii 3.

[65]) Hebr. *wdrshw hmshpṭ*, cf. vi 7; the phrase means 'study the Law or the Right' (DELCOR). In pl. v, as well as in our context, *'shr lw'* introduces a prohibition, and *'shr lw' yshpwṭ* .. may be taken as a quotation from the community's code of laws (cf. MILIK and others).

[66]) For the reading of the verb as Niphal, see note on vi 4.

[67]) See note on vii 18.

[68]) Hebr. *ttm*, with defective spelling; but perhaps the form was pronounced *tittam*.

[69]) For the restored text, cf. ix 2. The difficult syntactical construction of viii 25-ix 2 is, so it appears, due to an anacoluthon. BROWNLEE assumes that the main clause comes in ix 2 ('then ... he shall be enrolled ..'), the intervening material being paranthetical. REICKE supplies *yhy* in the beginning of viii 26, whereas SCHUBERT, at the end of that line, supplies: 'dann wird er wieder aufgenommen'. The unnecessarily lengthy wording appears to favour the assumption

that the author, or the scribe, had two versions of the same regulation in front of him, and (unsuccessfully) strived to unite them.

Pl. ix

[1]) Or perhaps: 'for acting' (*l'wśh*; for the form of the noun, see note on viii 3).

[2]) For the *plene* spelling, cf. note on vi 14.

[3]) Whereas in the penal code (vi 24-vii 25) it is difficult to realize how the various punishments were derived from scriptural passages (although we may rest assured of their biblical foundation), we have here a most instructive example of how periods of punishments for certain sins might be fixed. viii 26 ff deals with the possibility of rehabilitation in the society after some kind of misconduct, and puts down the general rule that if the member acts *bshggh*, he may be re-admitted to the society after a period of two years' repentance (i.e. the time it took for a novice to be acknowledged as a full member, see vi 13 ff). If, however, he acts *byd rmh*, he is to be expelled from the community. Both rules are derived from Num. xv. In that chapter, in v. 30, we read that the person, who acts *byd rmh*, is to be cut off from amongst his people—which corresponds to 1QS ix 1b: 'As for the one who acts with a high hand—he shall not come back again'. In v. 27—also of Num. xv—it is ordained that a person, who acts thoughtlessly, should offer up a one year old goat as a sin-offering—from which regulation our author derived the rule contained in 1QS ix 1a in the following way: (a) *'ḥt* was combined with *bshggh*, not with *npsh*, whereby the verse was taken to deal with a person who committed *one* thoughtless sin; (b) in *hqrybh* (Hiphil of *qrb* which is used constantly in 1QS of admission to the society) our author found it suggested that readmission was possible; (c) in *shnth* he found it intimated that the punishment should last for two years (whether this is simply due to the t-form in front of the suffix, which our author took suggestive of *shntym*, or whether he realized that, when pronounced without the *Mappiq*, the ending of the word was equal to the dual ending known from Arabic, is uncertain).

[4]) See note on viii 4.

[5]) The parallel passage in viii 13 reads 'by'; *Kaph* and *Bet* could easily be confused, and it is impossible to say which reading is the more original.

[6]) For the emendation proposed, see notes on vii 17 and 18. The translation given is supported by the parallel passage in viii

12 which reads *lyḥd*, cf. also iii 7: *wbrwḥ qdwshh lyḥd b'mtw* which provides a close parallel to our passage.

[7]) Cf. v 6, viii 6, 10. That the community is the subject for the atonement, is in line with the parallel passages mentioned, and is an interesting theological point, see note on v 6.

[8]) For the emendation proposed, cf. viii 3. *Taw* could easily in the course of copying be dissolved into *Waw* + *Nun* (cf. 1QIsa[a] xxviii 1, as compared with MT, and Ecclus. vii 6).

[9]) Hebr. *mbśr ʿwlwt wmḥlby zbḥy trwmt śptym lmshpṭ*. Presupposing BURROWS' reading (*zbḥ wtrwmt*) some scholars see in the passage a rejection of sacrificial cult and understand the preposition in *mbśr* and *wmḥlby* comparatively (thus e.g. VAN DER PLOEG). Amongst the first students of 1QS MILIK was the only one to realize that the text might be read in some other way and that, consequently, the preposition might be taken differently. His reading and translation, which we have adopted, reflects the spiritual attitude of the community with respect to sacrifices very clearly, and is in fact more in accordance with what the photograph shows than the reading of BURROWS. It also has the great advantage that the position of *trwmt śptym* becomes quite clear, whereas the syntactical position of these two words, with BURROWS' reading, and in spite of scholars' translations, is really very difficult. Although the sacrificial terminology is kept, the attitude is altogether spiritual, and there can hardly be any doubt that the religious circles behind 1QS did not practise sacrificial cult; there is in this respect an important difference from those behind CD (cf. CD xi 17 ff). HÖLSCHER has tried to interpret all the sacrificial laws in CD figuratively, but the attempt is rightly rejected by BAUMGARTEN (in *HTR*, xlvi (1953), p. 145, n. 10a). For the conception of prayer as a substitute for sacrifice, see e.g. Ps. lxix 31 f (BAUMGARTEN), cvii 22 and cxvi 17 (BROWNLEE).

[10]) For the usage of *mshpṭ* and *ṣdq* in this way, see Prov. xvi 11; Lev. xix 36.

[11]) For the idea of the perfect lives of the pious as the ideal sacrifice, see viii 3; Rom. xii 2.

[12]) Same expression in CD xi 21.

[13]) For the reading of *ybdylw* as Niphal (cf. BROWNLEE), see v 1, and especially viii 11, a passage which is closely related to ours. As for the orthographical peculiarity, cf. 1QIsa[a] xxx 29, xl 30, xlv 22, li 5; Ecclus. xxxvi 16; Prov. ix 11.

[14]) The following is closely related to the phraseology of v 6 and

viii 5 f: in all three passages the idea is that of the community as a spiritual temple, and in all three passages the community is said to consist of 'Aaron' (i.e. the priests) and 'Israel' (i.e. the laity), these two designations being used in parallelism. For the taking of *lyḥd* as the noun *hyḥd* + preposition, see note on i 8. The word is a gloss, added in the margin and later incorporated in the text; the reason for the variant may be that in the parallel passage in viii 5 the expression *byt qwdsh* was said to be made up of the lay members of the community, whereas in our passage the expression is connected with the clerical element.

[15]) Cf. Ps. lxxxiv 12.—The construction is *ad sensum*.

[16]) The expression is used of the priests of the community also in v 21; while, however, the priests according to pl. v functioned in collaboration with the laity, they appear in our passage to possess absolute power over the rest of the community. We may have here an old tradition, reflecting the absolute power of the clergy—a state of affairs which is different not only from the implications contained in pl. v and vi 1, 24, according to which the whole community took part in the government of current affairs, but also from viii 1, according to which a council, in which the clergy was in minority, was at the head of the community.

[17]) Hebr. *ymshlw bmshpṭ wbhwn*, cf. Ecclus. xlv 17 which deals with the control of Aaron over 'ordinance and regulation' (*bḥwq wmshpṭ*). The similarity between the two passages is so great that it seems justified to assume that our author was acquainted with Ecclus. xlv 17 and changed the passage deliberately to fit it into the particular context, in which he wanted to use it—a procedure he follows again and again in his use of Scripture. Cf. 1QSa i 2.

[18]) The text reads *yṣ' whgwrl*. The parallel passage in v 3 suggests that *hgwrl* is the subject of *yṣ'*. BROWNLEE would therefore emend to *yṣ' hgwrl* which may be right, but perhaps the emendation is not necessary, see e.g. 1QIsa[a] xxiv 20, also with an apparently redundant *Waw*.

[19]) The construction here of *tkwn* with a personal *nomen rectus* might suggest a usage similar to that in vi 4, 8, 9, 10, 22, vii 21, viii 19, ix 2, in which passages the word is used in the meaning 'definite rank (or seat)'; accordingly our phrase would state that the question of rank within the community was decided upon by the priests (cf. REICKE); on the other hand, interpreted thus the sentence does not naturally continue 7a; again, the parallel phrase in v 3 favours the meaning 'norm'. Taken in this way the figurative

use of the expression 'to cast lots' becomes evident, see note on v 3.

[20]) Hebr. *'nshy hrmyh*, by VAN DER PLOEG taken as 'people of negligence', i.e. people who are careless in money affairs. This translation appears to suggest that the expression alludes to *other members of the community* of lower rank—an interpretation which might perhaps be supported by reference to vi 17, 22, but is contradicted by the continuation in our context. The translation given is that of most scholars; it presupposes the identification of *'nshy hrmyh* with *bny ('nshy) h'wl* which is the term generally used in 1QS as a designation of the impious (see e.g. v 2).

[21]) Cf. viii 18, which makes it clear that *lhbdyl m'wl* is to be taken as belonging to what precedes (against MILIK).

[22]) Hebr. *'ṣt htwrh.* Scholars translate this expression by 'counsel of Torah', i.e. the counsel which has been elicited from the Torah by study; there is no doubt of this meaning in l. 17 below. On the other hand, the phraseology of our passage is closely related to that of vii 23 f which deals with departure from the community.

[23]) Cf. CD iv 8, xx 31 f. The expression 'the first ones' is in our passage, as in CD xx 31 f, combined with *mshpṭym* as an adjective, whilst in CD iv 8 it occupies the place of *'nshy hyḥd* in the two other passages. ROST draws attention to the meaning of *r'shwn* in Deutero-Isaiah, whereas COPPENS finds in the expression *hmshpṭym hrshwnym* an allusion to the Torah. *Nshpṭw* is correctly explained by YALON as denoting 'walking on the ways of the statutes and the regulations'; the verb is chosen because of *hmshpṭym* and should not be taken as designating subordination (against REICKE). As for *ysr*, cf. note on iii 6. YALON would read *ltysr* instead of *ltwsr* which is BURROWS' reading; that may be right.

[24]) Some scholars find difficulty in accepting the apparent dual or plural form in *mshyḥy* and suggest that singular be read (cf. e.g. DEL MEDICO). The question is linked up with the interpretation of the closely similar formula *mshyḥ 'hrn wyśr'l* in CD xii 23 f, xiv 19, xix 10, xx 1. That the *mshyḥ* alludes to the Messiah is certain, and BROWNLEE's suggestion that *mshyḥy* here alludes to members of the sect, is to be rejected. Scholars are, however, divided on the question of the interpretation of the phrase in CD. LAGRANGE and HVIDBERG maintain that 'Aaron and Israel' is a designation for the community and take the phrase to mean that the community expected their Messiah to arise from their own midst. Some students of CD, however, have maintained that the phrase *mshyḥ 'hrn wyśr'l* means that the

community expected two Messiahs, one from 'Aaron' and one from 'Israel', cf. especially GINZBERG, *Eine unbekannte jüdische Sekte*, p. 351, who equates the former with Elijah, and the latter with Messiah ben David, the two being the priestly and secular heads of the eschatological community. OTZEN draws attention to Test. Sim. vii 2 which speaks of two Messiahs. MILIK draws attention to the mention of a priest and 'the Messiah of Israel' in 1QSa ii 14, 20 in connection with the 'banquet' of the community, but is this to be taken as referring to two Messiahs (a priestly and a lay one), or is it to be taken in favour of the assumption that the community did, after all, expect only one Messiah (cf. *mshyḥ* in 1QSa ii 12)? The question cannot be decided with certainty at the present stage of scholarship. Perhaps 1QS and 1QSa reflect different stages in the development of the messianic doctrine of the sect. As for the coming of the prophet, cf. 1 Macc. iv 44, based on Deut. xviii 15, 18. RABIN, in note on CD vi 11, thinks that 'prophet' here should be taken in the meaning 'teacher', and he finds support for this interpretation in the context.

25) Cf. Lev. xxvi 46; Num. xxx 17; Deut. xii 1; CD xix 4.

26) Cf. note on iii 13.

27) Same phrase in CD xii 20 f; for *kwl ḥy*, cf. Gen. iii 20; Ps. cxliii 2 etc.

28) Hebr. *ltkwn ʿt wʿt*. In the parallel passage CD xii 20 f *tkwn* is replaced by *mshpṭ* (BROWNLEE), which appears to favour the taking of *tkwn* in the meaning 'regulation' (cf. VAN DER PLOEG). The idea may be that an action should take place at the moment 'destined' for it (cf. note on i 15), cf. Ecclus. iv 20, xx 5 f. Another interpretation is, however, equally possible when looking at the continuation *kkwl hnglh lʿt bʿt* in the next line; if that phrase is synonymous with *ltkwn ʿt wʿt*, the latter expression conveys the idea of the progressive flow of revelations to the community (cf. viii 4, ix 8).

29) For the use of *mshql* DUPONT-SOMMER compares Dan. v 27; Enoch xli 1. Our passage is dependent on Esther i 8, our author having taken *rṣwn* absolutely as referring to God's will (cf. note on v 1).

30) Hebr. *llmwd*, translated according to BROWNLEE. The phrase presupposes that the bulk of revelations was put down in writing and contained in a particular book, cf. note on viii 2.

31) Hebr. *lpy hʿtym*. The meaning of the phrase is not clear, and the expression *lpy hʿt* in CD x 5 is equally obscure. The translation is based on the assumption that the expression is parallel to, and syno-

nymous with, the preceding *kwl hnglh lʿt bʿt*. It may be relevant to draw attention to Greek κατὰ καίρους which has the particular connotation with which we are here concerned.

[32]) This phrase may be understood as a variation of what was perhaps already said in l. 12 with *tkwn ʿt wʿt*. The wise man must know, not only *what* to do, but also *when* to do it.

[33]) Cf. Job. xxxi 6a, on which passage our phrase seems to depend directly, our author having seen in the biblical *bm'zny ṣdq* an allusion to *bny ṣdq*. For the reading of our text as *bny hṣdyq*, see note on v 2.

[34]) Hebr. *rwḥwm*, see note on v 20.

[35]) The combination of 'righteous' and 'elect' is exceedingly common in Enoch (i 1, xxxviii 2, 3, 4, xxxix 6, 7, xlviii 1, lviii 1, 2 etc.).

[36]) Lit.: 'and everybody according to his spirit, thus to do his due', cf. GINSBERG.

[37]) Hebr. *lqrbw*, alluding to admission to the society; VAN DER PLOEG takes the verb as a cultic term and translates: 'et pour que chacun Le serve selon l'innocence', but the taking of the suffix as referring to God is unnatural as there is no support for this interpretation in the context.

[38]) Cf. Job ix 30, xxii 30; 2 Sam. xxii 21, 25 (BROWNLEE).

[39]) The suffixes are taken objectively, according to BROWNLEE.

[40]) Hitpolel of *ryb* is unprecedented in Hebrew. The prohibition of disputing with outsiders is also the thought underlying v 15 f; in that passage our community's halakic opponents were clearly alluded to; this may also be the case in our context in which the following line appears to intimate that the questions argued about were of halakic nature. As for the interpretation of *lhwkyḥ*, see note 43 below.

[41]) Hebr. *'nshy hshḥt*, cf. CD vi 15 and RABIN's note. For *shḥt* in the meaning of 'perdition', see note on iv 12.

[42]) For the emendation proposed, cf. l. 18 f, by way of contrast. *Bet* and *Mem* could easily be confused.

[43]) Hebr. *lhwkyḥ*, cf. v 24. It appears difficult to take the verb in the same meaning in l. 16 and here: in the former passage the impious were the object, in the latter the pious fellow members of the society; besides, whereas in our passage the reading of the verb as Hiphil is clear, its juxtaposition with *wlhtrwbb* in l. 16 suggests that *lhwkyḥ* there is meant reciprocally, i.e. we should point it as Niphal (as for the orthography, see note on vi 14).

[44]) Hebr. *lbwḥry drk*. Apart from the original text of viii 6 this

is the only passage in 1QS in which *bḥr* is actively used with a human subject (cf. CD ii 15). Cf. Ps. cxix 30 (BROWNLEE). The fact that *drk* is used here without any further explanation, even without the article, appears to show that the word is applied in pregnant meaning about the religious conviction of the particular community with which we are here concerned, cf. Acts ix 2 and the use of *fennōt* in Jub. xxiii 20.

45) Cf. CD iii 18; also 1Q27 i 7.

46) The original text is probably not due to dittography, as BROWNLEE suggests, but the *He* belonged to the preceding *lhm* (cf. *mhmh* in viii 21). By the present word division the *He* became redundant and was consequently effaced.

47) Cf. CD i 13 (BROWNLEE).

48) Cf. viii 12 ff. A literal translation must take into account that our passage reads *lmdbr* with viii 13, and not *bmdbr* with viii 14 (cf. VAN DER PLOEG: 'diriger le chemin vers le désert').

49) The phraseology implies that the revelations go on. For *hnmṣ' l'śwt*, cf. CD xv 10 (BROWNLEE).

50) As for the emendation proposed, cf. the parallel phrases in v 1 f, 10, ix 9, and especially vi 15; besides, in 1QS and CD *swr* is invariably constructed with *mn* in the meaning of 'away from' (see 1QS i 15, viii 17; CD viii 4, 16, xiv 1, xvi 5, xix 17, 19, 34). Cf. also RABIN, in his note on CD vi 16. YALON explains the confusion of *l* and *l'* as due to Aramaic influence, and refers to 1QIsa[a] xvi 6, xxix 9: both the negation and the preposition were pronounced *lā*.

51) Some dependence of the context on Eccles. ix 1 here is clear, and it seems therefore fairly certain that the expression describes a quality of the pious, not of their adversaries; this is also the way in which all scholars take the phrase, except DUPONT-SOMMER who interprets the phrase as alluding to *hoarding* (translating *b* as 'because of'), and as giving the reason for the following injunction against amassing riches.

52) The translation follows BROWNLEE and BURROWS. As for *'ml* in the meaning of 'outcome', 'gains', see Ps. cv 44; Eccles. ii 19.

53) Cf. VAN DER PLOEG. MILIK takes *mqn'* as meaning 'rousing the wrath of God', no doubt under the influence of the following *lywm nqm*. VERMÈS, separating *ḥwq* and *'tw*, understands the passage as being to the effect that the pious observe the Law, thereby speeding up the advent of the Day of Judgment.—The idea is that of viii 4; *'t* may perhaps be more suitably translated by 'occasion', 'opportunity' which is the connotation of the word in Ecclus. xii 16.

[54]) That *rṣwn* is used absolutely is due to influence from Isa. lxi 2, of which our author understood the first half as follows: 'to proclaim the year of doing the will of the Lord'—leaving out, of course, the Tetragrammaton.

[55]) Deut. xv 10, xxiii 21, xxviii 8, 20.

[56]) See note on iii 11.

[57]) Cf. Ps. xl 9. That *lw* is to be taken as equal to *lw'* is realized by BROWNLEE. The spelling is known from a number of passages in the Old Testament.

[58]) Cf. Hos. vi 5. In that biblical passage the suffix for 2nd pers. in *wmshpṭyk* is strange after the verbal forms in 1st pers., and MT may be due to wrong word division, cf. Sept., Pesh., and Targ., all of which presuppose the reading *k'wr*. That our author in *'wr yṣ'* saw the root *rṣh*, is obvious, and the form he gives the biblical passage is an interesting example of his ability to 'interpret' an otherwise unintelligible biblical passage. It appears natural to assume that he had in front of him a text similar to that of MT and, finding difficulty in *wmshpṭyk*, simply left it out. If he had had before him a text similar to that on which the old versions are based (i.e. if he had read *k'wr yṣ'*) he might not have found it suggestive of the interpretation which he gave it in our passage.

[59]) According to the context, the phrase *ṣph lmshpṭ 'l* does not mean 'to wait for the judgment of God', but *ṣph* here (as in CD i 18) alludes to the careful investigation and study of the Torah.

[60]) For the spelling *'wśyw*, cf. Ps. cxlix 2.

[61]) Between the reconstructed *ys*[*pr*] and [*trwmt*] *śptym* (cf. x 6) a word, the object of *yspr*, is lost.

Pl. x

[1]) Hebr. *'m qṣym 'shr ḥqq'*. This reading is reflected in the translations of all scholars except that of DUPONT-SOMMER who reads the third word as *'shyr* 'I will sing', assuming that the present hymn starts with *'m*, and not, as is generally assumed, with the last words of the previous plate. The basic idea of the ensuing hymn (ll. 1-8) is that of the pious' constant and unflagging worship which goes on during daytime (l. 1 as far as *tqwptw*), during night (l. 2 f as far as *lm'wn kbwd*), during months, as initiated by the new moons (ll. 3-6 as far as *kḥwq ḥrwt l'd*), during the seasons of the year (l. 6 f as far as *lmw'd dsh'*), during periods of seven years (l. 7), up to *mw'd drwr* (i.e. fifty years). The style of the hymn is turgid and stilted, but the

main thought is clear: every moment of the poet's life is occupied by adoration (days, nights, months, seasons, years). The hymn has a very close parallel in 1QH (*MG*, I, xii 4-11), to which DEL MEDICO has drawn attention. *Qṣym* is taken by BROWNLEE and others as denoting fixed times *for worship*, and the whole of the following lines is taken by DUPONT-SOMMER as containing the clue to the understanding of the festival calendar of the community to which he finds allusions also in i 8 f, 13 ff, iii 9 f. We have already discussed those passages and have seen that they should not be taken as alluding to some festival calendar of the society; besides, the preposition *'m*, which is used throughout the hymn in the meaning 'during' (cf. Ps. lxxii 5 and Dan. iii 33), suggests that *qṣym*, as in i 14, should be taken in the meaning 'periods', the word being qualified in the ensuing enumeration of days, nights etc. The meaning of *ḥqq'* is quite uncertain. Should it be taken as a verb, and if so, should the *Aleph* be taken as the suffix for 3rd pers. sing. (LAMBERT), or as an abbreviation of *'lhym* (BROWNLEE)? The latter scholar's ingenious suggestion that the *Aleph* forms an acrostic with the *Mem* in *hm* and the *Nun* in l. 2 is acknowledged by BURROWS, but DUPONT-SOMMER has drawn attention to the fact that there is no empty space in front of *Aleph*, the letter clearly belonging to the preceding word. For the translation given of *ḥqq'*, cf. SCHUBERT and HABERMANN.

²) Hebr. *mmshlt*, Gen. i 16; cf. the constant mention of 'dominion' in 'The Book of Celestial Physics' (Enoch lxxii-lxxxii). For prayer at dawn BROWNLEE refers to JOSEPHUS's description of the Essenes, in *Jewish War*, II, 128.

³) Scholars have discussed whether the section from *brshyt mmshlt 'wr* to *lm'wn kbwd* alludes to three or to two times for prayer. The former interpretation, which presupposes the taking of *tqwph* as 'middle of course', is preferred by VAN DER PLOEG and others, whereas the latter interpretation is proposed by DUPONT-SOMMER and BURROWS, these scholars taking the disputed word in the meaning of 'cycle', 'circuit'. Without sharing the view of DUPONT-SOMMER, that the text alludes to two times for prayer (for which he refers to PHILO's description of the Therapeutes, in *De Vita Contemplativa*, § 27), we have adopted the view that *tqwph* throughout the hymn is used in the meaning of 'completion of course', 'circuit'. In our passage the expression *'m tqwptw* simply means: 'as long as it is daylight'.

⁴) Cf. Ps. civ 22, which in its biblical context deals with the young lions' withdrawal to their dens at sunrise. Our author borrowed

'sp and *m'wn* from this passage, interpreting it as dealing with the withdrawal of sunlight.

5) Cf. Lam. ii 19. *'shmwry* is equal to *'shmwrwt* of classical Hebrew.

6) Cf. Deut. xxviii 12; Jer. l 25 in which passages also the suffix refers to God; in our context, however, it is more naturally understood as going back to *ḥwshk*, cf. Isa. xlv 3, and Dupont-Sommer.

7) In spite of the defective orthography the verb is to be derived from *shyt* 'to put', cf. Dupont-Sommer who points to the dependence on Ps. civ 20—a biblical context which has played the greatest rôle for the composition of the first lines of our hymn. As for the present reading *'lt*, it may be that the copyist in leaving the text unfinished was influenced by Ezek. xxxii 8 where *'rṣ*, and not *tbl*, is used. Lambert emends to *'lṭh*, Burrows to *l't*; others (Dupont-Sommer, Brownlee) suggest the word be taken as absolute infinitive of *'lh*; Habermann sees in the word the preposition *'l* and emends to *'lyw*.

8) I.e. when darkness is in retreat, being 'chased away' by the advancing light; the allusion is to the spell just before dawn when (l. 3) the 'luminaries' (i.e. the stars) shine from 'the holy abode' (i.e. heaven).

9) I.e.: 'when stars (for *m'wr* in this meaning, see Ezek. xxxii 8) shine forth from heaven' (cf. Isa. lxiii 15 (Brownlee)). The two passages *brshyt* ... *mpny 'wr* (ll. 1-2) and *b'wpy'* ... *lm'wn kbwd* are parallel and synonymous, cf. especially Lambert.

10) Cf. Ps. civ 19. Our author found in that passage an allusion to the regular recurrence of the days of the new moon, and he did so by translating the biblical passage thus: 'He maketh the moon *at fixed times*, the sun knoweth its (i.e. the moon's) entering'. The strange dependence on Ps. civ 19 here shows that *mw'dym* is not, as Dupont-Sommer thinks, applied in the sense of 'the four seasons'; his interpretation is also contradicted by the clear reference to the days of the new moon, which is most naturally taken as alluding to the monthly recurring days on which the new moon appears and not, as Dupont-Sommer wants it, to the four 'days of the seasons' mentioned in Jub. vi 23; our phrase is closely related to *brshyt yrḥym lmw'dyhm* in l. 5.

11) Hebr. *yḥd tqwptm 'm msrwtm zh lzh*. Dupont-Sommer translates this passage in the following way: '(par suite de) l'accord du circuit de celles-là (les saisons) avec les liens qui unissent celles-ci (les lunes, les mois) l'une à l'autre', taking it as alluding to the agreement of the solar cycle with the lunar one. The impossibility of this interpretation

lies not only in the lack of a preposition in front of *yḥd* which, in spite of Dupont-Sommer's reference to Isa. vii 25, is very striking, but also in the general absence of the ideas which Dupont-Sommer quite unwarrantably reads into it; besides, the translation given, which presupposes the taking of *yḥd*... *'m* in the meaning 'both during ... and during', is in accordance not only with classical usage (cf. e.g. Ps. xlix 3, 11), but also with the constant usage of *'m* in the present hymn in the meaning 'during' (cf. note 1 above). The suffix in *tqwptm* is most naturally taken as referring to the immediately preceding *ymy ḥwdsh*, and our passage seems to be to the effect that not only on the days of the new moon, which played a great religious rôle for the community, but also on the 'ordinary' days of the month, here called 'bonds' because they 'tie' the days of the new moon together, does the pious apply himself to adoration. This interpretation is based on the assumption that the phrase *zh lzh* refers to the ordinary days of the month, cf. the context of the identical expression in l. 7. For the spelling *msrwtm*, cf. Job xxxix 5 (Dupont-Sommer).

[12]) Hebr. *bhtḥdshm hm gdwl lqwdsh qwdshym w'wt* <.> *lmptḥ ḥsdyw*. This passage is the most disputed in the whole of the manuscript. That the verb *bhtḥdshm* alludes to the renewal of the new moons, mentioned in the immediately preceding clause, is clear (Dupont-Sommer), and is in fact another indication of the great awe in which those days were held by our community. The reading *hm* is not quite clear in the manuscript, and van der Ploeg and others would read *ywm*; the following *gdwl* is then taken as an adjective belonging to that substantive; the shapes of the letters are such that the reading cannot be established on purely palaeographical grounds, but Ecclus. xliii 2 ff may give us the clue to the correct interpretation. The subject-matter there is closely related to our context, as is the vocabulary: in both hymns we find the following significant key-words: *m'wr*, *gdwl*, *mmshlt*, *'wt*, *mw'd*, *ḥwq*, *tqwph*, *ḥdsh*, *htḥdsh*, *'wr*, *'shmrwt*. The number of identical words is very large, and it might be expected that the text in Ecclus. might help us to understand 1QS x 4 better. In Ecclus. xliii 5 *gdwl* is used with reference to the Lord which appears to recommend the taking of *gdwl* in our passage as connected with what follows, *qwdsh qwdshym* referring to God and not, as Dupont-Sommer suggests, to the supreme holiness of the letter *Nun*; his ingenious proposal is that the calendar of the community, which he finds reflected in our hymn, was based on Pythagorean speculations concerning the holiness of the number fifty (*Nun* = fifty), and he refers for this

to PHILO's description of the mystic character of that number in *De Vita Contemplativa*, § 65; in order to establish our line as referring to this, he separates *gdwl* from what follows (taking the word as the absolute infinitive of *gdl*), disregards the *Waw* in front of *'wt*, and takes the latter word in the meaning 'letter'. We have already given our reasons for interpreting *gdwl* as an adjective belonging to what follows, and it is very interesting and highly significant that the word *'wt* is used in the parallel passage Ecclus. xliii 6 about the moon which is said to be *'wt 'wlm*, 'an eternal sign'; this suggests that *'wt* also in our passage is used in the meaning 'sign', and not in the meaning 'letter'; the usage in Ecclus. as well as in our passage is dependent on Gen. i 14. The reader will appreciate that our objections to DUPONT-SOMMER's interpretation also apply to that of BROWNLEE, mentioned in note 1 above; as for this scholar's interpretation of *hm* which he renders 'the *Mem*', we may add that that translation would have required the spelling *hmm*, cf. DUPONT-SOMMER who refers to CD xv 1; besides, names of letters are feminine in Semitic languages. Palaeography supports the view that the *Nun* is not meant as the letter, but is the beginning of a word which the scribe began to write, but failed to finish (ZEITLIN): he was, for some reason or other, uncertain of the text and left a space for later completion. The word in the text before him was perhaps *nwr'* (VAN DER PLOEG) which occurs twice with emphasis in Ecclus. xliii (vv. 2 and 8), and the scribe may have hesitated to write it, because he found it unsuitable in a context dealing with 'the release of His mercy'. The translation given presupposes the taking of *hm* as giving emphasis to the preceding suffix (cf. DUPONT-SOMMER), and the taking of *gdwl* according to *GK* § 132c.

[13]) The translation presupposes the taking of *mptḥ* as a *nomen actionis* (cf. MILIK, referring to Prov. viii 6). BROWNLEE prefers the rendering 'key', finding support for his interpretation in the fact that the shape of the letter *Nun* is that of an ancient key.

[14]) Cf. xi 8 f. As for the meaning of participle Niphal of *hyh*, see note on iii 15.

[15]) That these words allude to the celebration of the new moons has been noticed by DUPONT-SOMMER; in fact, that is the sole theme of our hymn from *bmbw' mw'dyhm* in l. 3.

[16]) Cf. Isa. lviii 13, referring to the sabbath; this may also be the meaning intended by the author in our passage, the sabbaths marking the phases of the moon. DUPONT-SOMMER, who also takes the expression as alluding to the sabbaths, finds in our passage an indication

that 'the date of the sabbaths . . . is fixed according to the beginning of every season', but we have already seen (cf. note 10 above) that *mw'd* in the parallel expression in l. 3 does not allude to the four seasons of the year, but is most naturally understood as referring to the fixed, appointed times of the new moons.

17) Cf. Exod. xii 14, xiii 9; Ecclus. xlv 11. The biblical references show that the expression should be taken absolutely and disconnected with the following *trwmt śptym* (against VAN DER PLOEG).

18) The emendation proposed is generally accepted.

19) Scholars are divided on the question whether *ḥwq ḥrwt* should be taken as 'law of liberty' (*ḥōq ḥērūt*) or as 'inscribed law' (*ḥōq ḥārūt*). For the former, cf. Jas. i 25, ii 12; for the latter, cf. Exod. xxxii 16 and Ecclus. xlv 11.

20) Cf. Ezek. xl 1.

21) There is no reason for taking *bhshlm* as Hiphil with God as understood subject, as DUPONT-SOMMER does. The form is best taken as Niphal, cf. HABERMANN, and RABIN in note on CD iv 8; the word is Mishnaic.

22) Hebr. *ywm mshpṭw zh lzh*. The suffix is taken as referring to God by DUPONT-SOMMER; perhaps it is better taken as referring to the previous *ywm* (cf. MILIK). Allusion appears to be made to the definite measure of each day, rather than to the days on which the seasons of the year were initiated (against DUPONT-SOMMER).

23) Not even in this passage, which alludes to the four seasons of the year, does *mw'd* in itself mean 'season', as DUPONT-SOMMER thinks; the word is used in the classical way, cf. especially Hos. ii 11.

24) Lit.: 'the fixed times of years until their weeks', *shbw'* being used here in the meaning of 'period of seven years' as in Dan. ix. Cf. Lev. xxv 1 ff.

25) Cf. Lev. xxv 8 ff.

26) Cf. Prov. xviii 21; Sept. at Hos. xiv 3 (BROWNLEE).

27) The verb *zmr* implies music making as well as singing; that the following musical terms should be understood metaphorically is clear from the expression 'the flute of my lips', cf. Ps. of Sol. xv 5. *D't* refers to the technical skill of the artist (cf. e.g. Exod. xxxi 3; 1 Kings vii 14); the rendering of LAMBERT ('art'), therefore, is excellent and to the point. BROWNLEE refers to 1 Cor. xiv 15, but the implication of the purportedly corresponding Greek expression in that passage is quite different. In front of the beginning of our hymn a couple of words have been erased, and BARTHÉLEMY suggests that the

text originally read *'ś' bqw*, in anticipation of the identical phrase at the end of the line.

28) Hebr. *ltkwn qwdshw*. The phrase appears to be parallel with the following *bqw mshpṭw*.

29) Lit.: 'lift up', the object being 'the voice', for which 'the flute of my lips' stands.

30) Cf. Isa. xxviii 17. The meaning of l. 10b appears to be: 'My lips are adapted to, and fit for, the praise of His holiness and justice'.

31) Cf. Ps. lxv 9.

32) Hebr. *wbhywtm*. The context appears to make it clear that the preposition should be taken locally (cf. VAN DER PLOEG), in spite of the fact that *b*, in connection with an infinitive, is never used in this way in classical Hebrew.

33) The passage is an interesting homiletic application of Ps. civ 9, which deals with the boundary which God has laid down for the waters lest they should 'return'.

34) For the emendation proposed, cf. 2 Sam. vii 14 where *bshpṭ* by the author was taken as suggestive of *bmshpṭ* which, because of the fricative pronunciation of *Bet*, was copied erroneously. For the *plene* spelling of the verb (taken as Niphal), cf. note on vi 14.

35) Cf. Ps. iv 2; Jer. xxiii 6, xxxiii 16.

36) Cf. xi 3; Prov. xviii 4; Enoch xlviii 1 (TOURNAY).

37) The translation follows BROWNLEE in taking *ltp'rt 'wlm* to what precedes.

38) The parallelism with *ywrny* shows that *yshwpṭny* contains no allusion to the Judgment.

39) Cf. Deut. xii 7, xv 10, xxiii 21, xxviii 8 (BROWNLEE). In all the biblical passages mentioned the idiom is used together with *brk*, God being the author of the blessing throughout.

40) Cf. Ps. cxlv 1 f.

41) Cf. Deut. xxviii 6; Ps. cxxi 8; CD xx 27 f.

42) Cf. Deut. vi 7 (BROWNLEE); Ps. cxxxix 2. In 2 Kings xix 26 f our author no doubt read *qmk wshbtk*, an emendation which has been suggested by scholars and is supported by 1QIsa[a] xxxvii 27 f.

43) Cf. Num. xxx 13; Deut. xxiii 24; Jer. xvii 16; Ps. lxxxix 35.

44) The phrase alludes to the rows of men at worship. The military phraseology has an interesting parallel in Arab. صَفّ which means 'a row of soldiers or of worshippers' (cf. FISCHER, *Arabische Chrestomatie*, p. 68).

[45]) Cf. Gen. xli 44.

[46]) Cf. Ps. xxxvi 9; CD i 8. *Lhdshn* may be taken as Niphal or Hitpael. The translation given follows GINSBERG, and is supported by the Greek renderings of the verb in Ecclus. xxvi 2 and xliii 22 (εὐφραίνει and ἱλαρώσει respectively). The turgidity of the whole passage might suggest a messianic interpretation, in which case it alludes to the time until the messianic era as a time for praise.

[47]) BURROWS transcribes the text as *brshyt*, and his reading is adopted by most scholars. BROWNLEE reads *brshwt* because of the following *wbmkwn*, but cf. the phrase *wbhptḥ ṣrh* in l. 17 which is only a variation of what appears to be intended by *brshyt pḥd* in our line.

[48]) As for the emendation proposed, cf. the combination of *ṣrh* and *ṣwqh* in Isa. xxx 6; Prov. i 27.

[49]) Hebr. *bhpl' mwdh* which has been taken in many different ways. Most students take *mwdh* as a verb explaining the preceding *'brknw* (cf. e.g. VAN DER PLOEG); *bhpl'* is then regarded either as the object of that verb (VAN DER PLOEG), or as an adverbial expression (DEL MEDICO). RABIN, in note on CD ix 11, suggests *mwdh* taken as the equivalent of *m'dh* (read as *meʾōdōh*) 'His strength', an interpretation which is no doubt due to the following *wbgbwrtw*. DRIVER(orally) suggests *mwdh* taken as the equivalent of *twdh* and compares *mwṣ'h*—*twṣ'h* 'exit'. We have adopted that suggestion in our translation; for the meaning of the verb ('to pronounce distinctly)', see JASTROW's *Dictionary*, II, p. 1181. The translation given, which is closely related to that of BURROWS, is proposed with the greatest of reservations; the text may not be in order.

[50]) The translation follows BROWNLEE in taking the verb as Polel of *śyḥ*, cf. Ps. cxliii 5, and not as some form of *shḥḥ*, as DEL MEDICO proposes.

[51]) Hebr. *w'dʿh*. The verb is closely connected with what precedes, explaining and developing the theme of complete confidence in the divine mercy, as this was expressed in the immediately previous sentence. The use of voluntative forms after *Waw* consecutive is quite common in the Scrolls and in the Samaritan Pentateuch, but is also to be found in MT, cf. *GK* § 49e.

[52]) Cf. Job xii 10, our author having seen in *npsh* of that passage an allusion to the word *mshpṭ*.

[53]) Cf. Ps. cxi 7.

[54]) For the use of *ptḥ* in this way, cf. Jer. i 14 (IWRY). Our passage is dependent on 1QIsa[a] li 14 which reads *ṣrh* for *ṣʿh* of MT.

[55]) Conflation of Isa. lii 9 and Ps. xx 6.

[56]) Cf. Ps. vii 5 f. In the psalm the words are, in fact, a self-imprecation: *'m* is meant hypothetically and *yrdp* introduces the apodosis. The application of the biblical verses in our passage displays several interesting features: (a) *'m* was taken to introduce an oath, hence *lw'* in 1QS; (b) the *Shin* of *shwlmy* was combined with what precedes; (c) *npshy* was taken as the subject, and not as the object, of *yrdp*; (d) *'wyb* was found suggestive of *ṭwb*. The translation given follows VAN DER PLOEG. SCHUBERT objects to this interpretation because it seems to run counter to the hatred of the members of the community against outsiders, and he translates: 'Nicht werde ich dem Manne Böses mit Gutem vergelten, ich werde den Starken verfolgen'; but the object of *hshyb* (in the meaning 'to repay') is never introduced by the preposition *b*; besides, the dependence on Ps. vii 5 f suggests that *r'* is meant to finish the first half of the stichos.

[57]) Cf. Jer. li 56.

[58]) The construction of Piel of *qn'* in Prov. iii 31, xxiv 1, 19, whose phraseology is closely related to our context, might suggest that we should translate as follows: 'I will not be envious of a godless spirit' (cf. BROWNLEE), if it were not for the following *npsh* with which *rwḥ* appears to be synonymous. The translation follows VAN DER PLOEG.

[59]) Cf. *hwn rsh'h* in CD vi 15, viii 5; see also Enoch lxiii 10; Luke xvi 9, and *hwn 'nshy ḥms* in 1QpHab viii 11.

[60]) Reading *wryb*, with BURROWS. BROWNLEE reads *wrwb* and takes *rwb* in the meaning 'abundance'. In Prov. iii 30 f, on which 1QS x 18 f is obviously dependent, the consonantal text has *trwb*, whereas the Massoretes tell us to read *tryb* which is alone correct, as is clear from the context. That our author has read the verb in the same way as the Massoretes seems clear when the general dependence of our passage on Prov. iii 30 f is kept in mind, and when it is realized that with the reading *wrwb* the text, in spite of the apparent parallelism with *hwn*, must be taken to allude to the *multitude* of the men of Perdition, and not to their abundance, as *rwb* never, at any stage of the development of the Hebrew language, is used in the meaning 'riches'. The text, then, literally translated, is to the following effect: 'The trial of the men of Perdition I will not handle' (for *tpś* constructed with an abstract noun, cf. Num. xxxi 27; Jer. ii 8).

[61]) For the idiom, cf. Prov. xxiv 18, xxix 8. On the form of the suffix, see the Introduction.

[62]) The construction of *nṭr* (Lev. xix 18) with *b* introducing the object is remarkable.

[63]) Cf. Isa. lix 20; CD iv 2.

[64]) Cf. Exod. xxxii 8; Deut. ix 16; CD ii 6 (Brownlee).

[65]) The construction of *nḥm* (Piel) with *b* introducing the object is as remarkable as the identical construction of *nṭr* in l. 20. For the parallelism of *rḥm* and *nḥm*, see Isa. xlix 13.

[66]) Hebr. *nk'ym*. It is not possible to combine this word with *rwḥ nk'h* in Prov. xv 13, xvii 22, xviii 14 or with *nkh rwḥ* in Isa. lxvi 2 and translate: 'the humble ones', this translation providing a meaning contradictory to the statement in l. 26; besides, the following *'d twm drkm* would be unintelligible, humility being a fundamental virtue in the ethics of the community, cf. ii 24, iii 8, iv 3, v 3, 25, ix 22. The expression *'d twm drkm* appears to suggest that *nk'ym* must refer to some people who did not live according to the rules of the society (parallel with the previous *swrry drk*). Habermann refers to *nkym* in Ps. xxxv 15 which he understands as the equivalent of *rsh'ym* 'impious', cf. also Yalon who takes the word in Ps. xxxv 15 as the equivalent of *bzwym* 'despised ones', on the assumption that the passive participle of *nkh* may have this connotation. In the translation given we have ventured to propose the equation of the root in our passage with Syriac ܢܟܐ which is used in Pesh. in Gal. v 17 in the meaning 'to struggle (against)'.

[67]) Cf. Job iv 6; Prov. xiii 6.

[68]) Or: 'worthlessness' (cf. Brownlee who refers to Deut. xv 9).

[69]) Hebr. *nblwt* (cf. Hos. ii 12).

[70]) Cf. Lev. xix 24 (Brownlee, who also draws attention to the figurative use of 'fruit' in Prov. xii 14, xiii 2, xviii 20 f). From a comparison of the two passages it appears that our author treated the biblical passage in the following way: (a) *wbshnh* he found suggestive of *blshwny*; (b) he left *hrb'yt* out; (c) for *pryw* he read *pry* which he took as *nomen regens* of the following *qdsh*; (d) for *hlwlym* he read *ḥlwlym* (the Samaritan Pentateuch actually reads thus), connecting the word with the meaning 'profane', and taking it as the opposite of the previous *qdsh* (*ḥl* is used as the opposite of *qdsh* in Lev. x 10; Ezek. xxii 26, xlii 20, xliv 23); (e) *lYHWH* he read as *l' yhyh* (cf. note on i 18). In this way he understood the verse as conveying the following meaning: 'And on my tongue ... there shall be fruit of holiness; profane things shall not be (there)', and, putting this into language suitable for a poetical context he paraphrased: 'The fruit of holiness shall be

on my tongue, and abominations shall not be found on it'. *Ymṣ'* is probably to be read as plural.

[71]) Hebr. *bhwdwt*. The remarkable similarity here to Ps. lxxviii 2, however, raises the question whether we should not rather read *bhydwt* (= *bḥydwt* by weakening of the *Ḥet*), but absolute certainty cannot be attained here, as the author may very well have seen *hwdwt* in the biblical *ḥydwt*.

[72]) Lit.: 'and the faithlessness of man until the completion of his sin' (cf. BURROWS), or perhaps: 'until the end of their sin' (MILIK). The translation given presupposes the assumption of a stop after *psh'm*, thus most scholars. YALON draws *rqym* to what precedes and, assuming that the word is due to corruption of some form of *rḥq*, he translates: 'I will keep away from man until his sin is ended'. This interpretation founders on the word *rqym* which is *plural*; besides, the similar phrase *'d twm drkm* in l. 21 suggests a stop after *psh'm*, and recommends the taking of *rqym* to what follows. Also VAN DER PLOEG and LAMBERT take *rqym* to what precedes, the former scholar regarding the word as the predicate of *m'l*, the latter taking it as *nomen regens* of the preceding *twm drkm*; both suggestions are unsatisfactory.

[73]) Lit.: 'impure and tortuous things from the knowledge of my heart'.

[74]) Or: 'In the council of wisdom I will recount knowledge'. It is difficult to see whether *'ṣh* here means 'counsel' or 'council', but BROWNLEE is probably right when suggesting that the connotation of the word depends on whether the verb is read as *'str* or as *'spr*; with the former reading goes the meaning 'counsel' (cf. ix 17), and with the latter goes the meaning 'council' (cf. vi 9 f). REICKE points to the parallelism with the ensuing *wb'rmt d't* as favouring the former interpretation, cf. also VAN DER PLOEG; we have adopted this interpretation in our translation. As for the phrase *'ṣt twshyh*, cf. *'ṣh wtwshyh* in Prov. viii 14.

[75]) For the restoration proposed, cf. Job i 10 (REICKE). The suffix goes back to *d't*.

[76]) This passage aptly expresses the esoteric intellectualism of the society and is, in fact, an allegorical interpretation of Isa. xxvi 1-3 which deals with 'a strong city', protected by 'walls and bulwarks' (cf. note on vi 17). As a city is protected by walls, thus the secrets of the society should be protected by the members of the society against onslaught and dispersion by prudent, shrewd behaviour. The strange

expression 'the strong decision (or judgment) of God's righteousness' is satisfactorily explained as due to our author's dependence on Isa. xxvi 1 which he changed according to the context in his hymn.

[77]) The context seems to favour the view that *ḥlq* is not used here in the classical sense 'to distribute', but in the sense 'to decide the measure of something' (cf. Arab. خلق) which is the basic meaning underlying the application of the root in the meaning 'to create' in Ecclus. (cf. SMEND, on Ecclus. xxxi 13). For the conception of the close relationship between a commandment and its 'time', cf. note on i 15; accordingly, our passage appears to mean: 'I will fulfil an ordinance at the correct time'.

[78]) For the orthography, cf. e.g. *nytpśym* in CD iv 20.

[79]) Hebr. *wḥzyq* which appears to be construct infinitive Piel.

[80]) Cf. Isa. xxxv 4. YALON finds that our author, in his application of the biblical phrase, uses the expression *nmhry lb* in the meaning in which it was current at his time, viz. 'feeble of heart' (cf. Sept., Vulg., Pesh. in Isa. xxxv 4, and also Sept. in Isa. xxxii 4).

Pl. xi

[1]) The lacuna at the bottom of the preceding plate undoubtedly contained some word for 'teaching', parallel with *wlhśkyl* in our passage, cf. Isa. xxix 24. GINSBERG is justified in equating *rwknym* with *rwgnym*, on the assumption of confusion of *Kaph* and *Gimel* (cf. also MILIK), and it is a mistake when some scholars have suggested 'weak' or 'lowly' as alternative renderings (DEL MEDICO and others), although the context might seem to support it.

[2]) Hebr. *ʿnwh*, taken adverbially, or as the equivalent of *bʿnwh*, parallel with the following *wbrwḥ nshbrh*, with most scholars. Cf. ix 22 f.

[3]) See note on viii 3.

[4]) As the continuation shows, the expression *'nshy mṭh* is dependent on Isa. lviii 9. MT and 1QIsa[a] have *mwṭh* 'yoke', used figuratively of 'oppression'. The spelling *mṭh* might suggest a different interpretation, either 'injustice' (thus BROWNLEE who, referring to Ezek. ix 9, suggests that the consonantal text in Isa. lviii 9 is the word *muṭṭēh* written *plene*), or 'rod' (*maṭṭēh*), thus DUPONT-SOMMER, or 'down', 'downwards' (*maṭṭāh*), thus HABERMANN who explains the expression *'nshy mṭh* as alluding to people who stand on a lower level. We have no means of obtaining absolute certainty as to the meaning of the phrase in our passage, because we do not know how our author interpreted Isa. lviii 9.

[5]) Hebr. *wmqny hwn*. The translation follows MILIK in taking *mqny* as participle Hiphil of *qnh*, parallel with the previous *shwlḥy* and *mdbry*. BROWNLEE also regards *mqny* as parallel with the preceding participles, but prefers the meaning 'to be envious' or 'to be zealous'. DRIVER takes *mqny* as an infinitive, regarding it as the object of *mdbry*, parallel with *'wn* (cf. VAN DER PLOEG).

[6]) Cf. Isa. xlix 4. BROWNLEE takes *mshpṭ* in the meaning of 'justification'.

[7]) A lax allusion to Deut. ix 5, quoted in CD viii 14. For *yshwr*, see note on iv 9; for the defective spelling *ṣdqwtw*, see note on i 17.

[8]) Cf. Isa. xliii 25, xliv 22; Ps. li 3.

[9]) Hebr. *'wrw*, read by some scholars as *'wry* 'my light' (cf. MILIK, and others). The matter cannot be decided by palaeographical considerations.

[10]) Hebr. *'wrt lbby*. The translation given follows the majority of scholars in presupposing the taking of *'wrt* as a noun. VAN DER PLOEG appears to have seen a verb in the word, but the verb of the sentence is understood and is to be supplied from the first part of the stichos.

[11]) Hebr. *brz nhyh whww' 'wlm*. Cf. 1Q26 i 1, 4; 1Q27 i 3, 4. Some scholars make a stop after *nhyh* and regard *hww' 'wlm* as referring to God (thus e.g. DUPONT-SOMMER), but the phraseology of CD ii 10 and xiii 8 shows that *hww'* (Aramaic) should not be separated from *nhyh* (for the meaning of participle Niphal, cf. note on iii 15).

[12]) Cf. e.g. Ps. xviii 19, xl 3, lxxiii 23, lxxxv 14.

[13]) HABERMANN maintains the text, deriving the verb from *zyd*, cf. MOLIN; these two scholars also agree in drawing *mpny kwl* to what precedes. Already VAN DER PLOEG assumed that the text was not in order, and most scholars have adopted the emendation suggested (Hitpalpel of *zw'*; for the form, cf. viii 8). BROWNLEE inserts *r'* after *mpny kwl*; his suggestion might be supported by a reference to the phraseology of Ps. of Sol. xv 6: ὁ ποιῶν ταῦτα οὐ σαλευθήσεται εἰς τὸν αἰῶνα ἀπο κακοῦ.

[14]) The reading *mshpṭy* is generally accepted by scholars and has been interpreted either as *mshpṭ* + suffix for 1st person (thus VAN DER PLOEG), or as the construct state plural (thus MILIK); in either case the meaning is not clear; against the former suggestion speaks that we do not seem to want a mention of 'my right' or 'my justification' here; against the latter speaks the phraseology of l. 3 f. The translation given presupposes the reading *mshpṭw*, this word being a gloss of the

preceding *ṣdqtw* which, in the process of copying, has been incorporated into the text. For 'fountain of righteousness', cf. Enoch xlviii 1 (BROWNLEE).

[15]) The meaning of this long sentence is obscured by most scholars, because they have not realized (a) that *bhww' 'wlm* in l. 5 is the object of the ensuing *hbyṭh* (cf. the same construction in l. 3) and that (b) *m'nwsh* in l. 6 is parallel, not only with the ensuing *bny 'dm* in the same line, but also with *mswd bśr* in l. 7; accordingly, *d'h* in l. 6 should not be connected with the preceding *'nwsh*; on the other hand, *mswd bśr* is to be connected with what precedes, and not with what follows. MILIK has given the best translation of the passage. For *d'h wmzmt 'rmh*, cf. Prov. i 4.

[16]) The translation follows DELCOR: *l'shr bḥr* is *casus pendens*, resumed by the suffix in *ntnm*; the continuation supports this interpretation, as does the phraseology of Gen. xvii 8, xlviii 4; Lev. xxv 34, on which our author is dependent. Many scholars regard the suffix in *ntnm* as referring to the gifts mentioned in the previous sentence (thus e.g. BROWNLEE).

[17]) That both *qdwshym* and *bny shmym* refer to angels is realized by most scholars (except KUHN and VERMÈS); for *qdwshym* in this meaning, cf. CD xx 8. As a parallel to the entire passage BROWNLEE refers to Wisd. of Sol. v 5 whose phraseology is closely related to that of our passage.

[18]) The text is kept by many scholars (cf. BURROWS: 'a company of holy building'); HABERMANN, reading *mbnwt*, sees in the words a reference to 'daughters'. IWRY draws the *Mem* of *mbnwt* to what precedes and takes *bnwt* in the meaning 'in the abode'. The context is an almost word by word parallel of viii 5, which appears to justify the emendation proposed.

[19]) See note on x 5.

[20]) The translation follows YALON who takes *l* emphatically, referring to Eccles. ix 4; for the usage in general, see NÖTSCHER, in *VT*, iii (1953), pp. 372 ff.

[21]) For the construct state of *'dm* DRIVER refers to Prov. vi 12; Karatepe iv 1; the Ba'al Poem V ii 8.

[22]) Hebr. *bśr 'wl*, cf. 1QM (*MG*, i, p. 19). KUHN compares Rom. viii 3.

[23]) Cf. Prov. xii 8. See note on v 24.

[24]) Cf. l. 21 below; the idea stems from Job (vii 5, xvii 14, xxi 26, xxv 6).

[25]) Cf. Isa. ix 1; Eccles. vi 4.

[26]) Some scholars keep the text, thus VAN DER PLOEG and others. There is no doubt, however, that we have here a simple case of haplography (cf. 1QIsa[a] xxxi 8); not only the parallelism with the following sentence suggests this, but also the clear allusion in this line to Jer. x 23 (cf. MILIK).

[27]) For the emendation proposed, cf. x 16, xi 2.

[28]) Cf. iii 15.

[29]) Cf. l. 17 below; John i 3.

[30]) Echo of Ps. xiii 5 f.

[31]) For 'stumbling over sin', cf. Hos. v 5, xiv 2. VAN DER PLOEG explains the expression 'sin of flesh' as denoting a slight pardonable sin, cf. KUHN.

[32]) Many scholars take *mshpṭ* as the subject of *tʿmwd* (VAN DER PLOEG and others); but *mshpṭ* is masculine and the verb is feminine; *tʿmwd*, therefore, must be taken as a relative clause going back to *ṣdqt ʾl* (cf. MILIK).

[33]) The verb is Niphal, cf. x 17.

[34]) Cf. Ps. cxvi 8.

[35]) BURROWS refers to Ps. xl 2 f, lxxxv 14. Pesh. in Ps. cxix 133 provides an even closer parallel.

[36]) Cf. Job xiv 3; Eccles. xi 9, xii 14. These passages appear to recommend the reading of the verb as Hiphil (cf. MILIK).

[37]) Cf. Ps. ix 9, xcvi 13, xcviii 9.

[38]) Cf. Sept. in Ps. cxlv 7.

[39]) For *kpr bʿd*, cf. CD iii 18 and RABIN's note.

[40]) Cf. CD iii 17. RABIN's reference to Job xxxiv 3 is a printing error and should be corrected to Job xxxiv 6.

[41]) Cf. Ps. xcii 2. BROWNLEE suggests that the words be taken as the head-line of the ensuing hymn (starting with *brwk*).

[42]) After *tpʾrt* the scribe put down two dots, thus apparently indicating separation between the preceding and the following word, cf. note on v 22.

[43]) ZEITLIN suggests that this phrase is due to the scribe's ignorance: the biblical phrase *brwk ʾth ʾdny* was changed for fear of the Tetragrammaton, but the scribe thought the ending in *ʾdny* to be the suffix and wrote *ʾly* for *ʾl*. This argument is wholly unconvincing, if only because the ending of *ʾdny is* the suffix, the *Qameṣ* being a device in order to distinguish the divine lord from any human one.

[44]) Cf. Ps. cxvi 16.

[45]) The translation presupposes the taking of *hkn* and *hqm* as parallel imperatives (cf. SCHUBERT). For *bn 'mtkh*, cf. Ps. lxxxvi 16, cxvi 16 (BROWNLEE).

[46]) A cultic term, cf. e.g. 1 Sam. x 19.

[47]) The original text *hwdyth* is Hiphil of *yd'* with *Ayin* omitted.

[48]) Cf. 2 Sam. vii 22; 1 Chron. xvii 20, our author having replaced *'lhym* of these passages by *'ḥr*.

[49]) Several scholars translate *hshyb 'l* by 'reply to' (cf. e.g. VAN DER PLOEG and MILIK); the idiom means 'to oppose', 'to contradict', cf. YALON. Cf. 4 Ezra ix 18: *nemo contradixit mihi, tunc enim erat nemo.*

[50]) Cf. Rom. xi 33 (DELCOR).

[51]) Cf. Job xxxvii 14.

[52]) Cf. 1 Chron. xxix 12; 2 Chron. xx 6.

[53]) Cf. *gloria incomprehensibilis* in 4 Ezra viii 21.

[54]) Cf. Ps. viii 5; *m'śy yd* of Ps. viii 7 has been adapted to the usage of Ps. xxvi 7, cv 2 where *npl'wt* is used of the works of creation.

[55]) Cf. Job xiv 1, xv 14, xxv 4.

[56]) The original text has been emended to *mḥwshb* (IWRY); that suggestion has, however, been criticized, and the two dots have been taken to indicate *separation* (cf. MILIK). Most scholars take *yshb* in l. 21 in the meaning 'to sit' or 'to sit down', but the same scholars translate *yshyb* in l. 22 by 'reply'. That the two verbs in both lines are to be taken in one and the same meaning cannot be doubted, however, considering the great similarity of the contexts in which they occur, and it might be supposed that the present obscure text was caused by some textual corruption which started in one of the passages and by contamination spread to the other. It seems clear that *mh yshyb ḥmr wywṣr yd* in l. 22 is somehow dependent on Isa. xxix 16. Due to weak pronunciation of *Ḥet* (cf. note on iii 15) the letter might easily drop out (this actually happened in v 24); consequently we should read *yḥshyb* (Niphal; for the orthography, cf. note on vi 14) and the translation runs: 'As what is clay and that which is fashioned by hand, to be reckoned—and what counsel does it understand?' Almost every word is taken from Isa. xxix 16 which our author, in his characteristic way, used freely for his purpose. This interpretation holds good also in our passage which is to be translated: 'And as what can he, who is born of a woman, be reckoned before thee?'

[57]) Gen. ii 7. Pesh., in this passage, uses the root *gbl*.

[58]) Cf. Job iv 19.

[59]) I.e. earth, cf. Gen. iii 14.

[60]) The wording of the last half of the passage is clearly dependent on Job. xxxiii 6, and the idea expressed is identical with Gen. ii 7; Job iv 19, x 9 (where Sept. read *ḥmr* for *kḥmr* of MT); Wisd. of Sol. vii 1, ix 15; Ecclus. xvii 1; according to this conception primeval man (and his posterity) was, and is, created of earth, dust or clay. However, the doctrine soon arose that the actual creation of the individual man is brought about by means of *semen virile*; Wisd. of Sol. vii 2 may be regarded as the first evidence of this idea, to which rabbinic writings bear testimony, cf. Abot iii 1: 'Know from where you have come: from a stinking drop!'; in Sota 5a *srwḥh* alludes perhaps to the same doctrine; in Jer. Talm. Jeb. iv 5c the conception is called 'the first creation'; in Tanḥuma, Piqqude 3, this theme is treated at great length (see WEBER, *Jüdische Theologie*, pp. 225 ff); in some passages 'water' is used, equal to 'seed' (thus e.g. in Mekilta Shirata, commenting on the words *nwr' thlwt* (Exod. xv 11) God is referred to as the one who 'shapes forms of mere water' and the one who 'gives to a man a son out of a drop of water'); with this usage in mind a very interesting light is thrown on a passage in 1QH (*MG*, I, xiii 6 f): 'I am something fashioned of clay—what am I? —something kneaded with water—as whom can I be reckoned?' That in this passage *mym* means 'seed' is very probable, not only because of the parallels mentioned, but especially because the combination of 'clay' and 'water' strongly reminds us of several passages in the Quran, where these two elements are mentioned as the ones from which man is created, 'clay' alluding to primeval man and 'water' (= seed) to his posterity (see Sura xxi 31, xxiv 44, xxxii 6 f (that 'water' is not to be taken in a literal sense, but is an euphemism for 'seed' has been supposed by Muslim commentators (see e.g. TABARI and ZAMAKHSHARI on Sura xxiv 44 and xxxii 6 f), and can be proved by reference to Sura xxii 5, xxiii 12 f, and xxxv 12 where 'clay' and 'dust' are followed by 'drop of semen', and to Sura lxxxvi 6 f, where 'water' by the continuation: 'pouring forth from the loins and the ribs' is clearly used in the meaning 'semen'; cf. also Sanhedrin 91a)).—*Mṣy* I suggest be taken as a noun 'something which has been squeezed out, emitted', the following *nomen rectus* being explanatory. Thus we are able to translate the passage: 'He is saliva which has been emitted, clay which has been nipped off'—'saliva' being used as a metaphor for semen as in Nidda II iv 16b. BURROWS has adopted this interpretation in his translation.

[61]) The parallel phrase in 1QH (*MG*, II, x 2 f) might suggest the emendation of *tṣhwqtw* into *tshwbtw* (thus YALON); but cf. MT in Gen. iii 16, as compared to Sept. and Itala.

[62]) For *ʿṣt mh*, cf. e.g. Jer. viii 9: *ḥkmt mh*. For phraseology, cf. Mic. iv 12.

REFERENCE TABLES

The Zadokite Fragments continued

x 18	i 16, vii 9
xi 4	v 1, vii 24
xi 17 ff	ix 4 f
xi 18	v 15, 17, viii 14
xi 21	ix 5
xi 23	i 14
xii 1 f	iv 10
xii 3 ff	vii 3
xii 6	vii 18 f
xii 19	v 2, vi 8, vii 11, 18 f
xii 20 f	ix 12
xii 21	iii 13, ix 12, 21
xii 22	v 2, vi 8
xii 23 f	ix 11
xiii 1	iv 6
xiii 1 f	ii 21 f, vi 3
xiii 2 f	vi 4 ff
xiii 4	v 3, vi 16
xiii 5	iii 13, iv 3, 22, vi 15, xi 1
xiii 6	vii 3
xiii 7	v 1, vi 8
xiii 8	iii 15, iv 3 f, ix 18, xi 4
xiii 11	v 21, 23, vi 14, 18, viii 19
xiii 12	i 10, ii 23, iv 24, v 23
xiii 13	vi 14
xiii 15	v 17
xiii 18	ii 24, v 3 f, 25
xiii 20	v 2
xiv 1	ix 20 f
xiv 2	v 8
xiv 3	v 2, vi 8
xiv 3 ff	ii 19 ff, vi 8 f
xiv 6	vi 4
xiv 7	vi 14
xiv 10	xi 7
xiv 10 f	vi 11 f
xiv 19	ii 8, iii 6 ff, v 6, viii 6, ix 11, xi 14
xiv 21	vi 25, 26
xiv 22	vii 8
xv 1	x 4
xv 2	ii 15 f, v 8, 12, vi 27, viii 22
xv 3	vii 1
xv 4	i 23, iii 22, v 15
xv 5	viii 10
xv 5 f	v 7

The Zadokite Fragments continued

xv 8	vi 12
xv 9 f	v 8 f
xv 10	ix 20
xv 10 f	vi 15
xv 12	v 8, viii 22
xv 13	v 9
xvi 1 f	v 8
xvi 2	i 14, iv 11, v 8, viii 19, 22
xvi 5	iii 23, v 8, viii 22, ix 20 f
xix 1 f	i 8
xix 4	ix 12
xix 5 f	iii 1
xix 10	iii 18, v 6
xix 10 f	ix 11
xix 13	viii 19
xix 14	ii 6, v 1, 3, ix 14
xix 17	vii 18, ix 20 f
xix 19	i 6, ii 26, vii 24, ix 10, 20 f
xix 21	iv 19, v 11
xix 29	viii 19
xix 32	iii 6
xix 33	i 6, ii 26, vii 24, ix 10
xix 34	vii 18, 23, ix 20 f
xx 1	v 6, ix 11
xx 2	iii 1, iv 22, viii 20
xx 4	ix 13
xx 4 f	vii 18 f
xx 5	ii 25
xx 6	viii 15
xx 7	v 14, vi 2, viii 15, 20
xx 8	ii 4 f, xi 8
xx 8-10	ii 12
xx 17	v 8, x 20
xx 18	iii 9
xx 24	ii 20, iv 26, ix 15, 18
xx 24 f	ii 25, viii 21
xx 27	i 17, v 1, 3, ix 14
xx 27 f	x 13
xx 28-30	i 25 f
xx 29	viii 10
xx 29 f	iv 2, 24, v 3 f, viii 2, xi 14
xx 30 f	iii 1, iv 4, ix 17
xx 31 f	ix 10
xx 32	v 1, 2 f, vi 21, vii 24, viii 16, ix 5 f

The Zadokite Fragments continued

xx 34	ii 8, iii 6 ff, v 6, viii 6, xi 4

The Habakkuk Commentary

ii 4	v 8
ii 9	i 3
iii 2	viii 13 f
iii 4	i 17, x 15
iii 5	v 5
iii 13 f	viii 13 f
iv 7	i 17, x 15
v 4	iv 22, viii 6, ix 14, xi 7
v 6	viii 13 f
v 13	v 5
vii 5	i 3
vii 7	iv 16 f
vii 8	ix 18
vii 12	iv 16 f
vii 13	x 1
vii 14	iv 18
viii 10	iv 9, vii 18
viii 11	x 19
ix 1	viii 10
x 13	iv 22, viii 6, ix 14, xi 7
xi 6	i 14
xi 13	v 5
xi 13 f	ii 14
xii 3	ii 6 f
xii 4	iii 2, v 7, vi 3
xii 8	iv 10

The Thanksgiving Hymns

MG I,	
xii 4-11	x 1 ff
xiii 6 f	xi 22
MG II,	
x 2 f	xi 22

1*QSa*

i 1	v 1, vi 13
i 2	v 2, 9, ix 7
i 3	v 3, viii 6
i 4	v 20
i 5	vi 15
i 6	iv 15
i 7	ii 19
i 7 f	vi 14
i 8	vii 22

BIBLIOGRAPHY

ALBRECHT, K., 'Das Geschlecht der hebräischen Hauptwörter', in *ZAW*, xvi (1896), pp. 42-121.

ALBRIGHT, W. F., 'Editorial Note on the Jerusalem Scrolls', in *BASOR*, No. 111 (1948), p. 2 f.

——, 'On the Date of the Scrolls from Ain Feshkha and the Nash Papyrus', *ibid.*, No. 115 (1949), pp. 10-19.

——, 'Comments on Dr. Lacheman's Reply and the Scrolls', *ibid.*, No. 116 (1949), p. 17 f.

——, 'The Dead Sea Scrolls of St. Mark's Monastery', *ibid.*, No. 118 (1950), p. 5 f.

——, 'From the Acting President's Desk', *ibid.*, No. 126 (1952), p. 1 f.

——, 'From the President's Desk', *ibid.*, No. 129 (1953), p. 1 f.

——, 'New Light on Early Recensions of the Hebrew Bible', *ibid.*, No. 140 (1955), pp. 27-33.

——, 'The Phoenician Inscriptions of the Tenth Century B.C. from Byblos', in *JAOS*, lxvii (1947), pp. 153-60.

——, 'A Biblical Fragment from the Maccabaean Age: The Nash Papyrus', in *JBL*, lvi (1937), pp. 145-76.

——, and MORAN, W. L., 'Rib-Adda of Byblos and the Affairs of Tyre (EA 89)', in *JCS*, iv (1950), pp. 163-68.

——, 'Are the Ain Feshkha Scrolls a Hoax?' in *JQR*, N.S. xl (1949-50), pp. 41-49.

——, 'The Chronology of the Dead Sea Scrolls', *apud* BROWNLEE, W. H., *The Dead Sea Manual of Discipline*, 1951, pp. 57-60.

ALLEGRO, J. M., 'Further Light on the History of the Qumran Sect', in *JBL*, lxxv (1956), pp. 89-95.

ARENDZEN, J., see PASS, L. H.

AUDET, J.-P., 'Affinités literaires et doctrinales du 'Manuel de Discipline'', in *RB*, lix (1952), pp. 219-38, and lx (1953), pp. 41-82.

AVI-YONAH, M., 'The 'War of the Sons of Light and the Sons of Darkness' and Maccabean Warfare', in *IEJ*, ii (1952), pp. 1-5.

BACHER, W., 'Qirqisani, the Qaraite, and his Work on Jewish Sects', in *JQR*, vii (1894-95), pp. 687-710.

——, 'Zur Schechter's neuesten Geniza-Funde', in *ZHB*, xv (1911), pp. 13-25.

BARDTKE, H., *Die Handschriftenfunde am Toten Meer*, 2nd ed., 1953.

BARNES, W. E., 'Fresh Light on Maccabean Times', in *JTS*, xii (1910-11), pp. 301-03.

BARTHÉLEMY, D., 'Le grand rouleau d'Isaie trouvé près de la Mer Morte', in *RB*, lvii (1950), pp. 530-49.

——, 'Notes en marge de publications récentes sur les manuscrits de Qumran', *ibid.*, lix (1952), pp. 187-218.

——, 'Redécouverte d'un chainon manquant de l'histoire de la Septante', *ibid.*, lx (1953), pp. 18-29.

——, and MILIK. J. T., *Discoveries in the Judaean Desert I. Qumran Cave I*, 1955.

BAUCHET, J.-M., 'Une page d'une des manuscrits du désert de Judée', in *RB*, lvi (1949), pp. 583-85.

——, and SUTCLIFFE, E. F., 'The Sectarian Document', in *Scripture*, iv (1949), pp. 76-79.

GRAF BAUDISSIN, W. W., *Kyrios als Gottesname im Judentum und seine Stellung in der Religionsgeschichte*, 1929.

BAUER, W., *Wörterbuch zum Neuen Testament*, 3rd ed., 1937.

BAUMGARTEN, J. M., 'Sacrifice and Worship among the Jewish Sectaries of the Dead Sea Scrolls', in *HTR*, xlvi (1953), pp. 141-59.

BAUMGARTNER, W., 'Der palästinische Handschriftenfund', in *TR*, N.F. xvii (1948-49), pp. 329-46, and xix (1951), pp. 97-154.

BAUMGÄRTEL, F., 'Zur Liturgie in der 'Sektenrolle' vom Toten Meer', in *ZAW*, N.F. xxiv (1953), pp. 263-65.

BEEGLE, D. M., 'Proper Names in the New Isaiah Scroll', in *BASOR*, No. 123 (1951), pp. 26-30.

——, 'Ligatures with *Waw* and *Yodh* in the Dead Sea Isaiah Scroll', *ibid.*, No. 129 (1953), pp. 11-14.

BEER, G., *Der Text des Buches Hiob untersucht*, 1897.

BERTHOLET, A., 'Zur Datierung der Damaskusschrift', in *Budde Festschrift* (1920), pp. 31-37.

BICKELL, G., *Ephraemi Syri Carmina Nisibena*, 1866.

BIRKELAND, H., *Akzent und Vokalismus im Althebräischen*, 1940.

——, 'Some Linguistic Remarks on the Dead Sea Scrolls', in *Mowinckel Festschrift* (1955), pp. 24-35.

BIRNBAUM, S. A., 'The Date of the Isaiah Scroll', in *BASOR*, No. 113 (1949), pp. 33-35.

——, 'The Dates of the Cave Scrolls', *ibid.*, No. 115 (1949), pp. 20-22.

——, 'The Leviticus Fragments from the Cave', *ibid.*, No. 118 (1950), pp. 20-27.

——, *The Qumran (Dead Sea) Scrolls and Palaeography*, (*BASOR*, Supplementary Studies, Nos. 13-14), 1952.

——, 'The Date of the Habakkuk Cave Scroll', in *JBL*, lxviii (1949), pp. 161-68.

——, 'Notes on the Internal and Archaeological Evidence concerning the Cave Scrolls', *ibid.*, lxx (1951), pp. 227-32.

——, 'The Date of the Covenant Scroll', in *PEQ*, 1949, pp. 140-47.

——, 'The Date of the Hymn Scroll', *ibid.*, 1952, pp. 94-103.

——, 'How old are the Cave Manuscripts? A Palaeographical Discussion', in *VT*, i (1951), pp. 91-109.

BLACK, M., 'The Dating of the New Hebrew Scrolls on Internal Evidence', in *JJS*, i (1949), pp. 199.

BOCCACCIO, P., 'I manoscritti del Mar Morto e i nomi di Dio Yahweh, El', in *Biblica*, xxxii (1951), pp. 90-96.

BOUSSET, W., *Die Religion des Judentums im späthellenistischen Zeitalter*, 3rd ed. by GRESSMANN, H., 1926.

——, 'Literatur und Religion des Spätjudentums und des rabbinischen Judentums', in *TR*, *xviii* (1915), pp. 41-58.

BRAUN, H., 'Beobachtungen zur Tora-Verschärfung im häretischen Spätjudentum', in *TLZ*, lxxix (1954), cols. 347-52.

BROCKELMANN, C., *Grundriss der vergleichenden Grammatik der Semitischen Sprachen*, I-II, 1908-13.

——, *Lexicon Syriacum*, 1928.

BROWN, F., DRIVER, S. R., and BRIGGS, C. A., *A Hebrew and English Lexicon of the Old Testament*, 1906.

BROWNLEE, W. H., 'A Comparison of the Covenanters of the Dead Sea Scrolls with Pre-Christian Jewish Sects', in *BA*, xiii (1950), pp. 49-72.

——, 'Biblical Interpretation among the Sectaries of the Dead Sea Scrolls', *ibid.*, xiv (1951), pp. 53-76.

——, 'Excerpts from the Translation of the Dead Sea Manual of Discipline', in *BASOR*, No. 121 (1951), pp. 8-12.

——, 'Light on the Manual of Discipline (DSD) from the Book of Jubilees', *ibid.*, No. 123 (1951), pp. 30-32.
——, 'The Servant of the Lord in the Qumran Scrolls i-ii', *ibid.*, No. 132 (1953), pp. 8-15, No. 135 (1954), pp. 33-38.
——, *The Dead Sea Manual of Discipline* (*ibid.*, Supplementary Studies, No. 10-12) 1951.
——, 'Emendations of the Dead Sea Manual of Discipline and some Notes concerning the Habakkuk Midrash', in *JQR*, N.S. xlv (1954-55), pp. 141-58 and pp. 198-218.
Buhl, F., see under Gesenius, W.
Burrows, M., 'The Messiahs of Aaron and Israel', in *ATR*, xxxiv (1952), pp. 203-06.
——, 'Variant Readings in the Isaiah Manuscript', in *BASOR*, No. 111 (1948), pp. 16-24, and No. 113 (1949), pp. 24-32.
——, 'The Dating of the Dead Sea Scrolls', *ibid.*, No. 122 (1951), pp. 4-6.
——, '*Waw* and *Yodh* in the Isaiah Dead Sea Scroll', *ibid.*, No. 124 (1951), pp. 18-20.
——, 'Orthography, Morphology and Syntax of the St. Mark's Isaiah Manuscript', in *JBL*, lxviii (1949), pp. 195-211.
——, 'A Note on the Recently Discovered Manuscripts', in *JQR*, N.S. xl (1949-50), pp. 51-56.
——, 'The Discipline Manual of the Judaean Covenanters', in *OS*, viii (1950), pp. 156-92.
——, *The Dead Sea Scrolls*, 1955.
——, Trever, J. C. and Brownlee, W. H., *The Dead Sea Scrolls of St. Mark's Monastery I: The Isaiah Manuscript and the Habakkuk Commentary*, 1950; *II, Fasc. 2: Plates and Transcription of the Manual of Discipline*, 1951.
Büchler, A., 'Schechter's 'Jewish Sectaries'', in *JQR*, N.S. iii (1912-13), pp. 429-85.
Carmignac, J., 'Précisions apportées au vocabulaire de l'Hebreu Biblique par la Guerre des Fils de Lumière contre les Fils de Tenèbres', in *VT*, v (1955), pp. 345-65.
Charles, R. H., *The Apocrypha and Pseudepigrapha of the Old Testament I-II*, 1913.
——, *The Book of Enoch*, 1893.
——, *The Ethiopic Version of the Hebrew Book of Jubilees*, 1895.
——, *The Greek Versions of the Testaments of the Twelve Patriarchs*, 1908.
——, and Cowley, A., 'An Early Source of the Testaments of the Patriarchs', in *JQR*, xix (1906-07), pp. 566-83.
——, 'Aphraates and Monasticism', in *JTS*, vi (1905), pp. 522-39.
Cook, S. A., 'A Pre-Massoretic Biblical Papyrus', in *PSBA*, xxv (1903), pp. 34-56.
Coppens, J., 'La secte de Qumran et son attente eschatologique', in *NC*, v (1953), pp. 5-9.
Cowley, A., *The Samaritan Liturgy I-II*, 1909.
——, see under Charles, R. H.
Cross, F. M., 'The Manuscripts of the Dead Sea Caves', in *BA*, xvii (1954), pp. 2-21.
——, 'A New Qumran Biblical Fragment Related to the Original Hebrew Underlying the Septuagint', in *BASOR*, No. 132 (1953), pp. 15-26.
——, 'The Oldest Manuscripts from Qumran', in *JBL*, lxxiv (1955), pp. 147-72.
Dalmann, G. H., *Aramäisch-Neuhebräisches Handwörterbuch*, 1938.
Danby, H., *The Mishnah, Translated from the Hebrew with Introduction and Brief Explanatory Notes*, 1949.

Daniélou, J., 'La communauté de Qumran et l'organisation de l'église ancienne', in *RHPR*, xxxv (1955), pp. 104-15.
Davies, W. D., "Knowledge' in the Dead Sea Scrolls and Matthew 11 : 25-30, in *HTR*, xlvi (1953), pp. 113-39.
Delcor, M., 'Contribution à l'étude de la législation des sectaires de Damas et de Qumran', in *RB*, lxi (1954), pp. 533-53, and lxii (1955), pp. 60-75.
——, 'Le sacerdoce, les lieux de culte, les rites et les fêtes dans les documents de Khirbet Qumran', in *RHR*, cxliv (1955), pp. 5-41.
——, 'Des diverses manières d'écrire le Tetragramme sacré dans les anciens documents hébraiques', *ibid.*, cxlvii (1955), pp. 145-73.
——, 'L'éschatologie des documents de Khirbet Qumran', in *RSR*, xliv (1952), pp. 363-86.
——, Review of Vermès, G. *Les manuscrits du désert de Juda*, 1953, in *VT*, iv (1954), pp. 218-22.
del Medico, H. E., *Deux Manuscrits Hébreux de la Mer Morte*, 1951.
——, 'La traduction d'un texte démarqué dans le Manuel de Discipline (DSD x 1-9)', in *VT*, vi (1956), pp. 34-39.
Dhorme, E., see under Dupont-Sommer, A.
Diening, F., *Das Hebräische bei den Samaritanern*, 1938.
Diringer, D., 'Early Hebrew Writing', in *BA*, xiii (1950), pp. 74-95.
——, 'The Early Hebrew Book-hand', in *PEQ*, 1950, pp. 16-24.
Driver, G. R., 'New Hebrew Scrolls', in *HJ*, xlix (1950-51), pp. 11-21.
——, 'Hebrew Scrolls', in *JTS*, N.S. ii (1951), pp. 17-30.
——, 'New Hebrew Manuscripts', in *JQR*, N.S. xl (1949-50), pp. 127-34 and pp. 359-72.
——, 'Once again the Judaean Scrolls', *ibid.*, N.S. xliv (1953-54), pp. 1-20.
——, *The Hebrew Scrolls from the Neighbourhood of Jericho and the Dead Sea*, 1951.
Driver, S. R., *Hebrew Tenses*, 3rd ed., 1892.
Dupont-Sommer, A., *Aperçus préliminaires sur les manuscrits de la Mer Morte*, 1950.
——, *Nouveaux aperçus sur les manuscrits de la Mer Morte*, 1953,; English edition (*The Jewish Sect of Qumran and the Essenes*) 1954.
——, *Observations sur le Manuel de Discipline*, 1951.
——, 'Le probleme des influences étrangères sur la secte juive de Qumran', in *RHPR*, xxxv (1955), pp. 75-92.
——, 'La 'Règle' de la communauté de la Nouvelle Alliance. Extraits traduits et annotés', in *RHR*, cxxxviii (1950), pp. 5-21.
——, 'L'instruction sur les deux ésprits dans le 'Manuel de Discipline'', *ibid.*, cxlii (1952), pp. 5-35.
——, 'Contribution à l'exegese du Manuel de Discipline x 1-8', in *VT*, ii (1952), pp. 229-43.
Edelkoort, A. H., *De handschriften van de Dode Zee*, 1952.
Eissfeldt, O., 'Zahl und Art der in den Rollen enthaltenen Schriftwerke: ihre Entstehungszeit und ihre religionsgeschichtliche Einordnung', in *TLZ*, lxxiv (1949), cols. 95-98.
——, 'Varianten der Jesaia-Rolle', *ibid.*, lxxiv (1949), cols. 221-26.
——, 'Ansetzung der Rollen nach paläographischen Kriterien', *ibid.*, lxxiv (1949), cols. 226-28.
——, 'Der Anlass zur Entdeckung der Höhle und ihr ähnliche Vorgänge aus älterer Zeit', *ibid.*, lxxiv (1949), cols. 597-600.
Elliger, K., *Studien zum Habakkuk-Commentar vom Toten Meer*, 1953.
Finkelstein, L., 'Pre-Maccabean Documents in the Passover Haggadah', in *HTR*, xxv (1942), pp. 291-332, and xxxvi (1943), pp. 1-38.
Fischer, A., *Arabische Chrestomatie aus Prosaschriftstellern*, 1948.

FISCHER, J., *In welcher Schrift lag das Buch Isaias den LXX vor?* (Beihefte zur *ZAW*, 56, 1930).

FLUSSER, D., 'The Apocryphal Book of Ascensio Isaiae and the Dead Sea Sect', in *IEJ*, iii (1953), pp. 30-47.

VON GALL, A., *Der Hebräische Pentateuch der Samaritaner*, 1918.

GESENIUS, W., see under KAUTZSCH, E.

——, *Hebräisches und Aramäisches Handwörterbuch über das Alte Testament*, bearbeitet von BUHL, F., 17th ed., 1921.

GINSBERG, H. L., 'The Hebrew University Scrolls from the Sectarian Cache', in *BASOR*, No. 112 (1948), pp. 19-23.

GINSBURG, C. D., *The Essenes. Their History and Doctrines. The Kabbalah. Its Doctrines, Development and Literature*, 1864-65.

GINZBERG, L., 'Eine unbekannte jüdische Sekte', in *MGWJ*, lv (N.F. xix, 1911), pp. 666-98, lvi (N.F. xx, 1912), pp. 33-48, 285-307, 417-48, 546-66, 664-89, lvii (N.F. xxi, 1913), pp. 153-76, 284-308, 394-418, 666-96, lviii (N.F. xxii, 1914), pp. 16-18, 143-77, 395-425.

——, *Eine unbekannte jüdische Sekte*, 1922.

GOETZ, K. G., 'Ist der Mebaqqer der Genizafragmente wirklich das Vorbild des christlichen Episkopats?' in *ZNW*, xxx (1931), pp. 89-93.

GOOSSENS, R., 'L'état actuel des recherches sur les manuscrits de la Mer Morte et sur la secte de la Nouvelle Alliance', in *NC*, i-ii (1949-50), pp. 634-71.

GOTTSTEIN, M. H., 'Die Jesaia-Rolle im Lichte von Peshitta und Targum', in *Biblica*, liii (1954), pp. 51-71.

——, 'Studies in the Language of the Dead Sea Scrolls', in *JJS*, iv (1953), pp. 104-07.

——, 'Bible Quotations in the Sectarian Dead Sea Scrolls', in *VT*, iii (1953), pp. 79-82.

——, 'A DSS Biblical Variant in a Medieval Treatise', *ibid.*, iii (1953), p. 187 f.

——, 'Anti-Essene Traits in the Dead Sea Scrolls', *ibid.*, iv (1954), pp. 141-47.

——, 'A Supposed Dittography in DSD', *ibid.*, iv (1954), pp. 422-24.

GRESSMANN, H., Review of *Documents of Jewish Sectaries*, ed. by SCHECHTER, S., in *ZDMG*, lxvi (1912), pp. 491-505.

——, see under BOUSSET, W.

GUILLAUME, A., 'Mt. xxvii 46 in the Light of the Dead Sea Scroll of Isaiah', in *PEQ*, 1951, pp. 78-80.

——, 'Les manuscrits hébreux', in *RB*, lix (1952) pp. 182-86.

HABERMANN, A. M., *Edah we-Eduth*: *Three Scrolls from the Judaean Desert*: *The Legacy of a Community*, 1952.

HARDING, G. L., 'The Dead Sea Scrolls' ,in *PEQ*, 1949, pp. 112-16.

——, 'Khirbet Qumran and Wady Murabbaʿat', *ibid.*, 1952, pp. 104-09.

HEMPEL, J., 'Vorläufige Mitteilungen über die am Nordwestende des Toten Meeres gefundenen hebräischen Handschriften', in *NAWG*, Phil. Hist. Klasse, 1949, pp. 411-38.

——, 'Chronik', in *ZAW*, N.F. xxi (1950), pp. 246-72.

HIGGINS, A. J. B., 'Priest and Messiah', in *VT*, iii (1953), pp. 321-36 .

HÖLSCHER, G., 'Zur Frage nach Alter und Herkunft der sogenannten Damaskusschrift', in *ZNW*, xxviii (1929), pp. 21-46.

HVIDBERG, F. F., *Menigheden af den nye Pagt i Damascus*, 1928.

HYATT, J. P., 'On the Meaning and Origin of Micah 6 : 8', in *ATR*, xxxiv (1952), pp. 232-39.

JACOB, B., 'Das hebräische Sprachgut im Christlich-Palästinischen', in *ZAW*, xxii (1902), pp. 83-113.

JASTROW, M., *A Dictionary of the Targumim, the Talmud Babli and Yerushalmi, and the Midrashic Literature* I-II, 1903.
JAUBERT, A., 'Le calendrier des Jubilés et de la secte de Qumran. Ses origines bibliques', in *VT*, iii (1953), pp. 250-64.
JOHNSON, S. E., 'The Dead Sea Manual of Discipline and the Jerusalem Church of Acts', in *ZAW*, N.F. xxv (1954), pp. 106-20.
KAHLE, P., 'Ivan Engnell's Text och Tradition', in *Nötscher Festschrift* (1950), pp. 129-36.
——, 'Zur Aussprache des Hebräischen bei den Samaritanern', in *Bertholet Festschrift* (1950), pp. 281-86.
——, *Die hebräischen Handschriften aus der Höhle*, 1951.
——, *The Cairo Geniza*, 1947.
——, 'Die Auffindung der Rollen und ihr Ankauf. Die textkritische Bedeutung der Jesaia-Rolle. Der Anlass für das Verbergen der Rollen', in *TLZ*, lxxiv (1949), cols. 91-94.
——, 'Zu den Handschriftenfunden aus der Höhle', *ibid.*, lxxvi (1951), cols. 161-66.
——, 'Die Gemeinde des Neuen Bundes und die hebräischen Handschriften aus der Höhle', *ibid.*, lxxvii (1952), cols. 401-12.
——, 'The Karaites and the Manuscripts from the Cave', in *VT*, iii (1953), pp. 82-84.
KAUTZSCH, E., ed. *Gesenius' Hebrew Grammar*, 2nd English ed., 1910.
KITTEL, G., ed. *Theologisches Wörterbuch zum Neuen Testament*, 1933—,
KITTEL, R., ed. *Biblia Hebraica*, 1937.
KOHLER, K., 'Dositheus, the Samaritan Hesîarch, and his Relations to Jewish and Christian Doctrines and Sects', in *AJT*, xv (1911), pp. 404-35.
——, 'The Essenes and the Apocalyptic Literature', in *JQR*, N.S. xi (1920-21), pp. 145-68.
KUHL, C., 'Schreibereigentümlichkeiten, Bemerkungen zur Jesaiarolle', in *VT*, ii (1952), pp. 307-33.
KUHN, K. G., 'Über den ursprünglichen Sinn des Abendmahls und sein Verhältnis zu den Gemeinschaftsmahlen der Sektenschrift', in *ET*, 1951, pp. 508-27.
——, 'Die beiden Messias Aarons und Israels', in *NTS*, i (1954-55), pp. 168-79.
——, 'Zur Bedeutung der neuen palästinischen Handschriftenfunde für die neutestamentliche Wissenschaft', in *TLZ*, lxxv (1950), cols. 81-86.
——, 'Die beiden Messias Aarons und Israels', *ibid.*, lxxix (1954), cols. 760 f.
——, 'Die in Palästina gefundenen hebräischen Texte und das Neue Testament', in *ZTK*, xlvii (1950), pp. 192-211.
——, 'Peirasmos-hamartia-sarx im Neuen Testament und die damit zusammenhängenden Vorstellungen', *ibid.*, xlix (1952), pp. 200-22.
——, 'Die Sektenschrift und die iranische Religion', *ibid.*, xlix (1952), pp. 296-316.
LACHEMAN, E. R., 'Reply to the Editor', in *BASOR*, No. 116 (1949), p. 16 f.
——, 'A Matter of Method in Hebrew Palaeography', in *JQR*, N.S. xl (1949-50), pp. 15-39.
——, 'Can Hebrew Palaeography be called 'Scientific'?' *ibid.*, N.S. xlii (1951-52), pp. 377-85.
——, 'Hebrew Palaeography again', *ibid.*, N.S. xliv (1953-54), pp. 116-22.
LAGRANGE, M. J., 'La secte juive de la Nouvelle Alliance', in *RB*, xxi (N.S. ix, 1912), pp. 212-40 and pp. 321-60.
LAMBERT, G., 'Le Manuel de Discipline de la grotte de Qumran', *NRT*, lxxiii (1951), pp. 938-75.
——, 'Le Maître de Justice et la Communauté de l'Alliance', *ibid.*, lxxiv (1952), pp. 259-83.

LEHMANN, O. H., 'Materials concerning the Dating of the Dead Sea Scrolls I: Habakkuk', in *PEQ*, 1951, pp. 32-54.
LAUTERBACH, J. Z., 'Midrash and Mishnah. A Study in the Early History of the Halakah', in *JQR*, N.S. vi (1915-16), pp. 23-95.
LESZYNSKY, R., 'Observations sur les 'Fragments of a Zadokite Work', édités par Schechter', in *REJ*, lxii (1911), pp. 190-96.
LÉVI, I., 'Un écrit sadducéen antérieur à la déstruction du Temple', *ibid.*, lxi (1911), pp. 161-205, and lxiii (1912), pp. 1-19.
——, 'Notes sur les observations de M. Leszynsky', *ibid.*, lxii (1911), pp. 197-200.
——, 'Document relatif à la 'Communauté des Fils de Sadoc', *ibid.*, lxi (1913), pp. 24-31.
——, 'Le Tétragramme et l'écrit Sadoqite de Damas', *ibid.*, lxviii (1914), pp. 119-21.
——, *The Hebrew Text of the Book of Ecclesiasticus* (Semitic Studies Series, No. iii), 1904.
LIDELL H. G. and SCOTT, R., *A Greek-English Lexicon*, I-II, 1940.
LIEBERMAN, S., 'The Discipline in the so-called Dead Sea Manual of Discipline', in *JBL*, lxxi (1952), pp. 199-206.
——, 'Light on the Cave Scrolls from Rabbinic Sources', in *PAAJR*, xx (1951), pp. 395-404.
LIGHTFOOT, J. B., *St. Paul's Epistles to the Colossians and to Philemon*, 1886.
LOHMEYER, E., *Diatheke. Ein Beitrag zur Erklärung des neutestamentlichen Begriffs*, 1913.
LÖFGREN, O., 'Zur Characteristik des 'vormassoretischen' Jesaja-textes', in *Nyberg Festschrift* (1955), pp. 171-84.
MARCUS, R., 'Philo, Josephus and the Dead Sea YAHAD', in *JBL*, lxxi (1952), pp. 207-10.
——, 'Pharisees, Essenes, and Gnostics', *ibid.*, lxxiii (1954), pp. 157-61.
——, 'Textual Notes on the Dead Sea Manual of Discipline', in *JNES*, xi (1952), pp. 205-11.
——, 'The Pharisees in the Light of Modern Scholarship', in *JR*, xxxii (1952), pp. 153-64.
MARGOLIOUTH, G., 'The Sadducean Christians of Damascus', in *Athenaeum*, No. 4335, November 26, 1910, pp. 657-59.
——, 'The Sadducean Christians of Damascus', in *Expositor*, 8th series, ii (1911), pp. 499-517, and iii (1912), pp. 213-35.
——, 'The Calendar, the Sabbath, and the Marriage Law in the Geniza Zadokite Document', in *Expository Times*, xxiii (1911-12), pp. 362-65, xxiv (1912-13), pp. 553-58, and xxv (1913-14), pp. 560-64.
——, 'The Two Zadokite Messiahs', in *JTS*, xii (1910-11), pp. 446-50.
MARTI, K., *Kurzgefasste Grammatik der Biblisch-Aramäischen Sprache*, 3rd ed., 1925.
MEYER, E., *Die Gemeinde des Neuen Bundes im Lande Damaskus: eine jüdische Schrift aus der Seleukidenzeit* (in *APAW*), 1919.
——, *Ursprung und Anfänge des Christentums*, I-III, 1923-25.
MEYER, R., 'Zur Sprache von Ain Feshkha', in *TLZ*, lxxv (1950), cols. 721-26.
——, 'Zur Geschichte des hebräischen Verbums', in *VT*, iii (1953), pp. 225-35.
——, 'Probleme der hebräischen Grammatik', in *ZAW*, N.F. xxii (1951), pp. 221-35.
MICHAUD, H., 'Orthographe fonctionelle et orthographe de série', in *JA*, ccxxxix (1951), pp. 299-310.
——, 'Un mythe zervanite dans un des manuscrits de Qumran', in *VT*, v (1955), pp. 137-47.

MILIK, J. T., 'Note sui manoscritti di Ain Feshkha', in *Biblica*, xxxi (1950), pp. 73-94 and pp. 204-25.
——, 'Le Testament de Lévi en araméen. Fragment de la grotte 4 de Qumran', in *RB*, lxii (1955), pp. 398-406.
——, 'Manuale Disciplinae', in *VD*, xxix (1951), pp. 129-58.
——, see under BARTHÉLEMY, D.
MOLIN, G., *Die Söhne des Lichtes*, 1952.
——, 'Die Rollen von Ain Feshkha und ihre Stellung in der jüdischen Religionsgeschichte', in *Judaica*, vii (1952), pp. 161-213.
MOORE, G. F., 'The Covenanters of Damascus: a hitherto Unknown Jewish Sect', in *HTR*, iv (1911), pp. 330-77.
MORAN, W. L., see under ALBRIGHT, W. F.
MOSBECH, H., *Essaeismen: Et Bidrag til Senjødedommens Religionshistorie*, 1916.
NAUCK, W., 'Lex insculpta in der Sektenschrift', in *ZNW*, xlvi (1955), pp. 138-40.
NEMOY, L., 'Al-Qirqisani's Account of the Jewish Sects and Christianity', in *HUCA*, vii (1930), pp. 317-97.
——, *Karaite Anthology* (Yale Judaica Series, vii), 1952.
NEUBERG, F. J., 'An Unrecognized Meaning of Hebrew *Dor*', in *JNES*, ix (1950), pp. 215-17.
NORTH, C. R., *The Suffering Servant in Deutero-Isaiah*, 1948.
NORTH, R., 'Manuale Disciplinae et Liber Sapientiae', in *Biblica*, xxxv (1954), p. 138.
——, 'The Damascus of Qumran Geography', in *PEQ*, 1955, pp. 34-48.
NOTH, M., 'Die Heiligen des Höchsten', in *Mowinckel Festschrift* (1955), pp. 146-61.
NÖTSCHER, F., "Gesetz der Freiheit' im NT und in der Mönchgemeinde am Toten Meer,' in *Biblica*, xxxiv (1953), p. 193 f.
——, 'Heisst *kabod* auch 'Seele'?' in *VT*, ii (1952), pp. 358-62.
——, 'Zum emphatischen Lamed', *ibid.*, iii (1953), pp. 372-80.
OESTERLEY, W. O. E., *The Jews and Judaism during the Greek Period: the Background of Christianity*, 1941.
ORLINSKY, H. M., 'Studies in the St. Mark's Isaiah Scroll, i-vi', in *JBL*, lxix (1950), pp. 149-66, in *JNES*, xi (1950), pp. 153-56, in *JJS*, ii (1951), pp. 151-54, in *JQR*, N.S. xliii (1952-53), pp. 329-40, in *IEJ*, iv (1954), pp. 5-8, and in *HUCA*, xxv (1954), pp. 85-92.
OTZEN, B., 'Die neugefundenen hebräischen Sektenschriften und die Testamenten der zwölf Patriarchen', in *ST*, vii (1954), pp. 125-57.
PASS, H. L., and ARENDZEN, J., 'Fragments of an Aramaic Text of the Testament of Levi', in *JQR*, xii (1899-1900), pp. 651-61.
PETERMANN, J. H., *Versuch einer hebräischen Formenlehre nach der Aussprache der heutigen Samaritaner* (in *AKM*), 1868.
PFEIFFER, R. H., *History of New Testament Times, with an Introduction to the Apocrypha*, 1949.
PLOEG, J. VAN DER, 'Le 'Manuel de Discipline' des rouleaux de la Mer Morte', in *BiOr*, viii (1951), pp. 115-26.
——, 'Quelques traductions du 'Manuel de Discipline' des manuscrits de la Mer Morte', *ibid.*, ix (1952), pp. 127-33.
——, 'Les manuscrits du Désert de Juda. Études et découvertes récentes', *ibid.*, xi (1954), pp. 145-60.
——, 'L'immortalité de l'homme d'apres les textes de la Mer Morte', in *VT*, ii (1952), pp. 171-75.
——, 'La Regle de la Guerre. Traduction et Notes', *ibid.*, v (1955), pp. 373-420.
RABIN, C., 'The 'Teacher of Righteousness' in the Testaments of the Twelve Patriarchs', in *JJS*, iii (1952), p. 127 f.

——, 'The Dead Sea Scrolls and the History of the Old Testament Text', in *JTS*, N.S. vi (1955), pp. 174-82.

——, *The Zadokite Documents. I. The Admonition. II. The Laws. Edited with a Translation and Notes*, 1954.

——, 'Notes on the Habakkuk Scroll and the Zadokite Documents', in *VT*, v (1955), pp. 148-62.

Rabinowitz, I., 'A Reconsideration of 'Damascus' and '390 Years' in the 'Damascus' Fragments', in *JBL*, lxxiii (1954), pp. 11-35.

——, 'Sequence and Dates of the Extra-Biblical Dead Sea Scroll Texts and the 'Damascus' Fragments', in *VT*, iii (1953), pp. 175-85.

Ratzaby, Y., 'Remarks concerning the Distinction between *Waw* and *Yodh* in the Habakkuk Scroll', in *JQR*, N.S. xli (1950-51), pp. 155-57.

Reicke, B., 'Traces of Gnosticism in the Dead Sea Scrolls?' in *NTS*, i (1954-55), pp. 137-41.

——, *Handskrifterna från Qumran* (*SBU*, No. 14), 1952.

——, 'Die Taʿamire-Schriften und die Damaskus Fragments', in *ST*, ii (1949-50), pp. 45-70.

——, 'Die Verfassung der Urgemeinde im Lichte jüdischer Documente', in *TZ*, x (1954), pp. 95-112.

Reider, J., 'The Dead Sea Scrolls', in *JQR*, N.S. xli (1950-51), pp. 59-70.

Revel, B., 'Inquiry into the sources of Karaite Halakha', *ibid.*, N.S. ii (1911-12), pp. 517-44, and iii (1912-13), pp. 337-96.

Roberts, B. J., 'Some Observations on the Damascus Documents and the Dead Sea Scrolls', in *BJRL*, xxxiv (1952), pp. 366-87.

——, 'The Dead Sea Scrolls and the Old Testament Scriptures', *ibid.*, xxxvi (1953), pp. 75-96.

——, 'The Jerusalem Scrolls', in *ZAW*, N.F. xxi (1950), pp. 224-45.

Rost, L., *Die Damaskusschrift* (in Litzmann's *Kleine Texte für Vorlesungen und Übungen*), 1933.

——, 'Die Sektenrolle', in *TLZ*, lxxv (1950), cols. 341-44.

——, 'Das Verhältniss von 'Damaskusschrift' und 'Sektenrolle', *ibid.*, lxxvii (1952), cols. 723-26.

——, 'Der 'Lehrer der Einung' und der 'Lehrer der Gerechtigkeit', *ibid.*, lxxviii (1953), cols. 143-48.

Rowley, H. H., 'The Covenanters of Damascus and the Dead Sea Scrolls', in *BJRL*, xxxv (1952-53), pp. 111-54.

——, '4QpNahum and the Teacher of Righteousness', in *JBL*, lxxv (1956), pp. 188-93.

——, *The Dead Sea Scrolls and Their Significance*, 1954.

——, *The Relevance of Apocalyptic: a Study of Jewish and Christian Apocalypses from Daniel to the Revelation*, 2nd ed., 1947.

——, *The Servant of the Lord*, 1952.

——, *The Zadokite Fragments and the Dead Sea Scrolls*, 1952.

Rubinstein, A., 'Urban Halakhah and Camp Rules in the 'Cairo Fragments of a Damascus Covenant', in *Sefarad*, 1952, pp. 283-96.

Schechter, S., *Documents of Jewish Sectaries. Vol. I: Fragments of a Zadokite Work*, 1910.

——, 'Reply to Dr. Büchler's Review of Schechter's 'Jewish Sectaries', in *JQR*, N.S. iv (1913-14), pp. 449-74.

Shoeps, H. J., 'Ebionite Christianity', in *JTS*, N.S. iv (1953), pp. 219-24.

——, 'Handelt es sich wirklich um ebionitische Dokumente?' in *ZRGG*, iii (1951), pp. 322-36.

——, 'Das gnostische Judentum in den Dead Sea Scrolls', *ibid.*, vi (1954), pp. 1-4 and pp. 276-79.

SCHOUSBOE, J., *La secte juive de l'Alliance Nouvelle au pays de Damas*, 1942.

SCHUBERT, K., 'Die Texte aus der Sektiererhöhle bei Jericho', in *Nötscher Festschrift* (1950), pp. 224-45.

——, 'Zwei Messiasse aus dem Regelbuch von Chirbet Qumran', in *Judaica*, xi (1955), p. 216-35.

——, 'Bemerkungen zum Verständnis einiger Termini in den Handschriften von En Feshkha und im Damaskusdokument', in *TLZ*, lxxvii (1952), cols. 329-36.

——, 'Der Sektenkanon von En Feshkha und die Anfänge der jüdischen Gnosis', *ibid.*, lxxviii (1953), cols. 495-506.

——, 'Die jüdischen und judenchristlichen Sekten im Lichte des Handschriftenfundes von En Feshkha', in *ZKT*, lxxiv (1952), pp. 1-62.

SCHULTHESS, F., *Lexicon Syropalaestinum*, 1903.

SEELIGMANN, I. L., 'The Epoch-making Discovery of the Hebrew Scrolls in the Judean Desert,' in *BiOr*, vi (1949), pp. 1-8.

SEGAL, M. H., *A Grammar of Mishnaic Hebrew*, 1927.

——, 'The Promulgation of the Authoritative Text of the Hebrew Bible', in *JBL*, lxxii (1953), pp. 35-47.

——, 'Notes on 'Fragments of a Zadokite Work', in *JQR*, N.S. ii (1911-12), pp. 133-41, and iii (1912-13), pp. 301-11.

SILBERMANN, L. H., 'The Two Messiahs of the Manual of Discipline', in *VT*, v (1955), pp. 77-82.

SMEND, R., *Die Weisheit des Jesus Sirach*, 1906.

——, *Griechisch-Syrisch-Hebräischer Index zur Weisheit des Jesus Sirach*, 1907.

SMITH, R. PAYNE, *Thesaurus Syriacus*, 1868-97.

SONNE, I., 'A Hymn against Heretics in the Newly Discovered Scrolls', in *HUCA*, xxiii, Part i (1952), pp. 275-313.

SPERBER, A., 'Hebrew Based upon Greek and Latin Transliterations', *ibid.*, xii-xiii (1937-38), pp. 103-274.

——, 'Hebrew Based upon Biblical Passages in Parallel Transmission', *ibid.*, xiv (1939), pp. 153-249.

——, 'Hebrew Phonology', *ibid.*, xvi (1941), pp. 415-82.

——, 'Problems of the Massora', *ibid.*, xvii (1942-43), pp. 293-394.

STAUFFER, E., 'Das Gesetz der Freiheit in der Ordensregel von Jericho', in *TLZ*, lxxvii (1952), cols. 527-32.

STERN, S. M., 'Notes on the New Manuscript Find', in *JBL*, lxix (1950), pp. 19-30.

SUKENIK, E. L., *Megillot Genuzot*, I-II, 1948-50.

——, *Oṣar ham-Megillot hag-Genuzot sheb-bide ha-Universita ha-Ivrit*, 1954.

SUTCLIFFE, E. F., see under BAUCHET, J.-M.

SZYSZMAN, S., 'A propos du Karaisme et les Textes de la Mer Morte', in *VT*, ii (1952), pp. 343-48.

——, 'Sur la geniza du Caire', *ibid.*, iii (1953), p. 411 f.

——, 'Une visit au Caire', *ibid.*, iv (1954), pp. 201-05.

TALMON, S., 'The Sectarian Yahad—a Biblical Noun', *ibid.*, iii (1953), pp. 133-40.

TEICHER, J. L., 'The Dead Sea Scrolls—Documents of the Jewish-Christian Sect of Ebionites', in *JJS*, ii (1951), pp. 67-99.

——, 'Method in Hebrew Palaeography', *ibid.*, ii (1951), pp. 200-02.

——, 'Puzzling Passages in the Damascus Fragments', *ibid.*, v (1954), pp. 139-47.

THOMAS, D. W., 'The Root SNʿ in Hebrew and the Meaning of QDRNYT in Malachi iii 14', *ibid.*, i (1949), pp. 182-88.

Tournay, R. T., 'Les anciens manuscrits hébreux récemment découverts', in *RB*, lvi (1949), pp. 204-33.
Trever, J. C., 'Preliminary Observations on the Jerusalem Scrolls', in *BASOR*, No. 111 (1948), pp. 3-16.
——, 'A Palaeographical Study of the Jerusalem Scrolls', *ibid.*, No. 113 (1949), pp. 6-23.
——, Review of Birnbaum, S. A.: *The Qumran (Dead Sea) Scrolls and Palaeography*', in *JBL*, lxxii (1953), p. 258 f.
——, 'Some Comments on the Palaeography of the Dead Sea Scrolls', in *JJS*, ii (1951), pp. 195-99.
Trinquet, J., 'Les liens 'Sadocites' de l'Écrit de Damas, des manuscrits de la Mer Morte et de l'Ecclésiastique', in *VT*, i (1951), pp. 287-92.
de Vaux, R., 'Les manuscrits hébreux du désert de Juda', in *LVI*, 1949, pp. 583-96.
——, 'Post-scriptum. La cachette des manuscrits hébreux', in *RB*, lvi (1949), pp. 234-37.
——, 'La grotte des manuscrits hébreux', *ibid.*, lvi (1949), pp. 586-609.
——, 'A propos des manuscrits de la Mer Morte', *ibid.*, lvii (1950), pp. 417-29.
——, 'Fouille au Khirbet Qumran', *ibid.*, lx (1953), pp. 83-106.
——, 'Exploration de la région de Qumran', *ibid.*, lx (1953), pp. 540-61.
——, 'Fouilles de Khirbet Qumran. Rapport préliminaire sur la deuxième campagne', *ibid.*, lxi (1954), pp. 193-236.
Vermès, G., 'Nouvelles lumières sur la Bible et sur le Judaisme', in *CS*, iii (1949), pp. 224-33.
——, 'La secte juive de la Nouvelle Alliance, d'apres ses hymnes récemment découverts', *ibid.*, iv (1950), pp. 178-202.
——, *Les manuscrits du désert de Juda*, 1953.
Volz, P., *Die Eschatologie der jüdischen Gemeinde im neutestamentlichen Zeitalter*, 1934.
Waddell, W. G., 'The Tetragrammaton in the LXX', in *JTS*, xlv (1944), pp. 158-161.
Wallenstein, M., 'A Striking Hymn from the Dead Sea Scrolls', in *BJRL*, xxxviii (1955), pp. 241-65.
——, 'Some Lexical Material in the Judean Scrolls', in *VT*, iv (1954), p. 211-14.
——, 'A Hymn from the Scrolls', *ibid.*, v (1955), pp. 277-83.
Ward, W. H., 'The 'Zadokite' Document', in *BS*, lxviii (1911), pp. 429-56.
Weber, F., *Jüdische Theologie auf Grund des Talmud und verwandter Schriften*, 1897.
Weis, P. R., 'The Date of the Habakkuk Scroll', in *JQR*, N.S. xli (1950-51), pp. 125-54.
Wernberg-Møller, P., 'Some Passages in the 'Zadokite' Fragments and their Parallels in the Manual of Discipline', in *JSS*, i (1956), pp. 110-28.
——, 'Some Reflections on the Biblical Material in the Manual of Discipline', in *ST*, ix (1955), pp. 40-66.
——, 'Observations on the Interchange of *Ayin* and *Ḥet* in the Manual of Discipline', in *VT*, iii (1953), pp. 104-07.
——, 'Notes on the Manual of Discipline i 18, ii 9, iii 1-4, 9 ,vii 10-12, and xi 21-22', *ibid.*, iii (1953), pp. 195-202.
——, 'SDQ, SDYQ, and SDWQ in the Zadokite Fragments, the Manual of Discipline, and the Habakkuk Commentary', *ibid.*, iii (1953), pp. 310-15.
Wieder, N., 'The 'Law-Interpreter' of the Sect of the Dead Sea Scrolls: the Second Moses', in *JJS*, iv (1953), pp. 158-75.
——, 'The Term QES in the Dead Sea Scrolls and in Hebrew Liturgical Poetry', *ibid.*, v (1954), pp. 22-31.
——, 'The Doctrine of the Two Messiahs among the Karaites', *ibid.*, vi (1955), pp. 14-25.

WIESENBERG, E., 'Chronological Data in the Zadokite Fragments', in *VT*, v, (1955), pp. 284-308.
WILDBERGER, H., 'Die Sektenrolle vom Toten Meer', in *ET*, 1953, pp. 25-43.
WINTER, P., 'Notes on Wieder's Observations on the *Doresh hat-Torah* in the Book of the New Covenanters of Damascus', in *JQR*, N.S. xlv (1954-55), pp. 39-47.
——, 'Ben Sira and the Teaching of the 'Two Ways', in *VT*, v (1955), pp. 315-18.
YADIN, Y., 'A Note on DSD iv 20', in *JBL*, lxxiv (1955), pp. 40-43.
YALON, H., Review of SUKENIK, E. L., *Megillot Genuzot* II, in *KS*, xxvi (1950), pp. 239-48.
——, Review of BURROWS, M. (ed.), *The Dead Sea Scrolls* I, *ibid.*, xxvii (1951), pp. 163-75.
——, Review of BURROWS, M. (ed)., *The Dead Sea Scrolls* II, fasc. 2, *ibid.*, xxviii (1952), pp. 64-74.
YEIVIN, S., 'The Date and Attribution of the Leviticus Fragments from the Cache in the Judaean Desert', in *BASOR*, No. 118 (1950), pp. 28-30.
ZEITLIN, S., 'The Book of Jubilees, its Character and Significance', in *JQR*, N.S. xxx (1939-40), pp. 1-31.
——, 'A Commentary on the Book of Habakkuk. Important Discovery or Hoax?' *ibid.*, N.S. xxxix (1948-49), pp. 235-47.
——, 'Scholarship and the Hoax of the Recent Discoveries', *ibid.*, N.S. xxxix (1948-49), pp. 337-63.
——, 'The Alleged Antiquity of the Scrolls', *ibid.*, N.S. xl (1949-50), pp. 57-78.
——, 'The Hebrew Scrolls: Once More and Finally', *ibid.*, N.S. xli (1950-51), pp. 1-58.
——, 'The Hebrew Scrolls: A Challenge to Scholarship', *ibid.*, N.S. xli (1950-51), pp. 251-75.
——, 'The Essenes and Messianic Expectations', *ibid.*, xlv (1954-55), pp. 83-119.
——, 'The Dead Sea Scrolls: A Travesty on Scholarship', *ibid.*, xlvii (1956-57), pp. 1-36.
——, *The Zadokite Fragments, with an Introduction* (JQR, Monograph Series, No. 1), 1952.

ABBREVIATIONS

MSS are abbreviated in the following way (cf. BARTHÉLEMY and MILIK, *Discoveries in the Judaean Desert I. Qumran Cave I*, p. 46 f):

1QIsa[a] : The First Isaiah Scroll
1QIsa[b] : The Second Isaiah Scroll
1QpHab : The Habakkuk Commentary
1QS : The Manual of Discipline
1QSa : The Rule of the Congregation
1QSb : The Benedictions
1QM : The War between the Children of Light and the Children of Darkness.
1QH : The Thanksgiving Hymns
CD : The 'Zadokite' (Damascus) Fragments

References to biblical and apocryphal books are given according to HART, *Rules for Compositors and Readers at the University Press, Oxford*, p. 51.

Other abbrevations:

AJT : American Journal of Theology
AKM : Abhandlungen für die Kunde des Morgenlandes
ALBO : Analecta Lovaniensia Biblica et Orientalia
AO : Archiv Orientalni
APAW : Abhandlungen der Preussischen Akademie der Wissenschaften
Aqu. : Aquila
ATR : Anglican Theological Review
BA : Biblical Archaeologist
BASOR : Bulletin of the American Schools of Oriental Research
BCUA : Bulletin of the Catholic University of America
BDB : BROWN, DRIVER and BRIGGS, *A Hebrew and English Lexicon of the Old Testament*, 1906.
BH : Biblia Hebraica, ed. KITTEL
BiOr : Bibliotheca Orientalis
BJRL : Bulletin of John Rylands Library
BK : Bibel und Kirche
BS : Bibliotheca Sacra
CBQ : Catholic Biblical Quarterly
CS : Cahiers Sioniens
ET : Evangelische Theologie
ETL : Ephemerides Theologicae Lovanienses
GB : *Gesenius' Hebräisches und Aramäisches Handwörterbuch über das Alte Testament*, bearbeitet von BUHL, 17th ed., 1921.
GK : *Gesenius' Hebrew Grammar*, ed. KAUTZSCH, 2nd Engl. ed., 1910.
HJ : Hibbert Journal
HTR : Harvard Theological Review
HUCA : Hebrew Union College Annual
IEJ : Israel Exploration Journal
JA : Journal Asiatique
JAOS : Journal of the American Oriental Society
JBL : Journal of Biblical Literature
JCS : Journal of Cuneiform Studies

JJS	:	Jour[illegible]wish Studies
JNES	:	J[illegible] Near Eastern Studies
JR	:	[illegible] Religion
JSS	:	[illegible]f Semitic Studies
J[illegible]	:	Jewi[illegible] Quarterly Review
JT[illegible]	:	Journal of Theological Studies
KS	:	Kirjath Sepher
LVI	:	La Vie Intellectuelle
MG	:	Sukenik, *Megillot Genuzot* I-II, 1948-50
MGWJ	:	Monatschrift für Geschichte und Wissenschaft des Judentums
MT	:	Massoretic Text
NAWG	:	Nachrichten der Akademie der Wissensch[illegible]ten i[illegible] Göttingen
NC	:	La Nouvelle Clio
NRT	:	Nouvelle Révue Théologique
NTS	:	New Testament Studies
OS	:	Oudtestamentische Studien
PAAJR	:	Proceedings of the American Academy for Jewish Research
PEQ	:	Palestine Exploration Quarterly
Pesh.	:	Peshitta
PSBA	:	Proceedings of the Society of Biblical Archaeology
RB	:	Révue Biblique
REJ	:	Révue des Etudes Juives
RHPR	:	Révue d'Histoire et de Philosophie Religieuse
RHR	:	Révue de l'Histoire des Religions
RSR	:	Révue de Science Religieuse
SBU	:	Symbolae Biblicae Upsalienses
SEÅ	:	Svensk Exegetisk Årsbok
Sept.	:	Septuagint
ST	:	Studia Theologica
Sym.	:	Symmachus
Targ.	:	Targum
Theod.	:	Theodotion
TLZ	:	Theologische Literaturzeitung
TR	:	Theologische Rundschau
TWNT	:	Theologisches Wörterbuch zum Neuen Testament
TZ	:	Theologische Zeitschrift
VD	:	Verbum Domini
VT	:	Vetus Testamentum
ZAW	:	Zeitschrift für die Alttestamentliche Wissenschaft
ZDMG	:	Zeitschrift der Deutschen Morgenländischen Gesellschaft
ZHB	:	Zeitschrift für Hebräische Bibliographie
ZKT	:	Zeitschrift für Katholische Theologie
ZNW	:	Zeitschrift für die Neutestamentliche Wissenschaft
ZRGG	:	Zeitschrift für Religions- und Geistesgeschichte
ZTK	:	Zeitschrift für Theologie und Kirche